EUROPE EAST AND WEST

EUROPE EAST AND WEST

NORMAN DAVIES

JONATHAN CAPE
LONDON

Published by Jonathan Cape 2006

2 4 6 8 10 9 7 5 3 1

First published in Great Britain in 2006 by
Jonathan Cape
Random House, 20 Vauxhall Bridge Road,
London SW1V 2SA

Random House Australia (Pty) Limited
20 Alfred Street, Milsons Point, Sydney,
New South Wales 2061, Australia

Random House New Zealand Limited
18 Poland Road, Glenfield,
Auckland 10, New Zealand

Random House South Africa (Pty) Limited
Isle of Houghton, Corner of Boundary Road & Carse O'Gowrie,
Houghton 2198, South Africa

The Random House Group Limited Reg. No. 954009
www.randomhouse.co.uk

A CIP catalogue record for this book is available from the British Library

ISBN 9780224069243 (from Jan 2007)
ISBN 0224069241

Mixed Sources
Product group from well-managed
forests and other controlled sources
www.fsc.org Cert no. TT-COC-2139
© 1996 Forest Stewardship Council
FSC

Typeset by Palimpsest Book Production Limited
Grangemouth, Stirlingshire
Printed and bound in Great Britain by William Clowes Ltd, Beccles, Suffolk

Map by Reginald Piggott

CONTENTS

ILLUSTRATIONS

The Rape of Europa by Peter Paul Rubens, copy after a painting by Titian (*akg-images/Erich Lessing*).

Europa and the bull, Apulian vase painting, fourth century BC (*akg-images/ Erich Lessing*).

Magdalen College, *c.* 1928 (*Getty Images*).

Edward Gibbon pictured in Switzerland, lithograph by C. Constans (*Mary Evans Picture Library*).

The Venerable Bede (*Getty Images*).

Pierre de Ronsard (*Getty Images*).

William Blake, engraving by W.C. Edwards (*Getty Images*).

Juliusz Słowacki, anonymous wood engraving (*akg-images*).

The Black Madonna of Częstochowa (*The Granger Collection, New York*).

The Crucifixion, sixteenth-century Greek icon painting (*akg-images*).

Johann Wolfgang von Goethe (*Time Life Pictures/Getty Images*).

Rudyard Kipling, *c.* 1930 (*The Granger Collection, New York*).

The School of Athens by Raphael, 1508–11, detail showing central group with Plato and Aristotle (*akg-images/Erich Lessing*).

Llanfairpwllgwynggyllgogerychwyrndrobwllllantysiliogogogoch, the Welsh railway station with the world's longest place name, 1935 (*Getty Images*).

Hell, Purgatory and Paradise by Domenico Michelino, 1465 (*Time Life Pictures/Getty Images*).

Vladimir Mayakovsky, *c.* 1925 (*akg-images*).

Botany Bay, eastern Australia, *c.* 1800 (*Getty Images*).

Fort Ross, Bodega Bay, California, 1828 (*Getty Images*).

King Władysław Jagiellon at the battle of Grunwald, painting by J. Matejko (*Time Life Pictures/Getty Images*).

Reception of August the Strong in the Berlin Palace (by Frederick William I and Sophie Dorothea), painting by Antoine Pesne, 1728 (*akg-images*).

'In a Polish Jewish Town', postcard from a series photographed during the German occupation of Poland in the First World War, *c.* 1915–16 (*akg-images*).

Arthur James Balfour visits a Jewish settlement in the British Mandate of Palestine, 1925 (*akg-images*).

Abu Abdullah (Boabdil), known as 'The Unfortunate', the last Moorish emir of Granada (*Time Life Pictures/Getty Images*).

Europe Is Liberated from the Turks, Austrian educational picture from 1959 depicting the battle of Kahlenberg, 12 September 1683 (*akg-images*).

The Zaporozhye Cossacks Writing a Mocking Letter to the Turkish Sultan Mehmet IV by Ilya Repin, 1880–91 (*akg-images*).

RAF Westland Wapitis on a reconnaissance flight over the mountains of Kurdistan, Iraq, March 1934 (*Getty Images*).

Leopold von Ranke, *c.* 1880 (*Getty Images*).

Nikolai Mikhailovich Karamzin.

Heinrich Himmler (*Time Life Pictures/Getty Images*).

Lavrenti Pavlovich Beria, *c.* 1946 (*Getty Images*).

The snow-covered belongings of those deported to Auschwitz-Birkenau litter the railway tracks leading to the camp's entrance, *c.* 1945 (*Getty Images*).

Vorkuta, 1930s/1940s (*Nowosti/ullstein bild*).

Winston Churchill addressing the Congress of Europe, The Hague, 29 May 1948 (*Getty Images*).

Boris Yeltsin addresses the people outside the White House, 19 August 1991 (*Nowosti/ullstein bild*).

Robert Schuman (*Time Life Pictures/Getty Images*).

INTRODUCTION

THIRTY years ago, when I wrote my first book, the Cold War was at its height.[1] We lived under the threat of nuclear exchange between 'the West' and the Soviet 'East'. Britain had just joined a European Economic Community that did not reach beyond West Germany. The Iron Curtain ran in an unbroken line from Lübeck to Trieste. The countries to the east of the Curtain were ruled by grim, communist regimes controlled by Moscow. What is more, the Iron Curtain was making inroads into our minds. The name Europe no longer seemed to apply to the whole of the continent, but was increasingly used as a shorthand term for the European project in our western half. The deadlock looked insoluble. The USSR possessed the largest nuclear arsenal in the world and looked invincible. The idea of a free and united Europe had become a mirage.

The eastern half was increasingly forgotten or ignored. Throughout the following decades, therefore, I devoted much time and energy to contesting the prevailing attitudes. As a historian whose interests had moved from France and Italy to Poland and Russia, I was determined to keep the history of Eastern Europe in general view, to stop views about the present overwhelming approaches towards the past. As a regular visitor to the East, I wanted to draw attention to the rich cultural and intellectual life of countries like Poland, Hungary and Czechoslovakia, thereby demonstrating that the communist system, which most other Western commentators were interested in, was an alien imposition, an ephemeral excrescence. It was in this spirit that I wrote *God's Playground: A History of Poland*. And it was in this spirit, in the late 1980s, that I began to prepare *Europe: A History*.[2]

Oddly enough, though, the attitudes and priorities of the Cold War era did not collapse when the Berlin Wall collapsed. On the contrary, many people ploughed on regardless as if nothing much had changed. The European Union went ahead with the scheme devised in the 1980s for creating monetary union in Western Europe, whilst putting the scheme for enlargement to the east on the back-burner. Historians, who had been disposed throughout their studies and their careers to ignore the East, made little effort to mend their ways. Some of the worst examples of books published as 'histories of Europe' but confined to Western Europe appeared at the turn of the 1980s and '90s – in other words at the very time that a change of heart might have been expected.[3]

In this situation, I began to give lectures, to write articles and to sketch out essays that were all connected in one way or another to the theme of Europe East and West. Many of them dealt with topics that would appear in *Europe: A History* or would be used in talks prompted by that publication. Many of them owed their conception to the next big book I wrote, *The Isles: A History*.[4] When engaged with *Europe*, I had already realised that Anglocentric British history was divorced from general European history by the same sort of mental gulf that divorced prevailing views of European history from Eastern Europe. So, both *Europe* and *The Isles* may be regarded as crusades for comprehensive history writing.

The present selection of essays, therefore, is based on pieces that have all been prepared in the last ten years. Whilst holding to the general theme, it puts variety at the top of its priorities. Several items, such as 'Fair Comparisons, False Contrasts', which was presented as a special faculty lecture in Oxford, or '*Sicut Lilium*', which was the opening salvo of six Wayneflete Lectures, reflect the atmosphere of more formal occasions. Others, like 'The Politics of History', are more analytical. Some, like the 'lifetime ramble', 'History, Language and Literature', reflect the personal experiences and sentiments of a long academic career. I hope that the mixture will prove both *seriozny* and entertaining. The Prologue picked itself. It starts with the words 'In the beginning . . .' and comes from the opening pages of *Europe: A History*. It shows, among other things, that Europa's journey started in the east. The last item, 'Waiting for Dinner', was published many years ago in the late and lamented journal *Encounter*. It purveys the flavour of everyday life in the so-called Eastern Bloc. It recalls a moment from a world that one hopes is by now pure history.

Reading through this collection of pieces in preparation for publication, I have been struck by the speed with which comments can become obsolescent. The world never stands still. The context within which one writes is constantly shifting. And observations penned only a few years ago can already be showing their age.

The temptation, of course, is to update everything and to excise the anachronisms. Such a policy, however, has not been followed. For one thing, it was not very practical. For another, it seemed somewhat dishonest. To strip a narrative of the context in which it was conceived, is to rob it of an essential part of its flavour and identity. For this reason, little of importance has been changed. Some passages have been trimmed. Others have been slightly expanded to accommodate a few explanatory or illustrative sentences. But none of the pieces has been substantially re-written.

The decade which spans the turn of the twentieth and twenty-first centuries has witnessed numerous signal events in Europe. Many countries of the former Soviet Bloc have joined NATO; and NATO troops now manoeuvre in locations from Estonia to Crimea where not long ago their appearance could have sparked a Third World War. Europe's relationship with the USA has been rocked – first by the wave of sympathy triggered by the attacks on New York and Washington on '9/11' 2001, and subsequently by the wave of distrust caused by the US-led war on Iraq. In 2004, no less than ten new member states joined the European Union, mainly in the east, thereby extending the EU's presence into all regions of the continent: north, south, east, west and centre. And in 2006, the separation of Montenegro from Serbia completed the long disintegration of the former Yugoslavia.

As a result, everyday contacts between East and West, inhibited for two or three generations, have multiplied mightily. Traders, tourists, bankers, industrialists and cheap-flight trippers have appeared in Prague, in Cracow, in Petersburg, and in Budapest, Sarajevo and Dubrovnik in unheard-of numbers. Europeans envisaged the imminent accession of Bulgaria and Romania with equanimity; and they discussed the pros and cons of EU entry for Turkey and Ukraine as part of a familiar process.

Nonetheless, the problem of re-integrating Europe proved to be more complicated than the mere removal of political barriers. It turned out the Iron Curtain could not be as easily dismissed from people's minds as it was dismantled on the ground. Mentalities changed slowest of all. Citizens of the former West continued to view the East with a mixture of suspicion, neglect and quizzical surprise. And the former Easterners continued to believe all too often in a mythical West where all was sweetness and light. Above all, European History failed to escape from the old ruts; and the information required to understand the roots of a new present was hard to find. All in all, I remain unshaken in the conviction that the theme of East and West, as elaborated in this volume, has lost little of the urgency which it possessed thirty years ago.

Going through my files, I found that many more such essays and lectures are waiting to be published. Should the first selection meet with the general approval of all concerned, especially of readers, I shall be delighted in due course to serve up further helpings.

Norman Davies
Cracow
June 2006

PROLOGUE:
THE LEGEND OF EUROPA

In the beginning, there was no Europe. All there was, for five million years, was a long, sinuous peninsula with no name, set like the figurehead of a ship on the prow of the world's largest land mass. To the west lay the ocean which no one had crossed. To the south lay two enclosed and interlinked seas, sprinkled with islands, inlets and peninsulas of their own. To the north lay the great polar ice cap, expanding and contracting across the ages like some monstrous, freezing jellyfish. To the east lay the land bridge to the rest of the world, whence all peoples and all civilisations were to come.

In the intervals between the ice ages, the peninsula received its first human settlers. The humanoids of Neanderthal and the cave people of Cro-Magnon must have had names and faces and ideas. But it cannot be known who they really were. They can only be recognised dimly from their pictures, their artefacts and their bones.

With the last retreat of the ice, only 12,000 years ago, the peninsula received new waves of migrants. Unsung pioneers and prospectors moved slowly out to the west, rounding the coasts, crossing the land and the seas until the furthest islands were reached. Their greatest surviving master-work, as the age of stone gave way to that of bronze, was built on the edge of human habitation on a remote, offshore island. But no amount of modern speculation can reveal for certain what inspired those master masons, nor what their great stone circle was called.[1]

At the other end of the peninsula, another of those distant peoples at

I

the dawn of the Bronze Age was founding a community whose influence has lasted to the present day. The Hellenes descended from the continental interior in three main waves, and took control of the shores of the Aegean towards the end of the second millennium BC. They conquered and mingled with the existing inhabitants. They spread out through the thousand islands which lie scattered among the waters between the coasts of the Peloponnese and of Asia Minor. They absorbed the prevailing culture of the mainland, and the still older culture of Crete. Their language distinguished them from the 'barbarians' – the 'speakers of unintelligible babble'. They were the creators of ancient Greece.

Later, when children of classical times asked where humankind had come from, they were told about the creation of the world by an unidentified *opifex rerum* or divine maker. They were told about the Flood, and about Europa.

Europa was the subject of one of the most venerable legends of the classical word. Europa was the mother of Minos, lord of Crete, and hence the progenitrix of the most ancient branch of Mediterranean civilisation. She was mentioned in passing by Homer. But in *Europa and the Bull*, attributed to Moschus of Syracuse, and above all in the *Metamorphoses* of the Roman poet Ovid, she is immortalised as an innocent princess seduced by the father of the gods. Wandering with her maidens along the shore of her native Phoenicia, she was beguiled by Zeus in the guise of a snow-white bull:

> And gradually she lost her fear, and he
> Offered his breast for her virgin caresses,
> His horns for her to wind with chains of flowers,
> Until the princess dared to mount his back,
> Her pet bull's back, unwitting whom she rode.
> Then – slowly, slowly down the broad, dry beach –
> First in the shallow waves the great god set
> His spurious hooves, then sauntered further out
> Till in the open sea he bore his prize.
> Fear filled her heart as, gazing back, she saw
> The fast receding sands. Her right hand grasped

A horn, the other leant upon his back.
Her fluttering tunic floated in the breeze.[2]

Here was the familiar legend of Europa as painted on Grecian vases, in the houses of Pompeii and in modern times by Titian, Rembrandt, Rubens, Veronese and Claude Lorrain.

The historian Herodotus, writing in the fifth century BC, was not impressed by the legend. In his view, the abduction of Europa was just an incident in the age-old wars over women-stealing. A band of Phoenicians from Tyre had carried off Io, daughter of the king of Argos; so a band of Greeks from Crete sailed over to Phoenicia and carried off the daughter of the king of Tyre. It was a case of tit for tat.[3]

The legend of Europa has many connotations. But in carrying the princess to Crete from the shore of Phoenicia (now south Lebanon) Zeus was surely transferring the fruits of the older Asian civilisations of the east to the new island colonies of the Aegean. Phoenicia belonged to the orbit of the pharaohs. Europa's ride provides the mythical link between ancient Egypt and ancient Greece. Europa's brother Cadmus, who roamed the world in search of her, *orbe pererrato*, was credited with bringing the art of writing to Greece.

Europa's ride also captures the essential restlessness of those who followed in her footsteps. Unlike the great river valley civilisations of the Nile, of the Indus, of Mesopotamia and of China, which were long in duration but lethargic in their geographical and intellectual development, the civilisation of the Mediterranean Sea was stimulated by constant movement. Movement caused uncertainty and insecurity. Uncertainty fed a constant ferment of ideas. Insecurity prompted energetic activity. Minos was famed for his ships. Crete was the first naval power. The ships carried people and goods and culture, fostering exchanges of all kinds with the lands to which they sailed. Like the vestments of Europa, the minds of those ancient mariners were constantly left 'fluttering in the breeze' – '*tremulae sinuantur flamine vestes*'.[4]

Europa rode in the path of the sun from east to west. According to another legend, the sun was a chariot of fire, pulled by unseen horses from their secret stables behind the sunrise to their resting place beyond the sunset. Indeed, one of several possible etymologies contrasts Asia, 'the land of the sunrise', with Europa, 'the land of the sunset'.[5] The Hellenes came to use 'Europe' as a name for their territory to the west of the Aegean as distinct from their older lands in Asia Minor.

At the dawn of European history, the known world lay to the east. The unknown waited in the west, in destinations still to be discovered. Europa's curiosity may have been her undoing. But it led to the founding of a new civilisation that would eventually bear her name and would spread to the whole peninsula.

I

THE IDEA OF EUROPE[1]

FOR several centuries, the right bank of the River Danube formed the northern frontier of the Roman empire. This means that the Hotel Gellért is built on land that once was Roman imperial territory. The Budapest University of Economics, in contrast, which faces the Hotel Gellért across the river, is built on a spot that was never within the empire. When we walk over the Szabadság Bridge today, we go from Buda to Pest. Sixteen or seventeen hundred years ago, anyone crossing the Danube in the same direction would have been leaving the comfortable suburbs of Roman Aquincum and entering the open plains of barbarian Pannonia.

One can imagine many other similar crossing points. Some of them would have been downstream in present-day Serbia and Bulgaria, at Taurunum or Durostorum. Others would have been on the upper Danube at Vindobona (Vienna) or Regina (Regensburg). Further north, at Colonia Augusta (Cologne), one left the imperial, western bank of the Rhine in order to land on the non-Roman, eastern bank of Germania Barbarica. At Luguvallium on Hadrian's Wall, one marched north through the gate to leave the province of Britannia behind and to enter the lands of the supposedly wild Caledonian tribes. In those days there was no England and no Scotland.

Talk of 'Roman' and 'barbarian' draws attention to a recurrent idea which the Romans have bequeathed to all their successors. It is the highly simplified and dubious notion that everything associated with the empire

5

was civilised, and everything outside the empire was barbarous. The very word 'civilisation' derives from the Latin *cives* or citizen. It implies that Roman citizens alone possessed the attributes of high culture, and that high culture could not be associated with non-citizens. The word *barbaros*, which is Greek, began as an epithet for anyone who spoke 'blah, blah, blah' (as we would say) and not Greek. But in time it took on a pejorative turn and was used to denote uncouthness, backwardness and inferiority.

Studies on the origins of ideas of barbarity, as passed by the Greeks to the Romans, point to two historical moments. The first moment goes back to the eighth century BC, when the ancient Greeks encountered the Scythians and other nomadic peoples of the Pontic steppes. The other came 300 years later, when the Greeks were almost overrun by the invading Persians, and when, in the interests of Greek solidarity and survival, all the great poets and dramatists of that golden age represented the invaders as inferior. The point about the Persians, of course, is that they belonged to an ancient and sophisticated culture with which in other circumstances ancient Greece might have interacted with greater equanimity. As it was, the Greeks turned their backs on the outside world, developed what would later be called a chauvinistic or xenophobic streak, and launched a tradition where disdain for the 'non-Greek Other' became a lasting and damaging element in the total mix.[2] There can be no doubt, however, that the idea of Europe begins with the ancient Greeks, and that among the Greeks it was most frequently expressed through the legend of the same name.

Legends apart, the idea of Europe has grown organically over a very long period of time. The best way to approach it is to look first at the three recurring concepts which are associated with the term 'Europe', and then to examine their chronological evolution. The former operation is purely analytical: it answers the question, 'What is Europe?' The latter reminds me of the work of an archaeologist, sifting through the accretions of time, and defining the successive stages through which the present cumulative idea has grown. It answers the question, 'How have the different components of European identity been created?'

As explained in the Introduction to *Europe: A History*,[3] the concept of Europe has three overlapping variants – one is geographical, the second civilisational, the third political. The geographical one may seem very straightforward. It is Europe as the western peninsula of Eurasia; and Europe's history becomes everything that has taken place on that peninsula. And yet it is not quite that simple. Although the peninsula is bounded on the north and the west and the south by a clear maritime coast, its land boundary in the east has always been ambiguous and shifting. The present frontier of Europe on the ridge of the Ural Mountains is quite arbitrary. It is the result of a convention created in the eighteenth century by a Swedish surveyor working for Catherine the Great of Russia; and it was the Russian empress who decided that the ancient and traditional frontier of Europe on the River Tanais or Don – as established, of course, by the Greeks – should be moved far to the east in order to include the greater part of Muscovy. That convention has held good for the last 200 years but there is no reason to think that it is eternal.

The second variant of Europe, as the new civilisation of the West, is the most complicated, and is the one with the largest number of subvariants within it. Suffice it to say here that there is a very real spatial problem to this idea simply because the human bearers of this civilisation decided to spread themselves over every continent of the globe. In its early stages, Europe was located on that one peninsula of Eurasia. Since the sixteenth century, however, Europeans have migrated to the Americas, to Australasia and to parts of Asia, and it is now extremely difficult to say exactly what is the base and what is the periphery. For practical purposes, most people talk about the base as being strictly confined to the European peninsula. But there are others, especially American proponents of 'Western civilisation', who would argue that North America or Australia have always been an integral part of the same civilisation ever since the great transoceanic migrations began.

The third variant is political. For many centuries the idea of a political Europe was no more than a utopia, an unrealised ideal. But from the Second World War a political Europe, now the European Union, has been a living and growing reality. According to the Treaty of Rome of 1956, all signatories are committed to 'an ever closer union'.

It is worth adding, perhaps, that there are two further general concepts of Europe in circulation. They are not usually taken into consideration these days because one is patently false, and the other is based on negative criteria.

The concept of Europe as a racial entity is peculiarly persistent. Modern Europeans don't tend to think about such things until they find themselves the only European in the changing room of a Japanese swimming pool, or begin to ponder the implications of transcontinental migration. It's not that there aren't genetic characteristics clearly indigenous to Europe and rarely encountered elsewhere, except among people of European descent. The so-called Nordic type – tall, blonde and blue-eyed – for example is rightly associated with parts of northern Europe, especially with Scandinavia and with the destinations of Viking colonists. The objections start to arise on three grounds. Firstly, the 'racial types' which were once thought to be standard are far too crude to withstand close examination. White skin itself is a myth, except among albinos. There are 'pinkoes', as seen on British beaches; there is sallow skin, which often goes with blonde hair; and there are all possible gradations of brown or swarthy skin which overlap with skin types from North Africa or the Middle East. Secondly, none of the established types is typical for the whole of Europe. Thirdly, no European genetic group coincides with any of the other indicators of Europeanness. It used to be thought that the Indo-Europeans who brought in most of Europe's modern languages were also a racial grouping. But that is clearly a mistake, since Bengali-speakers and Hindi-speakers are also Indo-Europeans. One might as well say that all Europeans are actually Middle Easterners, whose language (but not racial characteristics) spread both south and west. The discovery of DNA has greatly expanded the field of historical genetics but there is no expectation of finding either a European gene or an exclusively European gene pool.[4]

Lastly, whilst on this track, a wide range of views of European identity functions outside Europe, and draws on features that non-Europeans, through comparison, regard as foreign to themselves. And yes, race is part of it. In North America, where the natives predominantly have skins of a magnificent chestnut hue, the European foreigners became 'palefaces'. In the Far East, where pale faces are part of a familiar range of skin colour, the Europeans become the 'round-eyes' or the 'long-noses'. And in Australia, where most people are of British descent, Europe is the lost home of the ancestors. In Africa or Latin America, it is the home of imperialism and colonialism. In China or India, it is just one more, and much younger, civilisation among many. These relative observations are interesting with regard to the interaction of peoples across the world, but they don't say much that is positive or comprehensive about the components of European identity.

Most scholars would agree that the roots of European civilisation lie in the classical world, often identifying three pillars of the nascent community which would later emerge. Those pillars are ancient Greece, ancient Rome and the Judaeo-Christian tradition. However, none of the three pillars was exclusively or even predominantly European. Ancient Greece, for example, though born on the Peloponnese, on a peninsula of the peninsula, spawned a Hellenic civilisation which spread south- and eastwards into Asia, so that Alexander the Great was founding cities in lands which are now in Egypt, in Afghanistan and even in northern India. The centre of gravity of that Hellenic civilisation was certainly more in what we would now call the Near East, in Asia Minor, than in the heart of the European peninsula.[5]

Rome, too, founded a civilisation in a peninsula of the peninsula. But having taken over the whole of the Mediterranean Sea which it turned into a Latin lake, it is quite clear that the Roman empire was not centred on Europe so much as in the Mediterranean, and towards the eastern end of the Mediterranean at that. The whole of North Africa, for example, was Roman; the Near East as far as Mesopotamia and the eastern parts of the Black Sea, including Armenia, were Roman, and the most populous province of the Roman empire was Egypt. It was no accident that in the fourth century the first Christian emperor, Constantine, decided to move the capital of his empire from Rome to Byzantium, which became Constantinople, on the very bounds of Europe and Asia.[6]

By the same token, the Judaeo-Christian religion was not European in its beginnings. Like all three monotheistic religions, it came out of the Orient – *ex Oriente lux*. It was born from Judaism, in Judaea, and it was only at a later stage that it found its main focus in Europe.[7]

To my mind, the aspect to be stressed in the origins of Europe is the interplay of late Christian antiquity with the native peoples and pagan cultures of the peninsula. For those pagan natives supplied the basic human material which was gradually imbued with the expanding civilisation. The outcome of that interplay, in the middle of the first millennium, was a recognisably civilised community which called itself Christendom. After that, the community evolved over the centuries, slowly accumulating a number of layers, each of which contributes to its present identity.

The first layer, therefore, is Europe as Christendom, and I would place the critical period in its formation between the fifth and the eighth centuries of our era – that is after the collapse of the western Roman empire and the subsequent rise of Byzantium. Absolutely vital was the defining role of Islam, which having overtaken the original home of Christianity in the Holy Land, determined both the ideological and the geographical limits of Christendom as a coherent religion-based community located on the peninsula. Two processes were at work simultaneously: one, as already mentioned, the interplay of late Roman Christianity with the pagan peoples, and the other the limiting of that interplay by the rise of a Muslim counter-civilisation in the east. One should always quote the famous words of the Belgian historian, Henri Pirenne, who wrote, 'Charlemagne without Muhammad would have been inconceivable.' Charlemagne, the first Christian emperor of the West, founder of the Carolingian empire, was crowned in Rome in AD 800. He was given the opportunity to found such an empire by the earlier collapse of the western Roman empire and by the rise of Islam.

The overall product of these processes was a medieval theocracy in which the Christian religion was the guiding principle not only of spiritual affairs but of all spheres of human activity including politics and economics, social life, morality, arts and music. Everything was theocratic, that is God-governed. Of course, one should not exaggerate; the medieval theocracy was never complete, and there continued to be important Jewish, Muslim and subterranean pagan strands within the body of Christendom.

One should also emphasise another outstanding fact which prevailed from the very beginning: the duality of East and West. Christendom was split between its two Churches – the Latin or Catholic Church in the west (the Roman Church) and the Greek or Orthodox Church in the east. These two branches of the Christian religion date back to the cultural division within the Roman empire itself, and they have never been fully conjoined. In the age of the Church councils, which basically continued to 787, the Western and Eastern Churches cooperated in founding the fundamental theological doctrines of Christianity. But thereafter the ideological schism widened, and in 1054 the moment came when the Roman and the Orthodox Churches no longer recognised a mutual communion. The West and the East in Christendom learned to reject each other and this rejection has its legacy right up to the present day.[8]

Nonetheless, pagan Europe thrived for much longer than most historians allow, and even after Christianisation survived in sufficient strength to stage several important revivals. The first country outside the Roman empire to accept Christianity, Armenia, did so in the fourth century AD. The last, Lithuania, followed suit in the early fifteenth. This means that pagan religion and pagan culture functioned alongside Christianity for 1100 years after the landmark conversion of Constantine. It's true that the pagan sphere was steadily shrinking throughout that millennium and more, but it is also true that its lasting impact was enormous. In England, for example, paganism was not fully eradicated by the mission of St Augustine in 597, as many were taught at school, but by the conversion of the Danelaw in the ninth century and by the suppression of the kingdom of Eric Blood-Axe in York in 954. It dominated Viking Scandinavia including outlying parts of the British Isles until the twelfth century, and Prussia until the crusades of the Teutonic Knights in the thirteenth and fourteenth centuries. It formally bowed out in the heart of the Lithuanian grand duchy in 1385, after the grand duke's marriage to the Catholic queen of Poland, but it was kept on ice for forty years more in a tiny enclave of Teutonic territory, presumably to justify the fund-raising of the knights.

At every step, the pagan groves were felled on the orders of Christian bishops, just as the groves of Celtic druids had been felled by the Romans at every point between Provence and Anglesey. But the memory, the poetry and the sagas lived long enough to be recorded by Christian monks. And the rites, thinly disguised with nominal Christian symbols, often continued as an essential element of European folklore. The gods of the Celts, the Slavs and of the Germanic tribes were never completely forgotten, and they were to rise again in the imagination of nineteenth-century Romantics. The operas of Richard Wagner were not just magnificent musical dramas. They were the last reworkings of traditions much older than Christianity. And it didn't end with harmless music-making. Through no fault of their own, Wagner and other pagan revivalists had admirers in a later political generation. When the Nazis held their rallies bristling with burning torches and swastika banners, they were consciously defying established political and religious norms, and ushering in an era of neo-paganism. Both the swastika and the lightning flash of the SS were ancient pagan symbols.

A similar story can be told about the afterlife of classical paganism. The last Olympic Games – the last festival of the gods – was held in AD 396; it was then suppressed by Emperor Theodosius. For several centuries pre-Christian culture was distinctly out of fashion. But it turned out that a large part of the amazing Greek and Roman repertoire of philosophy, poetry and drama had been preserved in the great library of Alexandria, in Arabic translations or in monkish copies. From the twelfth century onwards, the classical authors returned to their former position as an essential accomplishment of every educated person. Dante Alighieri (d.1321), the first and greatest of Europe's long line of vernacular poets, chose Virgil as his guide in the underworld, and called him *il maestro di lor chi sanno*, 'the master of those who know'. Henceforth, right to the twentieth century, every generation of educated Europeans received an education based on the Classics. The ancients were as much a part of Europe's intellectual world as the medievals and moderns. The Christian Church absorbed many ancient philosophers, from Aristotle to Marcus Aurelius, as its own, and the boundaries between Christian and non-Christian wisdom were blurred. Classical revivals occurred in every subject from art and architecture to literature and politics. When Mussolini's fascists strutted round Rome carrying the *fasces*, the rods of authority of the eternal city, they were fantasising about the reconstruction of the Roman empire, just as Hitler's Nazis were fantasising in Germany about the revival of the Germanic gods.[9]

The reaction against medieval theocratic Christendom came with the gradual rise of what one might call secular Europe – an international intellectual movement devoted to non-religious ideas and activities. The movement would never replace the Christian ideals of the previous era, but it created a fresh fusion of old and new, of Christian and secular. The Renaissance, for example, was a critical era when the civilisation of the classical world was systematically revived and moulded into every branch of culture; it posed a clear counterpoint to the previous, exclusively religious, theocratic view. Similar things can be said of the arts. Although all the arts in European civilisation are rooted in Christianity, whether one is talking about music or painting or sculpture or poetry or almost anything else, the exclusive religious focus of the arts was superseded at the time of the Renaissance by a new interest in secular, humanist matters. One of the key subjects in this new area of secular interest was the human body itself and the individual personality of people as revealed in their lives and appearance, in their faces, their emotions and their speech.[10]

Another stage can be found in the scientific revolution, usually dated from 1543 when the Polish astronomer Copernicus first received a printed copy of his *De Revolutionibus orbium coelestium* – a revolutionary work in all senses of the term. On his deathbed, Copernicus launched not just a new view of the universe – that is, that the earth revolves around the sun and not vice versa – but a new manner of thinking. He had only published his theory after exhaustive practical experiments. Standing on the tower of his church at Frauenberg (Frombork) in Warmia he had painstakingly measured and noted down the positions of the stars and the planets over almost three decades. This inductive method of reaching a conclusion on the basis of demonstrable fact was to give scientists a new, entirely secular and independent approach to knowledge. Henceforth, science would gradually be freed from the restrictions of Church-dictated convention.[11]

It is also important to realise the destructive effect of the Reformation, and in particular of the religious wars that followed, which discredited the very name of Christendom. In the sixteenth and seventeenth centuries, most parts of Europe were embroiled in the most vicious and extended religious conflicts, whether it was the Wars of Religion in France or the Thirty Years War between Catholics and Protestants in Germany or, in the east, the wars between the Catholic Poles and Orthodox Russians. These very unchristian conflicts had the effect of destroying the previous core of the civilisation's identity. Europeans ceased to see any unity in Christianity, and stopped calling their civilisation Christendom. They looked instead for a different label; and they found, of course, the old term 'Europe'. The last occasion where an official document talks about the 'princes of Christendom' as opposed to the princes of Europe, certainly in the diplomatic sphere, is to be found in the Treaty of Utrecht in 1713.[12]

At that time, in the early eighteenth century, European civilisation was moving towards what one might regard as the culmination of the secular trend, namely the cult of rationalism in the so-called Age of Enlightenment. The Enlightenment was a quite consciously secular movement which, while it did not reject Christianity outright, had many other philosophical priorities in mind. In particular, it propagated belief in the supreme power of reason in ordering human affairs. Many people today still look back with admiration to the Enlightenment as the launch pad of modern thought. But it would not be long before some of its shortcomings became all too evident. Human beings, alas, may be endowed with reason, but they are not just simple or exclusively rational creatures.[13]

The age of Enlightenment also saw the appearance of the Concert of Europe, the idea of Europe as a political community of powers. It was a concept where only powerful states and dynasties counted. It was not a concert of the peoples or the nations or even the states of Europe; it was an aristocratic, elitist construct of the community of the powerful. And the balance of power between the members of that community became, in the eighteenth century, the supreme aim of international affairs. The point was reached when the leaders of the club began to think of themselves as the embodiment of Europe itself. In the negotiations at Tilsit, on the River Niemen, between Napoleon and the Russian Emperor Alexander I in 1809, Napoleon had been arguing at some length that 'Europe needs this, Europe wants that, and Europe must have the other' when the tsar stopped him and said, 'What is this Europe that you keep talking about?' And then he answered himself: '*L'Europe c'est nous!*' In other words, we, the great leaders of the great powers, we are the incarnation of Europe.

Following the terrible decades of the Revolutionary Wars, the Concert of Europe continued on into the nineteenth century. The meetings of the powers, from the Conference of Vienna in 1815 to the Congress of Berlin in 1878, constituted the decisive international events of the European arena. One can also see that the great powers of that period did not simply project their political, diplomatic and military power; they consciously sought to project their cultures. Just as there were a small number of states which saw themselves as the only states that counted, there was a parallel belief in the exclusive validity of a small number of powerful cultures. Here in the making, of course, was the nefarious concept of Western civilisation, which provides one of the most serious obstacles to a proper under-standing of the full content of European achievements and European failings (see pages 46–60).[14]

At the end of its existence, the Concert of Europe moved into the phase of imperialism, where the great powers, mainly of Western Europe, were able to overrun large regions of the globe and to strengthen themselves by colonies sited on other continents. Europe in its imperialist version is a concept which has greatly affected non-Europeans, because it is in this period and through contact with the imperial powers that most inhabitants of the world came into contact with Europeans. The contact was not always felicitous. Added together, the empires of Britain, France, Belgium, the Netherlands, Spain, Portugal and Russia covered almost three quarters of the earth's surface. It is not uncommon, though manifestly unjust, for Europe to be equated with nothing but imperialism and colonialism.[15] After all, large numbers of Europeans as well as non-Europeans were the involuntary subjects of the empires.

An important aspect of imperialism is connected with industrialisation, social modernisation and economic progress. Indeed, in the eyes of many non-Europeans, European civilisation came to be closely identified with commercial industry – with 'Europe as the workshop of the world', to borrow a phrase from British history. What is absolutely clear is that the Industrial Revolution (as historians once called it)[16] began in Europe. From particular parts of the British Isles, it spread quickly to areas of north-western Europe, northern France, the Low Countries and northern Germany, and it was from there that imperial power was principally projected around the globe. In the eyes of some theorists, among them the Marxists, imperialism is a purely economic phenomenon, where the Industrial Revolution and socio-economic modernisation were the core and the driving force of all imperial activity. Europe, therefore, became the home base of heavy industry, whereas the overseas colonies were the suppliers of labour, raw materials and captive markets. This industrial Europe has another facet to it, namely the amazing development of science and technology, which for reasons which are not easy to define took place first in Europe and not elsewhere. Some historians think that this European precocity was due to a miracle, whereas Europeans at the time rather arrogantly thought that it was the natural birthright of a superior people. Certainly imperialism and the scientific and technological prowess of the nineteenth century went hand in hand, leading to some of the racial theories which were current at the end of the period.[17]

One should also point out that the European science of the nineteenth century caused very deep intellectual and religious worries, since some theories were thought by many to be incompatible with the basic tenets of the Christian religion. There was a famous debate in Oxford in 1860 between the then bishop of Oxford and a representative of Charles· Darwin, whose evolutionary theory had just been published. The bishop made fun of Darwin and his followers by asking whether their ape-like ancestors were to be found on the maternal or the paternal side. In due course, however, a consensus emerged, holding that scientific knowledge is not contrary to religious belief. On the contrary, many modern-day religious people see the glory of God expressed in the wonders of science and technology.[18]

In its geographical aspect, industrial Europe reveals an interesting pattern. Many historians have identified a 'western core' and a backward periphery in the east. This is extremely misleading. I have no doubt that the industrial core of late nineteenth- and early twentieth-century Europe was located in a section of north-western Europe. But what is quite false is to suggest that the whole of the west was advanced while the whole of the east was backward. One has only to look, for example, at the most advanced state of the nineteenth century, the United Kingdom, to see that Ireland was every bit as economically backward as parts of Eastern Europe. It is a simple fact that the most rapid industrial advancement and the most catastrophic famine of the age both occurred in the United Kingdom.[19] By the same token, certain parts of Eastern Europe, the industrial oases of Silesia, Łódź or the Donbass, saw impressive development. It is simply not true, as one can see it written, that there was no significant industrial development in Central and Eastern Europe prior to the 1930s. The complacent confrontation of superior west and inferior east does not entirely add up.

To conclude this argument, however, one observes that the industrialisation and the socio-economic modernisation which spread with imperial power came to be equated with 'Europeanisation'. Indeed, it is often so regarded in an unfavourable light, since it tended to undermine the foundations of existing society.

Brief reference was made earlier to the concept of Europe as a racial entity. This concept has been thoroughly discredited by the misdeeds of those who tried to validate it. None other than Adolf Hitler once declared, 'Europe is a racial entity, not a geographical one.' Nonetheless, it would be wrong to underestimate the strength of the convictions which such ideas once engendered nor the extent of the pseudoscience which reinforced them. Systematic European racism and the resultant science of eugenics were common enough in Hitler's formative years, and they were no less widespread in England than in Germany or France. They are most usually traced to the works of the Comte de Gobineau, and especially to his essay *The Inequality of the Human Races* (1855), where one can find the extreme statement, 'all civilisation derives from the white race'. Gobineau was a specialist in the history of Persia. It was this special interest which led him first to give the label Aryan (Iranian) to the 'white race' and then to make the false link between his Ayran racial group and the Indo-European language group. Some commentators prefer to give more prominence to Gobineau's predecessor, Johann Friedrich Blumenbach (1752–1840). A learned professor at Göttingen, Blumenbach had invented his influential Five Race Scheme – of white, black, yellow, brown and red – long before Gobineau's birth. He also adopted the term 'Caucasian' to describe Europeans. One of my own sons happened to be born in California, and I was greatly surprised to find that he was officially classed in the United States as a Caucasian. It is strange that in the age of modern genetics, some of the old pseudoscientific terminology can still have currency.[20]

Even so, it is undeniable that the idea of a superior white European race held sway for many decades in large parts of Europe, and for even longer in the American South and in South Africa. In part it was a product of imperialism, and one has to say that the German Nazis were only responsible for its last, most ghastly chapter. As the *Götterdämmerung* closed in, in late 1944, when the Jewish Holocaust was virtually complete,

Heinrich Himmler, the *Reichsführer SS*, called a meeting of his officers to explain that the next phase would be to defend Europe against the 'yellow peril'.[21] In the final months of the war on the Eastern Front, the Germans were appalled to find just how many Red Army soldiers had been drafted in from the central Asian republics. Since they always regarded the racial struggle as more important than the military one, they all too late suspected that 'Jewish Bolshevism' might be in league with the 'Asiatic hordes'.

Coming to contemporary times, one frequently meets the concept of Europe as a new political ideal. The pre-eminence of Europe as the world's first industrial centre has given way to industrial powers elsewhere, notably to the United States and Japan. What is more, Europe has ceased to dominate the world politically through the great tragedies of the First and Second World Wars, of which Europe was the principal casualty. It is this trauma which provides the essential background to the rise of the European Movement and to the determination to create a new community free from the conflicts and antagonisms of the past.

There have been many European utopias, some of them extremely high-minded, from that of Thomas More in the sixteenth century, the inventor of the word, to that of William Penn, the Anglo-Dutch thinker and statesman, founder of the state of Pennsylvania, who was the first to recommend the creation of a European parliament. Other utopias have been much less inspirational. One should not forget that both fascism and communism, the two great totalitarian movements of the twentieth century, were generated in Europe – fascism in the west, communism in the east – and that each of them had its own utopia. The fascists, certainly in their Nazi variant, imagined a utopia which would be a racially pure society run by Aryans; the communists dreamed of a classless utopia run by the self-appointed elite of the international communist parties. Both required the forcible elimination of undesirable elements: elimination by the Nazis of *Untermenschen* – subhumans – of whom the Jews were the frontline category, and the wholesale elimination by the Soviet communists of social groups such as the kulaks. Genocide and *classocide* – as some French commentators have dubbed it – form the two greatest moments of Europe's disgrace.[22]

Liberalism, it should be remembered, was only one of the products of nineteenth-century Europe, and it was the ailing 'third way' in European history until it was saved by American intervention in 1945. There can be by no means any certainty that totalitarian Europe could have been overcome by liberal Europe without the very great assistance of the United States of America. Since 1945, liberal European activists have been determined to find a way out of this terrible tragedy, but their triumph was not confirmed until 1989.

The founding congress of the European Movement took place at The Hague in May 1948, at the very time when the Berlin Blockade was about to fail, and when the Iron Curtain was dividing Europe. As a result the European Movement could only operate in Western Europe and not in the whole continent. Here one might consider two quotations, from Winston Churchill and Salvador de Madariaga, illustrating the extraordinary ideals of that Hague congress. Churchill's statement included the following:

> We must proclaim the mission and the design of a united Europe whose moral conception will win the respect and gratitude of mankind, and whose physical strength will be such that none will dare molest her tranquil sway . . . I hope to see a Europe where men and women of every country will think of being European as of belonging to their native land, and wherever they go in this wide domain will truly feel 'Here I am at home.'[23]

The Spanish diplomat and writer de Madariaga was not to be outdone:

> This Europe must be born. And she will [be born] when Spaniards say 'our Chartres', Englishmen 'our Cracow', Italians 'our Copenhagen' and Germans 'our Bruges' . . . Then Europe will live. For then it will be that the spirit which leads Europe will have uttered the creative words: *Fiat Europa*.[24]

Within a very short time, it was obvious that hopes of putting such ideals into immediate practice were premature.

For forty years, therefore, the European Movement grew exclusively in the West and in the inhibitive context of the Cold War. European identity could only be openly expressed in the West. Even so, the existence of the Soviet Bloc concealed the fact that in many ways the captive peoples of the east were more conscious of their European heritage than the Westerners were. To repeat an old truth, we are never so conscious of what is dear to us until we've lost it. It would be no accident that the most convincing declarations of attachment to Europe as a civilisation were to be made by dissident intellectuals from the Soviet Bloc like Milan Kundera. The Westerners in contrast were pushed onto what has been called the economic track, or into what one German commentator rightly called 'the economic trap'. All too often the European Economic Community was seen as a rich man's club, a means of securing wealth and prosperity without due regard to the much higher concerns for peace, culture and security which were the driving force of its founding fathers.

In 1989, the European Movement suffered a shock when it realised that its field of activity would no longer be constrained by the Iron Curtain. Henceforth it would be open to the whole of the continent, one half of which had been artificially excluded by the supremacy of the Soviets in the east for over forty years. The great test of the subsequent time was to see whether the achievements of the European Movement in Western Europe could be retained while extending them to those countries which had been denied them for so long. The situation demanded unusual foresight and generosity. The most harmful, selfish and short-sighted of attitudes was that which attempted to prolong the separation of west and east, and which, by appealing to the old stereotypes, intended to hold half of Europe at arm's length.

In this regard, a brief anecdote may not be amiss. In 1991, the first prime minister of a fully independent Poland, Jan Krzysztof Bielecki, visited London. According to Mr Bielecki's account, when he met the British prime minister, John Major boasted, 'Britain has the highest growth rate in Europe.' To which his Polish visitor apparently replied, 'Speaking on behalf of Albania, I can assure you that there are several countries in Europe which have a higher growth rate than Britain's.'[25]

*

Such, in outline, are the main layers which can be uncovered in the idea of Europe. But that is not to say there are no problems. On the contrary, problems abound. Few Europeans are familiar with the continent's history as a whole. Still fewer of them possess the sort of vision which hovered over the Hague congress fifty years ago and which might be used to mobilise the achievements of the past for the political purposes of the present. For a decade after 1991, the year both of the Maastricht Treaty and of the collapse of the USSR, the leaders of the European Union stuck to the old priorities and showed little enthusiasm for changing them.

Which, by way of conclusion, brings me back to the observation that people from the former Soviet Bloc are more likely to treasure the best aspects of Europe's heritage than their more comfortable neighbours in the west. There is a broad band of Europe, from the Baltic to the Aegean, which is enjoying its first spell of freedom for sixty or seventy years. Occupied by the Nazis and then by the Soviets, subjected for a lifetime by communist tyranny, the Poles, the Czechs, the Hungarians and others have lived through the eye of Europe's modern storms. They are fiercely attached to their national identities and through no fault of their own have borne the brunt of the oppressions and the humiliations. Budapest lies in the epicentre of that zone of hard experience. So it may well be, after all, that the 'barbarians' have much to teach those who are tempted to think of themselves as the sole bearers of civilisation.

Finally, another little Hungarian story. In 1835, the composer Franz Liszt – or rather Liszt Ferenc – checked into the Hotel de l'Union in Geneva. He was at the head of a walking party which included Chopin's partner, Georges Sand. When asked to register, they were faced with the question *Lieu de résidence*, and they decided to have a bit of fun. One of them wrote, 'Parnasse', the other, 'Europe'.[26]

II

FAIR COMPARISONS, FALSE CONTRASTS: EAST AND WEST IN MODERN EUROPEAN HISTORY[1]

IN September 1865, *The Times* of London published a short article on the recent disturbances in Ireland. In its opinion, what it called the 'Fenian sedition' amounted to no more than 'a piece of feeble mischief'.[2] Whatever the injustices of the past, the Irish were no longer judged to possess the slightest grounds for grievance in the present. A week later, a Russian newspaper, the *Journal de Saint-Petersbourg politique et littéraire*, alias the *Sankt-Petersburgski Zhurnal*, reprinted *The Times* article, adding a commentary of its own which drew a parallel between the position of Ireland within the United Kingdom and the position of Poland within the realms of the tsar: 'The analogy is so striking,' it wrote, and, 'the circumstances so identical ... that we believe it necessary to remind Russian readers of the fact that it is Ireland in 1865, and not Poland in 1863, that is spoken of.'[3] This, in its turn, provoked a fierce riposte from *The Times* on 10 October.

The mid-1860s did indeed witness events in Ireland and Poland which merited comparison. The secret Irish Republican Brotherhood of Fenians was attracting huge support, not least among the Irish in Britain and America; Professor Roy Foster estimates 80,000 supporters in Britain alone.[4] In September 1865, the British authorities had just sentenced a group of Fenians to penal servitude in Australia. The principal Fenian newspaper in Dublin, *The Irish People*, which had openly called for armed rebellion led by Irish-American soldiers from the US army, had just been suppressed. In Poland, the tsarist authorities were mopping up the last guerrilla fighters of the defeated January rising, and were deporting tens of thousands of Polish prisoners to Siberian servitude. Yet the conspiracies continued. The next year, 1866, would see an abortive Fenian raid on Fort Erie in Canada and the great Polish rising on Lake Baykal in Siberia.

As imperialists, the editors of *The Times* held scant sympathy for either the Polish or the Irish cause. 'The Poles are the Irish of the Continent,' they said, talking of 'their unstable character, their incapacity for self-government, and the futility of their schemes' – 'a very hot-headed and unreasonable people, who have quarrelled with their benefactors, the Russians, without any cause'. In support of their 'Imperial reasoning', as they put it, they accepted that 'Russia is made to govern', that Russia is 'a Power which has been, and always will be, successful', that 'the Poles have nothing left but to submit'. 'Poland,' they concluded, 'is now nothing, and can do nothing.' At the same time, these self-important Victorians were thoroughly outraged by the idea that British rule in Ireland was comparable in any way to tsarist rule in Poland.

> How many . . . tens of thousands [of Poles] have been dragged from their homes since 1830 and marched to the depths of Siberia or shut up in dungeons at home! Where is the parallel to this in Ireland? There is not such a being at present as an Irish political convict. Ireland has no religious disabilities . . . Ireland is not governed by military rule; Irishmen are not conscripted into the British armies, nor hunted down in caves and cellars when they seek to evade the service . . . Ireland is as free as England, and its assimilation to the more powerful country proceeds from natural causes, and is in no way the effect of force or of tyrannical laws.[5]

In other words, though Ireland was wonderfully governed, the destiny of the fortunate Irish was to be exactly the same as that of the miserable Poles – and quite right too! There was absolutely no sense that by assimilating Ireland the powerful, liberal, democratic English majority of the United Kingdom might possibly be committing a grave injustice. In the same way, one recalls that it was Russia's allegedly most liberal tsar, Alexander II, who perpetrated the most brutal oppressions in Poland. This was the time when that 'reactionary liberal', as Marc Raeff called him, Professor Mikhail Katkov, coined the notorious slogan, 'Either Russia, or Poland'.[6] *Polonia delenda est* – for her own good.

Ireland versus Poland is my first example of what I call 'fair comparisons' in modern European history. It is a comparison seen by contemporaries and by historians alike[7] and it could be applied on a much wider front than the national movements of the nineteenth century. Nor is it just a matter, as my senior colleague the late Hugh Seton-Watson once suggested, of a common predilection for potatoes, priests, poteen and conspiracy.

On St Patrick's Eve a few years ago, I had the great pleasure of opening an Irish festival in, of all places, Toruń, birthplace of Copernicus. I suspect that the main point of the occasion was to promote the virtues of Guinness in post-communist Europe, but the organisers gave me an hour to range freely over the remarkable resonances of Polish and Irish history. What sticks in my mind from that exercise is the fascinating discrepancy between the objective circumstances of modern Ireland and modern Poland, which are somewhat different, and the subjective psychology of the two nations, which is remarkably congenial. At one level, the modern predicament of the Irish less resembles the Poles than the Czechs – a relatively small nation, with no experience of modern statehood and vastly outnumbered in their lonely struggle against a single, relatively benign empire. And yet the temper of the Irish is indisputably close to the Poles. As I concluded my speech in Toruń: the Irish are distinctly *Polskowaci*, the Poles distinctly *irlandizujący*. I won't attempt to translate.[8]

A second example of fair comparison relates to the ongoing debate about totalitarianism. What I have in mind here is the fact that, whilst fascism was predominantly a Western phenomenon, communism was predominantly an Eastern one. I strongly suspect that this consideration has influenced the judgement of Westerners, especially of ivory-towered or Ivy League Western theoreticians, who carry the guilt of the West in their consciences but who have never felt the totalitarian lash on their own backs. Hannah Arendt made an allusion to this in a quote on the title page of her study *Totalitarianism*: 'The subterranean stream of Western history has finally come to the surface and usurped the dignity of our tradition.'[9] Fascism was established in Italy in 1922, in Portugal in 1928, in Germany in 1933–4, and in Spain by 1939. It gained a few independent admirers and imitators in other European countries such as the Hungary of Admiral Horthy, the Austria of Dollfuss and the Romania of the Iron Guard. Oswald Mosley's League of British Fascists dated from 1932. But its main phase of international expansion occurred in 1940–44, in the long list of Axis occupation regimes stretching from the Atlantic to Albania and Ukraine. From its beginnings in Rome in 1922 to its demise in Madrid in 1975 it lasted for fifty-three years. Communism, meaning the Marxist-Leninist system, took hold in Soviet Russia from October 1917, in Soviet Hungary in 1919–20 and even more briefly in Soviet Bavaria in April 1919. It gained a gaggle of activists and fellow travellers among intellectuals and workers in some Western countries, notably France and Italy, but its main phase of international expansion occurred in 1939–45 in the wake of the Red Army's conquests. Between 1917 and 1991, it lasted for seventy-four years. For present purposes, it is relevant to note that there is a broad zone of Central and Eastern Europe, from the vicinity of Magdeburg to the outskirts of Moscow, which was subjected to both fascism and communism in turn. In my experience, the inhabitants of that zone, whose opinions were formed by hard experience, have few doubts about the concept of totalitarianism as the common denominator of the two great evils of our times.

But not to rush to conclusions. My approach to the totalitarian debate has not been to favour either the sceptics or the enthusiasts, but rather to widen the basis for judging the issue. The pioneering analysis of the subject in the 1950s proposed a six-point totalitarian model.[10] Forty years later, political scientists are still arguing the pros and cons of this narrow definition. In *Europe: A History* I proposed eighteen points for comparison. These comprised the original six starting with the dual party-state, the *Führerprinzip* and utopian goals, plus twelve more including genocide, pseudoscience, the psychology of hatred and the aesthetics of power.[11]

One trend within the debate, however, must be resisted. Some scholars seem to have taken the position that the evils of fascism were so extreme that it is not acceptable to compare them with anything else. Some even talk of Hitler's 'crimes' but of Stalin's 'mistakes'. Some are convinced that the Jewish Holocaust, for instance, is not only unique but incomparable. Such an approach is surely misguided. For one can only substantiate the claim to the uniqueness of the Holocaust – which I personally believe to be eminently possible – by showing how it differed in nature from other horrors of our age. On this, I rest my case with the words of Sir Isaiah Berlin: 'If uniqueness of a phenomenon is examined ... we mustn't rush to the conclusion that it's unique before we have compared it to other events which in some ways resemble it. That's what's happening to the Holocaust ... It has a conspicuously political motive.'[12] One thing, I think, is undeniable. Whether as totalitarian rivals or as ideological opposites, fascism and communism lived off each other in an all-European monster duel. Once fascism was dead, the death of communism was only a matter of time.

My third example is drawn from the history of modern art. Here I must draw attention to the fact that public appreciation of the arts inevitably lags behind the work of artists by several decades. Manet, Monet and Renoir were making their first Impressionist experiments in the 1860s, but Impressionism did not become the most popular artistic movement of all time until the middle of the next century.

This story, too, has an interesting east–west aspect. Modernism in art took flight before the First World War when Europe was far more united than afterwards. Paris served as a mecca for painters from far and wide. On the list of 'great French painters', one finds the Dutchman Van Gogh, the Belgian Vlaminck, the Catalan Picasso and Chagall, who was a Russian Jew from Minsk. More importantly, if one looks at the chronology of modern art, political barriers began to divide and fragment the avant-garde movement long before its achievements were properly disseminated.

The onset of Stalinism suppressed modernism in the Soviet Union from the end of the 1920s. The rise of Hitler had similar effects in Germany in the 1930s. But official philistinism blighted the artistic life of the Soviet Bloc until the 1990s. The consequences were far-reaching. Prominent artists from Central and Eastern Europe were prevented from exhibiting their works, or even from working, for significant stretches in their careers. Museums and galleries hoarded unseen masterworks in their attics and cellars, waiting for better times. Western critics wrote their textbooks of avant-garde painting blissfully unaware of the hidden canvasses, individuals or even schools beyond the Iron Curtain. For instance, the Soviet abstract painters Casimir Malevich, Vladimir Tatlin and Alexander Rodchenko made a sensational international debut in exhibitions held in Berlin before 1928, whence their early works passed into the general corpus of the subject. But much of their later works remained in oblivion until the collapse of the Soviet Union long after their deaths. Or again, the Osma group of early Czech cubists including Antonin Próchazka and Bohumil Kúbista, who had been active in Habsburg Prague, did not have time to gain widespread recognition before the arrival of the Nazis and then the communists. They remained virtually unknown, except to specialists, until the fall of communism. The canvasses of the early Lithuanian symbolist, Mikolojus Ciurlionis, who died in 1911, were not seen abroad for eighty or ninety years. Władysław Strzemiński, theorist and practitioner of constructivism, died in his native Poland in 1952 in an official cultural climate profoundly hostile to his activities. Large collections of Jewish paintings, like Chagall's, were never put on show because the post-war cultural commissars did not identify with the Jewish heritage.

All these things came into the open in 1994 when the richness and variety of Eastern Europe's avant-garde was assembled in a joint exhibition organised by the Museums of Modern Art of Łódź and Duisburg in the Bundeskunst- und Ausstellungshalle in Bonn.[13] Here was an artistic treasure trove never assembled in public. Only then could comparisons be made to establish an overall view of Europe's avant-garde art.

At this point, it may be convenient for me to pause and to signal an impression, a hypothesis even, about a set of negative stereotypes of Eastern Europe. These stereotypes were greatly strengthened by the artificial divisions of the Cold War, and they still obscure our understanding of many pan-European issues. Much as Western studies of the Middle East have been said to be distorted by views of the Islamic or Arabic Orient as the alien, exotic and inferior 'other',[14] so, I would argue, studies by Western scholars of the Eastern half of our continent have often been discoloured by deep-seated assumptions about the extent and permanence of Eastern Europe's 'otherness'. This is nothing new. Perhaps 'the alien East' in all its variants is an in-built necessity within the peculiar intellectual construct that is called Western civilisation. At all events, instead of the fair comparisons that I have just been recommending, it is all too easy to find a series of false, exaggerated or unwarranted contrasts between East and West. Again, I shall tender three or four examples, each drawn from a different social science.

The most extreme example that I have encountered comes from the realm of family history. In the 1970s, a group of Cambridge sociologists made their name by establishing a typology of family and household structures in the past. One of their collective studies, published in 1983, put forward a four-region hypothesis for family types across the whole of Europe in the nineteenth century. Based on data from four villages – Elmdon in Essex, Grossenmeer in north Germany, Fagagna in Lombardy and Krasnoe Sobakino in the depths of Russia – it purported to offer a refinement of an older scheme, said to be 'universally accepted', which had divided European families into two simple types, 'Western' and 'Eastern'. This latter scheme had given rise to something called the Leningrad–Trieste Line, to the west of which families were supposed to be relatively modern and increasingly nuclear, to the east of which families were supposed to be traditional and extended. Anything more artificial it would be hard to imagine.[15]

This is not a field which I am inclined to follow closely, and I trust that suitable modifications have been made in recent years. What I do know is that Eastern European social historians, who know their own countries well, often feel affronted by the casual not to say amateurish theorising of their ill-informed Western colleagues. The notion that one serf-bound Russian village could serve as the model for the intensely complex social conditions in countries as different as Latvia, Poland, Ukraine, Romania or Bulgaria is reductionism reduced to absurdity.

A strong sense of indignation of this sort can be discerned in a recent study of the Balkan *zadruga* or 'joint patrilinear household' by the Bulgarian scholar, Dr Maria Todorova. Dr Todorova, who once studied at St Antony's College, Oxford University, tears into the widespread assumption among Western sociologists that the *zadruga* has been the standard form of social organisation among the Balkan Slavs since time immemorial. *Zadruga*, she argues, is a Serbian neologism dating from only 1818. Its relevance to the pattern of family types in the Balkans is extremely patchy. It is common enough in the mountainous, stock-breeding zones of the Rhodopes, Macedonia, Bosnia, Montenegro and central Albania, and was present in sectors of the Serb Kraina in Croatia and among the non-Slavic Vlachs; but it is virtually unknown in most of Bulgaria, on the Adriatic littoral, in Greece or in Romania. In short, she suggests, the *zadruga* is a worthy partner to that other figment of the Western imagination, 'the Slav soul'.[16]

Another example of exaggerated contrasts between East and West comes from the field of economic history. Immanuel Wallerstein's thesis on 'the origins of a European world-economy' was published in 1974 at a time when another long-running academic debate over the Brenner thesis on 'Agrarian Class Structure in Pre-industrial Europe' was still in progress. Robert Brenner built his theory on a narrow foundation confined to England and France, but Wallerstein took a broader view, identifying a dominant core region in north-west Europe and a dependent periphery in the east. Using the techniques of systems theory, he argued that the core region had possessed only a slight advantage over the periphery, when the dependent relationship came into being in the fifteenth century. With time, however, favourable trading relations enabled Western entrepreneurs to exploit their advantages and to turn the 'slight edge' into a yawning gulf. They transformed the feudal nobility of the East into a client class of agrarian capitalists. What is more, they projected their economic power into the New World, where a zone of 'coercive, cash-crop capitalism' grew up in parallel to the corresponding zone in Eastern Europe.[17] I trust that is a fair summary.

It is my impression, however, that debates engendered by this sort of grand theorising rapidly degenerate into exchanges of technicalities more designed to keep professional historians amused than to establish a final resolution. Wallerstein substantiated his description of the periphery by examples drawn very largely from Poland, and from the work of communist Poland's official Marxist historians. Detailed criticism of his observations suggest that if the agrarian capitalists he describes existed at all in early modern Poland, they existed only in very circumscribed localities and for a rather limited period. In short, if the Polish-based foundations are full of holes, the entire theory is bound to leak copiously.

Nonetheless, what concerns me here is not Wallerstein's theory as such but rather the assumption that Eastern Europe as a whole – half the European continent – can be characterised by a small spread of samples from parts of just one country in a limited span of time. Once again, this is reductionism running wild. Personally, though unqualified to judge, I rather like Wallerstein's theory. But surely some of the main implications need stating. One is that the greater part of Eastern Europe in the early modern period lay beyond even the periphery of the world economic system. The second is that most of Western Europe lay well outside it as well. In other words, the areas of backwardness and dependence had very little correlation with either East or West.

Another example of false contrasts comes from political science, in particular from the rich and fashionable field of theories of nationalism. In recent years, a wide consensus has formed, putting modern nationalisms into one of two basic types. I myself chose to call these types state nationalism and popular nationalism, although numerous other labels can be found. As I see it, state nationalism refers to those movements where the ruling elite or establishment of a state seeks to imbue the population at large with the civic values, the political culture and the national identity that the elite prefers. France, the United Kingdom and above all the USA provide clear illustrations of this. Popular nationalism, on the other hand, refers to the opposite: to grass-root movements where the common people, or groups of people within the population, seek to create or to reinforce their culture, values and national identity against the aims and wishes of the state authorities. For this, I cite the instances of the Irish within the nineteenth-century United Kingdom and the Ukrainians within the Russian and Austrian empires.[18]

So far, so good. The trouble begins to arise from the fact that the commonest labels for these two types of nationalism are not 'state' and 'popular' or 'civic' and 'ethnic' (as I would equally approve) but – wait for it – 'western' and 'eastern'. What is more, the political scientists who propagate the dichotomy of western and eastern nationalisms have a marked proclivity for adding their own value judgements. Western or civic nationalism is allegedly constructive, progressive, peaceful and stabilising. Eastern or ethnic nationalism is presented as destructive, regressive, disruptive, divisive and destabilising, not to say murderous, xenophobic, anti-Semitic, hateful and generally nasty.

I first encountered this model of nationalism in the works and lectures of Dr John Plamenatz, who taught at Oxford in my student days. I now know that it has a much longer pedigree, traceable, I am told, to Friedrich Meinecke in the 1920s, and elaborated by Hans Kohn, Louis Snyder, Ernest Gellner and Anthony Smith, and others.[19] Plamenatz was born in Montenegro, and I have a sneaking suspicion that his views may have been coloured by a half-remembered and rejected association with the land which he had left. At all events, he recorded his reasons for adopting the label 'eastern nationalism' in these words: 'What I call eastern nationalism has flourished among the Slavs as well as in Africa and Asia, and . . . also in Latin America. I could not call it non-European and have thought it best to call it eastern because it first appeared to the east of Western Europe.'[20] What a gem! 'I couldn't call it non-European,' he says. But he would have done if he could possibly have got away with it! 'East European' is classed with African, Asian and Latin American.

Plamenatz, who stressed the culture factor, went on to define his view of western nationalism by reference to Germans and Italians, who, he said, were 'culturally well equipped':

> They had languages adapted . . . to progressive civilisation. They had universities and schools . . . imparting the skills prized by that civilisation. They had . . . philosophers, scientists, artists and poets . . . of world reputation. They had legal, medical and other professions . . . with high . . . standards. To put themselves on a level with the English and the French, they had little need to equip themselves culturally by appropriating what was alien to them . . .[21]

Is the message clear? 'The case with the Slavs,' concluded Plamenatz, 'as with the Africans and Asians, has been quite different.'[22]

One should not speak ill of the dead, but I know that I can cause Dr Plamenatz no embarrassment. Which Slavs did he have in mind, I wonder – apart, that is, from the Montenegrins. Certainly not the Poles or the Russians. And which languages? Polish was an established literary and governmental language in the sixteenth century, before even German was.

And which universities? Presumably he knew that the universities of Prague (founded 1348) and Cracow (founded 1364) are both senior to Vienna, Heidelberg, Cologne, Leipzig, Freiburg, Tübingen, Göttingen, Berlin or Munich? And which philosophers, scientists, artists and poets? Take Comenius, Copernicus, Chopin and Pushkin for a start. Please excuse me, but a more cockeyed and patronising view of European culture would be hard to find.

The really odd thing, though, if one seriously applies the prevailing typology of nationalism to Europe east and west, is that one finds the best example of eastern-type ethnic nationalism emerged in Ireland, the most westerly of western nations. And the largest example of state-sponsored, western-type nationalism is to be found in Russia. Stalin, after all, considered himself very progressive; and he seduced a distressing number of Western intellectuals into thinking likewise.

The last example comes from ethno-religious studies, and in particular from the field of Christian–Jewish relations. For obvious reasons, anti-Semitism and its history has become a major topic for study and discussion in recent decades. And quite right, too. Yet one can hardly say that it is always discussed in a fair or impartial manner, especially as concerns its geographical distribution. The fact is: anti-Semitism has been rife in Western Europe for centuries, whilst for a long period it hardly existed at all in the east. In Russia, for example, there was no Jewish settlement and hence no anti-Semitism prior to the late eighteenth century. The Jews were unceremoniously expelled from England in the thirteenth century, from Germany in the fourteenth century, from France on several occasions, especially in the early fifteenth century, and from Spain at the turn of the sixteenth century. Throughout this long era, they were invited to settle in Poland-Lithuania, until the old Polish Commonwealth became by far the largest refuge for Jews in the world. Prior to the abolition of the commonwealth, they enjoyed far-reaching autonomy, including their own parliament, and freedom of religious practice. Indeed, this large Polish-Jewish community mainly stayed in place right up to the Second World War, even though it had frequently passed under the rule of the Russian, Austrian or German empires, and in the modern period it largely avoided the mass pogroms that were perpetrated in Russia and Ukraine. It was finally destroyed

FAIR COMPARISONS, FALSE CONTRASTS

during the Holocaust of 1941–5, when the organs of the German Nazi party and of the German state used German-occupied Poland as the site for their genocidal killing fields. Yet which among the nations of Europe is routinely labelled as being 'incorrigibly' or 'historically' or 'traditionally' anti-Semitic? Who, according to an Israeli prime minister, 'imbibes anti-Semitism with their mothers' milk'? I can tell you the answer is not the Germans, who perpetrated the Holocaust, or the Russians, who were largely responsible for the worst of the pogroms. What is more, one can state with confidence that this cruel slander obstructs all rational analysis of the subject. No informed person can argue that anti-Semitism has *not* been a stain on modern Poland or that 'Polish anti-Semitism' is somehow the invention of 'anti-Polonites'. At the same time, no one should be allowed to get away with loose talk about 'Polish concentration camps' or of Poles as a 'collaborator nation'. There is a limit to which honest language can be stretched. The facts are: that wartime Poland was an Allied nation, unwaveringly loyal to the struggle against the Third Reich; that the Poles raised the largest anti-Nazi underground army in Europe, which fought the German occupiers, particularly during the Warsaw Rising of 1944, with unparalleled heroism; and finally, that despite the forced segregation of Jews in their Nazi-built ghettos, the Poles supplied a record number of 'Righteous among the Nations', honoured at Yad Vashem for their courage and humanity in rescuing Jews. The balance sheet is not as the stereotypers would have us believe. And fair comparisons in these matters, as in all others, are essential if accurate conclusions are to be reached.[23]

By all accounts, the trend whereby Western social scientists pondered the patterns and sources of the innately retrograde nature of Eastern Europe reached its culmination in a conference held on the beautiful shores of Lake Como at Bellagio in 1985. The conference was dedicated to 'The Origins of Backwardness in Eastern Europe' and its centrepiece was apparently a paper by Hampstead's leading communist luminary, Eric Hobsbawm, which contrasted the development of Switzerland with that of Albania.[24] If ever there was a loaded comparison, this was it. No doubt Good King Zog missed his cue by not launching cuckoo clocks and numbered bank accounts!

*

For the historian, the prime question must be to explore how these tendentious attitudes arose. What are the roots and motors of a mindset which seems to distort so much of contemporary thinking? I have found ten headings, best discussed in chronological order.

1. The concept of a gulf dividing the civilised west from the barbarous east in Europe is at least as old as the Greeks and Romans. As Dr Edith Hall has shown so convincingly, the crystallisation of Greek identity in the Persian Wars of the fifth century BC went hand in hand with 'the invention of the barbarian' as the alien outsider.[25] And that alien barbarian could be a refined, sophisticated Persian or Indian, not just a wild Scythian nomad of the early steppes. The same mental divide was set in stone by the Romans when they built the empire's *limes*, with civilisation inside the lines and savage barbarism beyond. It declined and fell no doubt as the empire did, but it was reborn and restored by Renaissance scholars and by the generations of Europeans who, from the sixteenth to the early twentieth century received a classical education. It is hard to deny that for all its glories the classical tradition contained a set of dismissive judgements about non-classical cultures. As a close colleague of mine put it, 'It was this particular encounter [of Greeks and barbarians] that began the idea of "Europe" with all its arrogance, all its implications of superiority, all its assumptions of priority and antiquity, all its pretensions to a natural right to dominate.'[26]

2. When the Roman empire adopted Christianity, the division between civilisation and the barbarian world was supplanted by a new division between Christendom and paganism. The thousand-year process of Christianising pagan Europe, from the fifth to the fifteenth centuries, could not fail to leave a deep imprint. Christianity came from the south and west; the last bastions of paganism lay in the north, in Scandinavia, or in the east. The final pagan stronghold, in Teutonic Lithuania, held out until 1418. One of the curiosities of this story lies in the sleight of hand whereby the modern descendants of pagan, barbarian invaders like the English and the Magyars who had destroyed the Christian civilisation of the countries they invaded, nonetheless appropriated the Romano-Christian tradition as their own. On this point, look carefully at Holman Hunt's painting in the Ashmolean entitled *A Converted British Family Sheltering a Christian Missionary from the Persecution of the Druids* (1850).[27]

3. Yet European Christendom has never been fully united. The separate customs of the Latin and Greek Churches hardened by 1054 into a permanent schism. This 'scandal in Christ' has not yet been healed. Repeated attempts to end the schism, from the Council of Florence onwards, have failed. Militant attitudes towards the East in Counter-Reformation Catholicism have been matched by the xenophobic stance of the Russian Orthodox Church, which was created as a separate patriarchate by Ivan the Terrible in the late sixteenth century as an arm of Muscovite expansion. No strand in this theme is more pitiful than that of the Greek-Catholic Uniates, who chose to combine their non-Russian Orthodox tradition with loyalty to the Roman pope. They were forcibly suppressed at every stage of Russia's advance, from the first Muscovite conquest of Kiev from Poland in 1662 to Stalin's capture of western Ukraine at the end of the Second World War.[28] More recently, nothing better illustrates the persistent bitterness of Europe's ancient religious divide than the war in Bosnia.

4. The Enlightenment of the eighteenth century was deeply imbued with a sense of Western superiority over the East. Indeed, a brilliant study by the American scholar Larry Wolff has argued that it is the *philosophes* of the Enlightenment who must be held responsible for inventing the synthetic intellectual construct called Eastern Europe. This construct encapsulates all the West's negative stereotypes of the East and exerts an insidious influence to this day.[29] The Enlightenment coincided with a period of history when one of the largest states of Eastern Europe, Poland-Lithuania, was in terminal decline, when the Ottoman empire still overlay most of the Balkans, and when serfdom was still in place, even in Prussia and Austria. As a result, the stream of travellers' tales retailed in France or Britain contained a melange of the repulsive and the exotic. 'Swarms of Jews', peasant hovels, dirt, wolves and lice were among the universal complaints.[30] But much of it was sheer prejudice. When the Marquis de Ségur railed bitterly in 1789 over the state of the lavatory in his Warsaw hotel, he did so as if Versailles were fitted with flush toilets. Similarly, the notorious libertine Giovanni Casanova, who bought a slave girl for his pleasure in St Petersburg in 1764 for 100 roubles, complained of the brutality of the Russian knout as if the penal principles of the Marquis Beccaria, newly published in that same year, were somehow the norm back

home. Anyone who has read Michel Foucault's sickening account of the torture and dismemberment of Robert Damiens in Paris in 1757 will know that barbaric cruelty was hardly an Eastern monopoly.[31]

No less influential were the widely publicised opinions of the Enlightenment's most representative figures. (Rousseau and Herder, who both expressed interest in and admiration for Eastern Europe, were exceptions to the rule.) Edward Gibbon, who never set foot east of Switzerland, loved to make play of the 'despicable' peoples of the East. Diderot, who travelled once to St Petersburg, used the occasion to flatter the despotism of Catherine the Great. And Voltaire, who never travelled beyond Berlin, fantasised to great effect about the misery and bigotry of the nations in order to justify the depredations of his patrons in Potsdam and the Peterhof.[32] His *History of Charles XII* (1731) presented a detailed and colourful account of the Swedish campaigns in the Baltic, Poland and Ukraine with little attention to verity while his mordant jokes mocked the laws and customs of the region. Yet no one was so unkind or so unfair as Frederick the Great, who joined the mockery of his *philosophe* friends with relish. He once talked of 'that multitude of imbeciles whose names end in —ski'. On the eve of the First Partition of Poland in 1771, he talked of a country 'that has not changed since the Creation':

> La même encore qu'à la Création
> Brute, stupide, et sans instruction
> Staroste, juif, serf, palatin ivrogne,
> Tous végétaux qui vivaient sans vergogne.[33]

One does not have to ask with what *ivrogne* and *vergogne* are intended to rhyme.

The final word must rest with an American visitor, John Ledyard, who in 1788 compared Poland favourably with Russia only to contrast it mercilessly with 'those Angels of Civilisation in the Godlike regions of the West'.[34] Much of this crude Western bias stuck. The East was the defenceless outsider against which the Enlightenment defined its own achievements. And the influence of the Enlightenment is still alive today.

5. The prejudices of the Enlightenment were greatly reinforced by two

interlinked developments of the nineteenth century, industrialisation and imperialism. It is indisputable that socio-economic modernisation proceeded faster and further in certain parts of north-western Europe than anywhere in the east, so for those who think that economics constitutes the main criterion of civilised life, the countries of Eastern Europe can easily be dismissed as incurably backward. It is also indisputable that, with the exception of Russia, all the great colonial empires of the nineteenth century were based in Western Europe. This fact served to propagate the notion of historic and unhistoric nations, some of them, mainly in the west, born to rule, and others, mainly in the east, born, like the Irish, to be assimilated. Europe's empires may have passed away, but many of the entrenched attitudes of the imperial legacy are still with us. The greater the empire, the longer its aftershadows.

6. Throughout modern Europe, misguided concepts of race have exercised a powerful influence on the way Europeans think about themselves and others. Although the old pseudoscientific racial theories have been discredited for good by the excesses of fascist racism during the Second World War and by the rise of modern genetics since the discovery of DNA in 1953, nonetheless I suspect that popular attitudes can often lag behind scientific advances and that a residue of racial and ethnic prejudice still operates. After 200 years of misinformation it could hardly be otherwise. In the United States it appears that the pseudo-racial classifications of Professor Johann Friedrich Blumenbach, first presented in Göttingen in 1797, are still alive and well. One has to remember that the racial ravings of the Nazis were solidly grounded in long-standing Western scholarship and in widespread eugenic theories. Their repellent association of Jews with dirt and disease, for example, follows that long line of travellers' tales chronicled by Professor Wolff. Their false identification of the Slavs as a racial group, classed as a sub-category of *Untermenschen*, had many antecedents from the Enlightenment onwards. Even the great Gibbon could not resist that one. His description of the Slavs living 'like beavers' in the watery wastes of the east[35] is a nice parallel to the phoney contention, still found in *The Times Atlas of World History*, that the Slavs originated in the Pripet Marshes,[36] or to the English habit of thinking of the Irish as 'bog-dwellers'.

Two quotations almost 200 years apart will make the point. One opinion, published by a Frenchman dismissed from the Polish army in 1780, described the Poles as 'the orang-utans of Europe': 'The Pole', he opined, is 'the worst, the most contemptible, the vilest, the most hateful, the most dishonourable, the dumbest, the filthiest, the falsest, the most cowardly creation *among the apes*.'[37] A second, from the leader of Germany, was uttered in October 1939: 'The Führer's verdict on the Poles,' reported Goebbels, 'is damning. More like animals than human beings, completely primitive and amorphous. And a ruling class that is an unsatisfactory result of mingling between the lower orders and the Aryan master-race. The Poles' dirtiness is unimaginable. Their capacity for intelligent judgement . . . absolutely nil.'[38] This drivel can best be countered by the famous Polish observation about the Aryan master race – 'as tall as Goebbels, as slim as Göring, as blond as Hitler'.

7. Unfortunately, one has to admit that many East Europeans, especially the intelligentsia, have often adopted Western prejudices for themselves. It has long been the fashion for Poles, Czechs, Hungarians and Romanians to look to Paris, London, Berlin or New York for their models of excellence, whilst despising or ignoring their neighbours in the east. Here again west was automatically equated with best.

8. These habits of thought have been greatly magnified by the huge waves of migration from Eastern Europe in the nineteenth and twentieth centuries. Successful migrants tended to cultivate the culture, language and values of their adopted countries with enthusiasm, whilst keeping no more than a mythological memory about their countries of origin. One fascinating study about immigrants to North America, for instance, explains how America's immigrant society set up the East European as a stereotype of 'the alien other'.[39] This finding coincides very much with my own observations of numerous American books and academic courses on so-called Western civilisation, which are almost totally lacking in an East European element. The point here is, whilst the starving Irish or Sicilian peasants who flocked to America in the mid-nineteenth century differed little from the subsequent wave of starving Poles and Ukrainians, Britain and Italy have not been struck off the American syllabus as countries about which contemporary students may remain uninformed. Another study, this time of Jewish immigrants to imperial Germany, shows not only how Central European Jews assimilated with

great alacrity into German language and culture, but also how assimilated German Jews turned their backs with distaste on the traditional, ultra-religious *Ostjuden* of Poland, Russia and Ukraine.[40]

9. The Allied victory in 1945 clearly affected attitudes to Eastern Europe in a major way. On the one hand, it reconfirmed the pre-war impression that the smaller nations of the East were too weak and fractious to stand on their own feet. Few people in the West drew the concomitant conclusion that the Western powers had proved too weak to defend their East European partners and clients. At the same time, in the euphoria of victory the Western powers had no interest in advertising the salient facts of the war in Europe – namely that the great bulk of the fighting against Hitler had been shouldered by the Soviet army (which inflicted 75 per cent of the *Wehrmacht*'s casualties) and that the great Stalin, the ally to whom in large measure we owed our victory, was implicated in mass crimes on a scale not inferior to those of the defeated enemy. The military and moral dilemmas posed by Soviet conduct were so acute that the line of least resistance for the West in 1945 was to write Eastern Europe off as a hopeless case.

One East European country, significantly, was *not* written off. It has been well argued that the Western leaders were preconditioned to abandon Eastern Europe to Stalin at Yalta and Potsdam because 200 years of cultural propaganda had desensitised Western opinion to the loss of Warsaw, Budapest or Sofia. But Athens was a different matter. The mythology of Western civilisation insisted that Greece was 'ours'. Greece was not seen as Eastern, alien, exotic or backward, and she had to be saved at all costs. In the Percentages Agreement of 1944, Churchill made Greece the sole exception. In his Fulton Speech in 1946, where he warned of the Iron Curtain, he also boasted that 'Greece with its immortal glories is free'.[41] Similar sentiments were expressed forty years later to support Greece's entry to the European Community.

10. Nonetheless, nothing reinforced the negative image of Eastern Europe so effectively as the Cold War. For four long decades, a new 'Western world' developed under American hegemony in direct confrontation with the Soviet Bloc on the other side of the Iron Curtain. Two whole generations of westerners grew up with little direct contact and still less understanding of Europe's eastern half. For these were the generations

when west Europeans were taught to believe that they alone were the true Europeans, when they basked complacently in their new-found affluence, and when in common parlance 'Europe' was taken to refer exclusively to the (west European) Common Market, to the (west) European Economic Community or to a narrow, parochial (west) European Union. Still worse, these were the generations when the social sciences rose to a prominent position in the study and analysis of European affairs, and when, as a result, the ephemeral political, social and economic systems imposed on Eastern Europe were made to look and to feel permanent. I may be wrong but, for all its virtues, my strong impression is that the social science approach was lacking in two important dimensions. One of the deficiencies relates to a weak sense of history, the other to a limited awareness of the independent, self-perpetuating power of culture – including religion, literature and national traditions. In varying degrees, in different countries it is these cultural traditions which pre-dated, resisted, undermined and in the end outlived the artificial grafts of communism.

Yet these were exactly the cultures pushed into the backwaters of Western consciousness. Any number of prestigious, well-funded 'schools of European studies' grew up with no interest beyond the principal languages and cultures of Western Europe. Any number of history graduates were produced who had immersed themselves deeply in courses of so-called European history but who could not tell you the first thing about the histories of the Baltic States, Poland, Bohemia, Hungary or the Balkans. Where Eastern Europe was studied at all, it was studied in small, over-specialised and above all separate institutions which lived behind an intellectual Iron Curtain of their own. Every Western country has had its 'Slavic departments', its 'Slavonic schools' and its *instituts de langues-O'* – where Eastern Europe was put on a par with the Orient, where experts laboured not only in isolation from European studies as a whole, but also in danger of ingestion by the dominant Russian interest. Many are the so-called Slavic departments, especially in the United States, where Russian and Russian alone is taught and where the dictates of tsarist pan-Slavism are still observed. It is only the most enlightened universities, like Oxford, where the title 'Professor of European History' can be bestowed on a distinguished scholar of Hungarian and Habsburg history, who is given to conversing in Welsh.[42]

Not surprisingly, therefore, it was left to intellectuals from the half-forgotten cultures of the Soviet Bloc to insist that 'Europe' had a wider and deeper meaning than the West imagined. The revival of the concept of Central Europe was launched by the Czech writer Milan Kundera in the mid-1980s as an antidote to the ethos of the Soviet Bloc. And it was an English writer now in Oxford, Timothy Garton Ash, who publicised the event most effectively.[43]

If I may, I will interpose a brief personal anecdote to illustrate the estrangement which grew up between Western social scientists and the realities of Eastern Europe. In 1986 I guided a large group of students from Stanford University in California on a month's visit to Cracow in Poland. All the students had been thoroughly briefed by the Political Science Department on the 'communist system', and all had to write up a project paper. One eager young woman had chosen a project which involved interviewing members of the ruling communist party on their beliefs. After a week, she complained to me that she couldn't find anyone in Cracow who would admit to being a communist. I told her to keep looking. At the end of the month, she actually cornered a member of the Polish politburo and cabinet minister, and she put the question to him direct: 'Sir, are you a communist or not?' There was a deathly silence before he replied, '*Proszę Panią, ja jestem pragmatykiem*' – Dear lady, I'm a pragmatist.

At all events, the net result of our experiences during the Cold War was something close to a black hole in the east which was known only superficially and which all too often was simply avoided. If anything was more damaging than the hostile image of Eastern Europe, it was the well-established convention of ignoring Eastern Europe completely. I have likened this convention to that of writing a textbook of human anatomy which makes no mention of the right leg. Any number of textbooks and courses gave themselves the label 'European history' whilst bypassing one half of the subject in its entirety. I can see no justification for this policy. I can't decide whether to call it one-legged, one-sided or one-eyed.

I shall confine myself to one of the most blatant examples – written by a Frenchman, subsidised by the European Commission and published in 1989. Jean-Baptiste Duroselle's *Europe: A History of Its Peoples* took the twelve members of the then EEC as the basis of his study and projected his selection back into the past. Fortunately, the Cold War ended just as the book was published; the political division of Europe collapsed; and this strange, one-eyed, Western perception of Europe collapsed with it.[44]

In discussing East and West in modern European history, I have presented you, magpie-fashion, with numerous specific, shiny examples. But an attempt should be made to outline a number of general conclusions.

Firstly, in exploring a subject which the Enlightenment called 'philosophical geography', one has to put aside the physical map of Europe, or at least to treat it with considerable elasticity. For on the mental map which people carry in their heads Western Europe and Eastern Europe are not just determined by points of the compass. They are terms of orientation in a shifting intellectual landscape, where all bearings are relative and paradoxes abound. In this vein, I once heard a Pole trying to explain why 'Poland was a Western country which happened to be in Eastern Europe'.

In the last analysis, a great deal turns on one's definition of 'backwardness'. If one takes the materialist view, in which civilisation is measured in terms of GNP, technology or standards of living, then most parts of Europe east of the Elbe have undoubtedly trailed many (though not all) parts of Western Europe. It is exactly in this economic sphere that the Soviet east imposed its own ideology of historical materialism and failed utterly in its own terms. Yet I see no good reason why economic or materialist criteria should be accepted as the main, let alone the sole mark of success. Surely, civilisation, enlightenment and human well-being have to be gauged against a much wider spectrum of values. Societies which have been led to believe that 'lifestyle' or the economic 'feel-good factor' constitute the ultimate goal are sorely mistaken. The European Union, if it continues to give priority to economic and monetary matters, is heading nowhere. It is a nice irony, but sixty years of deprivation under fascism and communism gave the peoples of the former Soviet Bloc not just a taste for the good life but also a more rounded vision of the Europe to which they wish to return.

Secondly, to compare and to contrast is an essential part of the historian's craft. It is only by gauging differences and similarities that we can put our judgements into focus. I have talked elsewhere of overspecialisation as the *déformation professionelle* of contemporary historians, and geographical parochialism is one aspect of that failing. Nor is it a sin confined to specialists in Western Europe. There is nothing more parochial than the outlook of that substantial cohort of the Sovietological or Russianist confraternity which rarely learned any language other than Russian, which takes no interest in the rich plurality of cultures within Russia itself and which never lifts its gaze beyond the gilded roofs of the Kremlin.

In this regard, historians of the so-called small nations or minor cultures possess a distinct advantage. They have no choice but to study the affairs of the great powers, which dominate neighbouring peoples. Historians of the great powers, however, like the statesmen of great powers, don't always feel the need to reciprocate and to interest themselves in the goings-on of the lesser fry. Yet it is a simple fact that within the great diversity of Europe the throng of less powerful nations is more numerous, and in that sense more representative, than the small circle of the high and mighty. And to comprehend diversity, comparisons are essential.

Thirdly, by insisting on the eastern component of European history, one is not necessarily making a value judgement. One is not saying that east European music is more or less melodious, that east European literature is more or less profound, or that east European agriculture is more or less perfumed. The contention is very simple: that the east European component exists and cannot be ignored.

For ignorance takes its toll. One of the more unpleasant consequences of the low public awareness of Eastern Europe is that numerous demeaning collective stereotypes can circulate with impunity, even in academic work. Just as not so very long ago all Welshmen were thieves and all Jews swindlers, so one still hears collective slurs go unchallenged about east Europeans being peasants or anti-Semites, about Poles being work-shy, Romanians vagrants, or Ukrainians being wartime collaborators. If only the truth were known, what is remarkable is how few of the forty million-plus Ukrainians actively collaborated with the Nazis, compared with, say, the Danes, the Dutch or the Belgians. On this score, the full list of volunteer Waffen SS divisions is a good starting-point for discussion.[45]

In reviewing *Europe: A History*, one critic started a hare by claiming that I had equated East with West.[46] That is not so. There is no such equation. All there is, is juxtaposition, where appropriate, and comparison. The instance given proves my point, I think. It was said that I had equated the events surrounding the Polish constitution of 1791 with the events of the French Revolution. Well, I hadn't. All I did was to indicate that events in Warsaw, like those in Brussels and Amsterdam and indeed in the Dauphiné were, alongside the events in Versailles and Paris, part of the terminal, continent-wide crisis of the *ancien régime*. Proportions here are important. The Polish constitution of 1791, with Burke's eulogy of it, was allotted forty-five lines in a chapter of eighty-two pages on the French Revolution – in other words, 1.22 per cent.[47] That is probably about right.

Finally, I should stress that by expounding the resonances of east and west in modern Europe, I do not discount the reverberations of other axes or of other geographical patterns – the relationship between north and south, for instance, or that between the margins and the centre, between various cores and peripheries. Thanks to the particular layout of the European peninsula and its contiguity with Eurasia, I do hold that the dynamics of the east–west axis are particularly important. But it is not the only one. Here, I would give the last word to the great Goethe. I mentioned earlier that derogatory Western attitudes to Eastern Europe have sometimes been likened to similar Western attitudes to the Islamic or Arabic Orient. So a few cautionary lines from Goethe's *Orientalische Divan* may be specially fitting:

> Gottes ist der Orient!
> Gottes ist der Okzident!
> Nord- und südliches Gelände
> Ruht im Frieden seiner Hände.[48]

> God's is the east!
> God's is the west!
> Northerly and southerly lands
> All of them rest in the peace of his hands.

The intellectual construct of 'Eastern Europe' has been present throughout modern times. Invented by the ancients and elaborated by the Enlightenment, it saw its greatest revival during the late and unlamented Cold War. To echo the sentiments of Churchill's Fulton speech once again, 'The dark line of the Iron Curtain was drawn on the maps of the mind.'[49] 'The shadowed lands of backwardness, even barbarism' were conjured up like chiaroscura to highlight those 'godlike regions of the West'. But today the Iron Curtain has collapsed, and the shadows are shortening. At last, there is reason to hope that the mental divisions of Europe can now dissolve, that the pernicious perceptual chasm between East and West will soon become a mere historical curiosity.

III

WESTERN CIVILISATION VERSUS EUROPEAN HISTORY[1]

LIKE many people, I had always assumed that 'Western Civilisation' and 'European History' were more or less the same thing. I gradually became convinced that they are conflicting, and incompatible concepts. What, one might ask, is Western civilisation? Whatever it is, it is not in my considered view an honest attempt to convey a full sense either of European history or of European civilisation. On the contrary, it is something that is highly reductive and shamelessly selective. It may be unwise to present the answer before the arguments substantiating it have been discussed. But, from all the evidence, Western civilisation is a metaphysical construct, an ideology, a conceit, an identity game, an intellectual invention designed to promote the interests of its inventors. It abstracts everything from Europe's past that is compliant with those interests, and consigns the rest to oblivion. If one wanted to be mischievous, one could say that it was neither western nor civilised.

My introduction to the phenomenon occurred in the early 1990s when I went to New York to talk to the editors of my forthcoming book, *Europe: A History*. The editors were keen to impress on me the size of the American market in the field and they showed me an old card index listing some 4000 colleges and universities in the USA where 'Western civ' was taught. They also explained that the market was in turmoil due to the widespread student revolt against the courses, and that all publishers were waiting and praying for the 'golden tome' that would fill the growing gap.

As a result, I made a number of forays into New York bookstores, both new and second-hand, and within a couple of days I had collected between thirty and forty textbooks all directed in one way or another at 'Western civ'. They varied from slim, succinct items to elaborate, multi-volume works containing both prepared readings and thematic commentaries. I cannot possibly recall all the titles, but a sample from my notes has produced the following:

- W.H. McNeill, *History of Western Civilisation: A Handbook*
- R.E. Herzstein, *Western Civilization*
- John B. Harrison et al., *A Short History of Western Civilization*
- J. Russell Major, *Civilization in the Western World*
- J. Kelly Sowards (ed.), *Makers of the Western Tradition*
- R.M. Golden, *A Social History of Western Civilisation*
- F. Roy Willis, *Western Civilization*
- Mark Kishlansky, *Civilization in the West*
- Marvin Perry, *Western Civilization: Ideas, Politics and Society*
- Glenn Blackburn, *Western Civilization: A Concise History*
- R.I. Greaves, *Civilisations of the West* (2 vols)[2]

Reading through these textbooks was nothing short of fascinating, but fascinating in the main for what one couldn't find. For example, there was very little, if anything, about the United States. There were periodic references to Christopher Columbus and to European overseas expansion, but it was clear that these were not studies of today's 'Western world' and how it came together. The focus was very obviously European, and narrowly European. Yet most of Europe was missing – vanished, AWOL! I remember wondering how a publisher out of Boston could possibly produce a history book that said nothing about Ireland or the Irish. One might have thought that an editor from New York, formerly New Amsterdam, might have included a bit about the Netherlands or about Dutch civilisation, but where Holland might have been there was a blank. At the start of my own student career I had been told to read Gibbon's *Decline and Fall of the Roman Empire*, which covers all the ground between the Emperor Augustus and the fall of Constantinople to the Turks in 1453. But where in these American textbooks was Byzantium? The answer was nowhere, or perhaps as an afterthought in Chapter 32. It was all extremely odd. It's not just that there were many omissions. Far more was omitted than was included.

It was equally obvious that the propagators of 'Western civilisation' had never made the mental effort to define their subject. William McNeill, for example, who was a very respected figure among American historians, uses 'Western civilisation' interchangeably with terms such as 'the civilisation of Western Europe' or 'European civilisation' or 'our civilisation' or 'European history'. In his chronological scheme, he relies on two main distinctions: 'Classical civilisation' and then, from *c*. AD 900, 'European civilisation', the latter being equated with 'Western Christendom'.[3] One is tempted to pose the old question, 'Where is Rome, and where is home?'h

Some time later, I made the attempt to acquaint myself a little with the background of what was evidently a major feature of American educational practices. I found out about the original Great Books Seminar, which had been organised at Columbia University in 1921 by Professor J. Erskine and which was transferred from Columbia to Chicago in 1930 by J. Mortimer Adler. This seminar was organised round a list of 104 authors which supposedly formed the canon of Western civilisation, and another list of 102 ideas, which provided the essential subject matter. The former started with 'Homer, Old Testament, Aeschylus and Sophocles ...' The latter proceeded from 'Angel, Animal and Aristocracy ...' to 'Wealth, Will, Wisdom and World'.[4] The list had been revised and expanded over the years, but two things were self-evident. Firstly, the content matter was overwhelmingly English, French, Greek, Latin and German – in that order of priority. And secondly, the seminars had become a widely imitated staple of the US university system. In effect, they were the ancestors of the very popular and widespread course called 'Western Civ 101'. They reminded me of another discovery made during that visit to New York – namely a condensed crib sheet of the entire contents of human knowledge crammed onto two sides of a pink plastic board.

Both the textbooks and the Great Books Scheme reeked of drastic selectivity. Yet the selectivity was not random. After a while, one became aware of a pattern of preferences, not to say of prejudices, that was repeated over and over again. Three processes could be observed: reductionism, excision and relentless glorification.

As I know very well from my own experience, no historical survey, no synthesis, no compact summary of history, can be designed without reducing the infinite accretions of the past to simplified schemes. Authors cannot follow all the byways. And excessive detail soon becomes a burden. The task is to decide what the main topics are, and what weight is to be given to each of them. And to this end the criteria for making choices become crucial. What is more, it is reasonable to accept that if the results of the choices are the same, the criteria by which they were made are likely to have been the same. So it can be no accident that the contents pages of the textbooks of Western civilisation are remarkably similar. Typically they include: Ancient Greece and Rome, the Judaeo-Christian Tradition, the Germanic Invasions, Latin Christendom, the Italian Renaissance and the continental Reformation, the Scientific Revolution, Absolutism and Enlightenment, the Romantic Movement, the French and Russian Revolutions, and Modern Art. At first sight, this can look fair enough until one realises what has been rejected.

The purging of unwanted topics appears to be pursued both by geographical and by arbitrary judgement. On the one hand a huge bias operates in favour of western and southern Europe to the detriment of northern, eastern, central and east central Europe. Russia is often the only eastern country to warrant a mention, and one would have to ask why. On the other hand, automatic priority is given to positive and uplifting aspects of the past, whilst negative or disturbing subjects are systematically avoided. The end product tends to be very curious – physically deformed yet mindlessly benign.

Let me use just one example: the history of Christianity in Europe. One knows that it is pretty complicated, but if one confines oneself to the Catholic and the Protestant strands and forgets the Orthodox story altogether, one cannot possibly claim to be drawing even a recognisably accurate caricature. Similarly, if one sketches out the theology of the Church Fathers, or the wonderful growth of monasticism, cathedrals and universities but forgets to mention the persecution of heretics, the Crusades and the degrading frequency of religious wars, one is not giving elementary justice to a serious subject.

Almost all educators of young children would agree that they should be encouraged to adopt a positive view of the world. Purveyors of 'heritage' also follow the same line, presenting a homogenised, quaint and dinky view of the past for the benefit of tourists and pensioners. One might have hoped, therefore, that study at university level might be willing to take a rather more sophisticated approach. After all, if real history is not made up exactly of Gibbon's recipe of the crimes and follies of mankind, it is a very mixed bag containing a fair share of conflicts, pain and distress. Yet everything points to the fact that 'Western civilisation' shuns a realistic image of Europe's past, preferring instead a mail-order catalogue of all that is wise, beautiful and strong.

Of course, there may be a case for the wise and the beautiful if one is studying aesthetics. Few people will see much sense in studying stupid philosophers or ugly art – even though the promotion of beauty isn't art's sole purpose. Yet it is not appropriate if one is seeking a realistic view of the past. For the key sense which Western civilisation sharpens is admiration for strength and power. The more one thinks of it, 'Western civ' is a power cult. Its business is that of publicising powerful states and powerful cultures, and, by extension, of depreciating all others. The reason why the spotlight is constantly shone on England, Germany and France is not because they are 'Western' but because they were the imperial powers of the day when 'Western civ' was invented. And since they all happened to be located in Western Europe – or rather in a particular part of Western Europe – 'the West' has become a synonym for 'the seat of power' and is duly lauded.

Several things flow from this realisation. One is that 'the West' does not really mean the west. It is not a purely geographical expression but belongs more to the distorted mental map of those who imagine it. One can do a simple test. Take the three countries on Europe's western border – Portugal, Ireland and Norway – then see what role they play in those schemes of Western civilisation. The answer is virtually none – because they were not perceived as powerful or influential, and hence could be safely dismissed.

'Europe of the powers' is an old idea, and is not lacking in reality. In the eighteenth and nineteenth centuries the balance of power supplied the guiding principle of international relations. Only those states which could compete militarily and politically took part, and they alone sent representatives to the various diplomatic 'Concerts of Europe' that determined the fate of the continent. All other states were the passive objects of the powers' decisions. In this context, it does make sense to describe modern international relations in terms of the wars and treaties of the established powers.

At least – and these are important reservations – one must concede that powers rise and fall and that countries possessing the rank of 'great power' were in the very nature of things untypical. Any faithful picture of Europe's past must shine the spotlight on different powers in different periods – on Spain and Portugal in their 'golden age', on Poland in its time, on Sweden, on Austria, on France, and on Britain and Russia only in modern times. Also, if the aim is to give a sense of the whole, it must pay some attention to countries which at any given moment were in decline or were of necessity clients of the great.

European culture, however, poses a very different proposition. Here, variety and diversity are of the essence. Although some cultures like Greek, Latin, French and in recent times English have exerted exceptional influence, one cannot possibly reduce the rest to a rump selection. Italian, for example, the fruit of the established vernaculars, had launched a wonderful literature in the pages of Dante, Petrarch and Boccaccio long before French, German and English had crystallised into their final form. In later centuries it was less influential. (To their credit, the authors of the 'Great Books' do at least include Dante.) Polish culture, too, was an early starter with a Renaissance pedigree and a broad sphere of influence. The point is: what is a survey of Western civilisation trying to demonstrate? If it aims to trace the roots of English, French and German greatness, or to outline the cultural interests of late imperial Englishmen, Frenchmen and Germans, it is on the right track. If it wants to explain what the European cultural scene looked like at various stages of its development, then it falls seriously short of requirements.

However, a further consideration would seem to be crucial. It is surely the case that the design of the Western civilisation scheme corresponds very closely to the prejudices of the American academics who created it in the early twentieth century. This was still the era in the USA of the WASP elite. The focus on modern English traditions – as opposed to those of the Catholic Irish, for example, or those of the pre-Reformation English

– is self-explanatory in this context. The emphasis on French culture is certainly bound up with the values of the Enlightenment, which had triumphed over the earlier Protestant–Catholic divide and was very influential. And the admiration for German culture answered very much both to the USA's second-largest immigrant group and to the German-Jewish intellectuals, like Mortimer Adler himself, who were coming to the fore in American academic life. By the same token, the members of that elite held many other aspects of history and civilisation in manifest disdain. They had no intention of promoting Black or African culture, which might have thrown light on America's principal social and racial problems. They would not have wished to promote a positive view of modern Catholic Europe still less of the countries whence the latest waves of downtrodden Irish, Polish, Italian and Hispanic immigrants were coming. And, above all, despite the extraordinary ethnic, religious and racial diversity of American society, they were vehemently opposed to the virtues of diversity. They stood at the forefront of Americanisation – a coercive educational process which aimed to deprive the new immigrant masses of previous cultural connections and enforce strict conformity both with anglophone supremacy and with cultural and social conventions as defined by the dominant elite.

For much of the twentieth century, therefore, Western civilisation appears to have reigned supreme in American education, and for many decades few protests were recorded. The various minorities who might have been offended were too committed to the demands of assimilation to notice. The first signs of revolt which emerged in the 1970s were linked to the rise of Black studies and of feminism. They resulted in the realisation that large swathes of the population had been deliberately divorced from their roots. The first expressions of the view that the Western civ scheme was 'a typically American invention' that might be misguided or outdated appeared in the 1980s.[5] But a coherent exposé of the fact that Western civilisation really belongs to the category of 'imagined histories' did not appear until the very end of the century.[6]

The particular American dismissiveness towards east European histories and cultures had been long in evidence, but had been greatly reinforced by the Cold War. It can probably be traced less to the Anglophile tendency than to long-standing German and German-Jewish attitudes which were provoked by the stresses of immigration from the east to imperial Germany[7] and which were subsequently replicated in American academia. Oddly enough, US government schemes to address the deficit during the Cold War only served to strengthen existing stereotypes. Almost three quarters of American studies of Eastern Europe in the 1960s, '70s and '80s referred to Russia or the Soviet Union, thereby again consigning all non-Russian languages, cultures and histories of the region to a barely visible minority within a minority. 'The Idea of Eastern Europe,' wrote Professor Larry Wolff in 1993, 'has become a pedagogical convenience in our curriculum, creating a category for quick generalisations to serve as a fig leaf for our scant attention to that historical terrain.'[8] One might add that the 'quick generalisations' are almost invariably pejorative, using Eastern Europe as a foil for positive assessments of 'the West'. Serious works of history, where developments in Eastern Europe are properly integrated with those in Europe as a whole, are an extremely rare species.[9]

It should cause no surprise, therefore, that studies devoted to checking textbooks on Western civilisation for the accuracy of information concerning the individual countries of Eastern Europe discover a plethora of yawning gaps, comical errors, basic misunderstandings and insulting comments. One such recent study, which concentrates on the image of Poland as presented by six current textbooks, describes their references to Polish history as 'infrequent and minuscule dots'.[10] Professor John Kulczycki concludes: 'Fifteen years after the fall of Communism ... the emphasis in Western Civilisation textbooks on Western Europe plus Russia remains at best merely "a pedagogical convenience" [and] fails to present the full panoply of the history of Western Civilisation in all its variety.'[11]

It may not be amiss to give a few concrete examples of the mechanisms employed. Trawling through the offerings on 'Western civilisation', one may observe a dozen variants of 'the West' which have merged over the last three millennia into a multi-layered phenomenon of considerable complexity. Built on the original division of the ancient world into the Greek east and the Roman west, these variants of 'the West' recur and reappear in new forms over the ages. But the essence of the operation lies in the fact that each positive western variant is defined against a correspondingly negative variant of the east. Hence the western Roman empire is

defined against the Byzantine empire, Latin Christendom against Orthodox
Christendom, and eventually the NATO alliance against the Soviet Bloc.

Time and space permit mention of only three. Take, for example, the
following paragraph that purports to introduce the political framework
of medieval Europe:

> In political terms, the Middle Ages witness the transition of England
> and France from decentralised feudal states to emerging national
> monarchies, but the course of German and Italian history was stir-
> ringly different because of the imperial ambitions of the German
> rulers and the determination of the papacy to re-juvenate the church
> by controlling episcopal appointments. Although the Popes won the
> struggle, destroying the Hohenstaufens in the process, they in turn
> succumbed to growing secular concerns and the forceful resistance
> of the French and English monarchs.[12]

After reading those sentences the student would be left with the strong
impression that medieval politics consisted of the interplay between the
papacy in Rome and the monarchs of France, England and Germany. The
chapter is entitled 'The Rise of Europe' and there is nothing else in sight.
If it were possible one would like to ask the authors directly, 'How many
monarchies did medieval Europe contain?' Even if one accepts that it is
Latin Christendom, not the whole of medieval Europe that is at issue, the
next question would have to be, 'What was the largest state in Latin Christendom?' Interestingly enough, the authors *do* know the answer. It appears
en passant, sixty-two pages later in a section of the chapter called 'Crisis
and Recovery in Europe'. 'Poland was an immense state,' we read, 'the
largest in Europe after its union with Lithuania in the late 1300s.'[13] So
ignorance is not the explanation. Poland is not excluded from the outline
description of the Middle Ages because no one has heard of it. As proven
by several side sections in the book, the authors are perfectly capable of
presenting useful summaries on Russia, the Mongols, Poland, Hungary
and the Ottomans. Yet they suffer from that strange compulsion which
besets all who are beguiled by 'Western civilisation': they close their mind
to the full picture and, in making their generalisations, put exclusive
emphasis on the chosen parts of a predetermined story.

In the nineteenth century one comes to what has been called 'the imperial variant' of the West. By this, one refers to the complex of developments, including the Industrial Revolution, social modernisation, technological advance and colonial expansion, which first enabled Britain to become 'the workshop of the world' and which then pushed France and Germany into leading and rival positions on the continent. One suspects that it was the prestige of this imperial-industrial triangle that gave rise to the mania for 'Western civilisation' in the first place.

No serious historian would dispute the assertion that by 1900 Britain, northern France and north-west Germany had risen to pre-eminence in many spheres. Cultural power was linked to economic, political and military power. London, Paris and Berlin were world capitals. And it is not difficult to see why young American scholars at the turn of the century should have been mightily impressed. Yet one can only hold up the imperial variant to sustained admiration by two parallel acts of amnesia. One is to forget the fact that unbridled imperialism, not democracy, lay at the heart of the successful project. The other is to close one's eyes to the fact that Europe's pre-eminence was eroded rapidly by two world wars and by the rise of new superpowers. Within the space of barely thirty years, between 1914 and 1945, the old imperial supremacy was shattered. Britain was hopelessly weakened, and the empire could not be defended. France had been soundly defeated and left with mere illusions of post-war greatness. Germany was crushed, ruined, forced into unconditional surrender and split into two for nearly fifty years. By 1945 the world's new superpowers were the USA and USSR, and the ex-imperials had fallen from grace.

As I see it, the purveyors of 'Western civilisation' fail to cope in any sensible way with the catastrophe that was twentieth-century Europe. Since they are more concerned with ideals than with reality, they presumably feel reluctant to let anything rock their cosy little scheme. In his 'Great Ideas' as updated in 1958, for instance, Mortimer Adler finds no room for fascism or for communism, nor for totalitarianism or even for militarism. Instead, he goes for a long line of positive ideas, including 'Democracy', 'Eternity', 'Family', 'God' and 'Happiness'. The only negatives permitted are 'Evil' (as part of 'Good and Evil'), 'Pain' (as part of 'Pleasure and Pain'), 'Vice' (as part of 'Virtue and Vice'), 'Sin', 'Slavery' and 'Tyranny'. Splendid! Yet no one could pretend that such a biased selection of ideas could lead to even an elementary understanding of 'Western civilisation' in our own time. For the central paradox of the subject lies in the stark contrast between what Europeans thought they stood for and what they actually inflicted on each other. Let no one be in doubt, both Hitler and Stalin, both record-breaking monsters, were Europeans. Both the Gulag and the Holocaust were products of the same civilisation of which some people still like to boast so unreservedly.

Finally, on this line of thought, a word about 'the WASP variant' of the West is called for. In recent years the White Anglo-Saxon Protestants who long supplied the backbone of the American elite have somewhat passed under a cloud. The symbolic moments when their near-monopoly was broken came in 1960, when a Catholic senator from Massachusetts was elected president, and in 1964, when the civil rights movement of Martin Luther King Jr forced through the abolition of public discrimination and segregation. Both Kennedy and King were assassinated for their pains. Since then, the scandalous discrimination against Afro-Americans and Native Americans has been curbed, human rights have come to the fore, and other ethnic groups including Hispanics, American Jews and Asian-Americans have made their presence felt. Even so, since 'Western civilisation' is essentially a conservative exercise, one can still expect to find the old WASP values fighting their corner hard. Black studies, or 'Afrology' as it is sometimes called, does not seem to have had much impact in wider circles, even though multiculturalism has become a subject of prime concern in Europe itself. Nor has the traditional Anglo-Saxon landscape, which was always coloured by French concerns and by admiration for Prussia (if not for all of Germany), been seriously dented by fresh, more exotic European interests. As always, medieval Catholic Europe is displayed, but it is typically presented in chronic crisis as it staggers towards the happier chapters of Renaissance, Reformation and Enlightenment.

Of all the new educational directions, therefore, feminism alone seems capable of making common cause with Waspism. After all, White Anglo-Saxon Protestant women have been no less numerous than their male counterparts. A recent volume, *Women Warlords*, which runs through a list from Artemisia and Zenobia to Boudicca and Eleanor of Aquitaine, may point to new avenues.[14] Oddly enough, since the Crusades are no longer fashionable in these politically correct times, no inhibitions are shown in portraying the doughty Eleanor as a Crusader in her own right, entering Constantinople on a par with her kingly husband. Her role in the ensuing massacre, if any, is however not stressed.

The Jewish strand of the story is especially interesting (see pages 223–39). A sizeable cohort of the American advocates of 'Western civilisation' have a Jewish background themselves, and it is natural that they should opt for their forebears' inclusion. Indeed, several textbooks actually start with the Hebrews, who as founders of the Judaeo-Christian tradition have good grounds for pride of place. The early history of the people of Israel certainly has chronological precedence over 'the glory that was Greece'. On the other hand, it could be argued that distant doings on Mount Sinai belong more to the chronicles of the Near East than to the heart of Europe. In that case, the Jews would only become part of 'Western civilisation' at a later stage, when the Jewish diaspora was dispersed throughout many Roman provinces and many countries of Europe:

No discussion of medieval life and culture can fail to acknowledge the significant contribution of the Jews. During the period of the Roman Empire, they had migrated as far afield as Spain, France, Dalmatia and the Crimea ... Many of the earliest Jewish settlers in the West were farmers, an occupation in which they continued for centuries in southern Europe, but most Jews who settled further north engaged in commerce as town life developed. Charlemagne's government welcomed Jewish immigrants by granting them charters that granted them protection and privileges. The Capetian kings continued this policy, making France a centre of medieval Jewry. The German Jewish communities were founded by immigrants from France and southern France beginning in the ninth century. By 1100 there were numerous Jews in the Rhineland. Few Jews emigrated to Scandinavia, and England was the last major European country where they settled, mostly after the Norman Conquest in 1066. The extensive Jewish settlements in Europe, and their contributions to culture ensured that in the future the Jews would be fundamentally European in outlook.[15]

So far so good. Some details might be contested, not least the reference to England as 'the last major European country' of Jewish settlement. With Russia and several other major countries in the offing, this looks gratuitous. But the main point is taken. Since the Jews had lost Judaea, and were largely Europe-based, they had become an integral element of the European scene.

Then came the catastrophes: usury, the blood-libel, anti-Semitic friars, the Crusades, endemic persecution, the Black Death and the Lateran Decrees:

> English authorities seized synagogues on trumped-up charges that Jewish chanting disrupted Christian church services. The Holy Roman Empire asserted proprietary rights over its Jews, making them virtually the property of the Crown, and other states followed suit. Many Jews fled to Poland and Lithuania only to become the legal property of the nobility ... When Edward I banned the Jews from England in 1290, as many as 16,000 emigrated. Louis IX had decreed their exile from France in 1249 but the order was not implemented. In 1306, however, Philip IV ordered ... their ouster. Twice they were allowed back, only to be banned again in 1394. Because of political disunity in Germany, there was no general expulsion, but many local governments forced the Jews to flee. Spain and Sicily followed in 1492, Portugal in 1497, Naples in 1510 and again in 1541, Milan in 1591. The expulsions forced the Jews eastward – particularly to Poland.[16]

Readers may regard this passage as a welcome outbreak of realism in the middle of 'Western civilisation's' prevailing enthusiasms. In fact, it repeats one of the most enduring and tiresome characteristics of the genre. Events in England, France and Germany are given relatively detailed treatment, whilst, when the action moves east, all interest stops. The information about Poland is either wrong – Jews did *not* become the legal property of the nobility – or simply non-existent. In reality, Poland was the country where the largest community of Jews in Europe found their longest period of refuge. It gave them local autonomy, courts of law, and in 'The Council of the Four Lands' their own parliament. In the schemes

WESTERN CIVILISATION VERSUS EUROPEAN HISTORY

of 'Western civilisation' it is faceless. Yet it deserves to be given prominence. For without it all sorts of myths and misinformation can flourish
unchallenged. As the late and legendary 'courier from Warsaw' once
remarked, Americans can say 'anything they like' about Poland.[17] Thanks
to their courses on 'Western civilisation', they are largely unhampered by
knowledge.

Of course, if the Jews are to be included, claims arise for the inclusion
of the Muslims. There are no two ways about it: Islam has maintained a
continuous presence in Europe from the early eighth century to the present
(see pages 203–22). Everyone favouring the pluralist view will welcome
the idea. Yet Islam, whether one likes it or not, has to be put in a different
category. Unlike Judaism it does not possess the same symbiotic relationship with Europe's Christian majority. Indeed, it has usually been seen as
'the Other' against which European Christendom defined itself. In most
surveys of 'Western civilisation', the most it can hope for is an honourable
mention:

> The Nasrids were noted patrons of education and the arts, and their
> court attracted numerous learned Muslims. Mathematics, science,
> medicine and literature flourished. A university was founded in the
> mid-1300s, and [Granada] had no less than three important libraries.
> A hospital for the sick and insane was founded in 1365–6. But
> perhaps the greatest monuments of the golden age are the Alhambra
> and the Generalife. The former, constructed mostly between 1238
> and 1358, was a palatial fortress replete with barracks, stables,
> mosques and gardens ... It is richly decorated in ornate Arabesque
> style with coloured tiles and marble, geometric figures, and floral
> motifs. Its horseshoe arches, delicate columns, and graceful arcades
> are the culmination of Islamic architecture in Iberia. The nearby
> Generalife resembles the Koran's description of paradise as 'a garden
> flowing with streams'.[18]

One thing is certain: students of 'Western civilisation' are sometimes given
a peek at Islam in Spain; they are never given the chance to learn about
European countries, like Bosnia or Albania, where Muslims form the
majority. And the Ottomans are treated as rank outsiders.

All these examples point to the prevalence of some unwritten assumptions which seem to underpin the construct of 'Western civilisation'. The unwritten needs to be written down so it can be examined. A fair start might be made with five such assumptions:

1. That the western and eastern halves of Europe are separate entities with little or nothing in common.
2. That Eastern Europe is not really part of Europe, or not part of 'the real Europe'.
3. That the East–West division of Europe, which can be observed in different manifestations at different times, is fixed and permanent.
4. That 'the West' is superior.
5. That all summaries of Western civilisation/European history can safely omit anything which belongs to the different and inferior East. (The only exception to this rule is Russia, which, being powerful, automatically qualifies for inclusion.)

One of the curious aspects of this phenomenon is that millions of Americans, whose heritage belongs to the excluded categories, have shown few signs of demanding their place in the sun. For most of the twentieth-century courses on 'Western civ' were served up as obligatory fare for freshmen in most US universities. Thousands upon thousands of Irish-Americans, Italian-Americans, Greek-Americans, Polish-Americans, Ukrainian-Americans and Hispanic-Americans have sat through those courses, written their term papers and passed the exams without ever learning anything about themselves or their families' heritage. It says a great deal about America's ability to enforce cultural and social conventions, and to crush the wellsprings of unconventional thought. For what it all boils down to is a narcissistic exercise in self-admiration. Young Americans have been taught to admire the wisdom, beauty and strength of the roots of their own derivative civilisation. And woe betide the awkward customer who dares to believe otherwise.

IV

ROLLER COASTER:
THE INSIDE STORY OF *EUROPE:*
A HISTORY[1]

W HEN *Europe: A History* was almost ready for publication, I was asked by the publishers for one sentence that summarised my view of the book and that could be used to head the blurb on the jacket. What I came up with was, 'I set myself the impossible task of writing a total history of the whole of Europe in every period.' The sentence became a sort of totem or slogan repeated at all the publicity events and book festivals which I subsequently addressed. In due course, through much repetition, the wording evolved slightly. The second half of the sentence became 'a total history of European life in all aspects, in all countries and in all periods'.[2] But the sentiment remained unchanged. The key words were 'total' and 'impossible'.

As I remember, the first of many 'meet-the-author' sessions took place one evening in October 1996 in Southampton Town Hall. Before it started, I jotted down five points which explained my aims in greater detail and which seemed to go down quite well at the official book launch. These five points soon established themselves as a regular routine, to be trotted out every time someone asked me to talk about the book. They have stood the test of many airings.

Aim 1 was to contest the convention in European history of concentrating on Western Europe to the exclusion or denigration of the rest: in other words, to present a comprehensive survey. In my considered view, most so-called histories of Europe did not deserve the title. They were histories of only part of Europe, usually of only part of Western Europe. And as far as I could see no one had ever seriously challenged them. This myopia, this obdurate refusal to look at the full expanse of the subject, had set in many decades before and had become the accepted fashion among teachers and authors dealing with European history. It was certainly in evidence in Hal Fisher's well-established *History of Europe* (1936), which was still on sale sixty years after publication and which I was hoping to knock off its perch.[3] For me, with my interests in Poland and Russia, it looked very peculiar, not to say grotesque. I likened it to a textbook of human anatomy which fails inexplicably to mention the left leg and the left arm. One can possibly imagine an anatomist who for some reason develops an antipathy for certain parts of the frame, but one can't accept that the offending parts be erased from standard diagrams of the human body.

The attitude which I had decided to confront was deeply rooted – indeed, it was the norm – and anyone who had the temerity to dissent was thought to be somewhat abnormal. For historians in general had no mental map of Eastern Europe in their heads at all. If, in a class on medieval Europe, a querulous student had ever raised a hand to ask whether it was true that the kingdom of Hungary was the second-largest of all Catholic realms, the professor would have been hard put to respond, because he, like everyone else, was unlikely to have encountered medieval Hungary in any form. He might have said, 'Don't be ridiculous,' or, hopefully, 'I shall have to look that one up.' What he couldn't say, and save face was, 'Quite right. Our course on medieval Europe is a dog's breakfast because many of the basic ingredients are missing!'

I had discussed this problem with the then history editor of OUP, Ivon Asquith, before accepting the commission. His starting-point had been the idea of publishing an updated version of *The Oxford History of Europe*, a title that had first appeared in 1929 from the pen of Revd Plunkett.[4] Having already sponsored my own *Oxford History of Poland*, *God's Playground*, Asquith knew that large chunks of Europe's past were overlooked in the standard histories, and he conceived a plan for preparing a radical history of Europe that would cover the whole of the subject. He then told me of his troubles with the history faculty, to whom he had earlier turned for advice. None of the distinguished Oxford dons who described themselves as European historians knew anything about the lands beyond the Elbe. And, though two of them were invited to submit a book proposal, both of them gave it up as a bad job. That was when he turned to his historian of Poland. He called me in and asked somewhat apologetically if I knew anything about west European history. His face lit up when I said France and Italy had been my first loves. He, too, had doubted whether a 'specialist' in one part of Europe could be conversant with the other parts. It turns out that east Europeanists, whom everyone imagined to be very narrow specialists, carry a much broader range of languages and interests than the so-called Europeanists. So I, to cut a long story short, was given the commission.

Aim 2 was to overturn the notion that European history is only concerned with the great powers: in other words, to find space for all countries great and small, for nations as well as states, for stateless nations and for religious and ethnic minorities – in short to prepare an inclusive overview of Europe's diverse communities. Since much of the writing on European history has dealt with international relations, it is inevitable that the wars and diplomacy of the powers have been given prominence. Indeed, the impression has been created that 'national histories' looked after internal affairs whilst 'general' or European history was left in charge of external, international affairs. Many educational schemes were based on this idea. Schoolchildren typically spent part of their time on their particular national history, and part on general, international history. As a result, there was little place for the internal history of other countries, and no space for the smaller states that could not compete with the beasts of the jungle.

Naturally, small states and less fashionable regions of Europe featured regularly on the agenda of the powers. Studies of nineteenth-century history, for example, would introduce students to all sorts of issues from Greek independence and the Polish risings to the Straits, Schleswig-Holstein and the Bulgarian horrors. Yet if one thinks of it, these topics only came up when the great policy-makers were interested in them. As soon as the crisis passed, the topic ceased to exist. Greece materialised out of the blue, and stayed on the agenda as long as the chancelleries were vying with each other to place their candidate on the throne. Then it disappeared. Bulgaria grabbed the headlines because Gladstone was upset by the conduct of the Turks. It then dropped off the table. By the same token, Poland was seen as a function of Russian and Prussian policies; Ireland as a function of British affairs; and nineteenth-century Spain as a backwater of no interest to anyone. Between the revolt of the South American colonies in the 1820s and the Spanish Civil War more than a century later, Spain was hardly visible.

In the last analysis, the issue is one of respect. If historians do not cast their nets far and wide, they leave themselves open to the charge that they are only concerned with the survival of the fittest. They need to show that Greek or Polish or Spanish history is valuable in its own right, indeed that it is just as worthwhile as the history of Britain, France or Germany. Of course, they also need to keep a sense of proportion. It would be a strange history of Europe that gave the same weight to Liechtenstein as to the Soviet Union. Priorities have to be worked out, and conflicting demands reconciled. In the case of *Europe: A History*, I ended up allotting the highest number of pages to Russia, whilst still managing to write a little about Andorra, Estonia, Monaco and Luxembourg.

One would face exactly the same difficulties if asked to write a history of English football. The task could be accomplished by writing exclusively about the Premiership champions of recent years. One would have to write about Crystal Palace or West Bromwich Albion if only to say that Manchester United beat them. Alternatively, one could sketch out the structure of the professional and amateur leagues, summarise the various cup competitions, and analyse the main changes in the game over the past century. One would then discover how clubs rise and fall, and learn that the 'great powers' of today were not necessarily the top dogs of yesteryear. In this context, teams like Blackburn Rovers or Bolton Wanderers gain kudos. And one realises that long-forgotten formations like Corinthian Casuals or Accrington Stanley have claims to fame no less than those of Arsenal, Chelsea or Liverpool.[5]

Aim 3 was to combine academic competence with literary merit: in other words, to overcome the prevailing distinction between academic and popular history. Ultra-specialisation is the besetting sin of today's historical profession. Faced with overwhelming torrents of information, historians have taken refuge in ever-narrower subjects, hoping against hope to master the ever-increasing data relevant to ever-shrinking areas of competence. Thirty or forty years prior to the Internet, to electronic journals and to the proliferation of obligatory conference papers, a scholar could be confident of keeping on top of all the most important material appearing on, say, sixteenth-century England or Renaissance Italy or the Second World War. Nowadays, the same level of expertise is impossible unless the boundaries of one's focus are drastically reduced. Young academics are encouraged to prepare doctorates on 'The ecclesiastical policy of Charles I towards Scotland 1637–8' or 'Women, warmongering and the water supply in Leonardo's Florence'. If anyone dares to enquire about Charles II's policy to Scotland, or about the women of Siena, they are more than likely to earn the universal response, 'That is not my field.'

Worse still, historians trained to write PhD theses and to prepare conference papers soon begin to talk in the stilted jargon of their professional circles. They rarely teach in ordinary schools and rarely meet the average public. They inevitably lose the ability to address a non-specialist audience, to expound general historical themes or to speak common sense. Worst of all, since some of them imagine that their brand of history is superior to that of the great classics, they have heralded an era in schools and universities when the stock of Gibbon, Macaulay or Trevelyan has never been lower.

Fortunately, a number of doughty individuals have succeeded in bucking the trend. Simon Schama, Martin Gilbert and Felipe Fernandez-Armesto are household names. Television programmes featuring lively presenters talking intelligently about history have proved highly popular. *Europe: A History* appeared on the scene at a moment when the *New York Times* was already announcing in tones of amazement, 'Big Books Can Be Popular.'

The trouble with *Europe* lay in the sheer size of the project. It was competing with tomes often of similar size but usually of much smaller scope. It is one thing to write a massive tome about the Russian Revolution, like Orlando Figes's excellent *A People's Tragedy* (1996).[6] It is something else to tackle a subject where the Russian Revolution occupies five out of 1365 pages or 0.366 per cent of the whole. As the size of the acreage to be covered increases, the smaller details fall out of focus and the overall precision inevitably decreases. It is a simple mathematical sum.

In the nature of things, the *grand simplificateur* must also be a great risk-taker, a shameless cutter of corners. Academic colleagues who have never undertaken the same sort of exercise are likely to be upset. All one can do, apart from writing with passion and clarity, is to know one's limitations, to hand one's typescript to more specialised colleagues for careful checking and to rely on the good sense of one's readers.

Aim 4 was to devise a literary structure which could make light of the sheer weight of material and which, at the same time, could do justice to the huge variety of subject matter.

At the outset, I found it very difficult to comprehend exactly what 'the whole of European history' meant. I would visualise the map of the peninsula and its constituent parts, and then try to imagine a virtual model where 'time-boxes' of 500, 1000 or 2000 years sat on top of each of the constituents. It was then possible to build up a series of these imaginary cubic 'time–space' containers, which could be calibrated into centuries, and into which convenient packages of political, economic, social, cultural and international history could be stacked. Finally, when the overall time parameters had been fixed, from prehistory to the present, the general mountainous outline of the project became apparent. I won't say that it was 'awesome', but it was.

The next step was to establish the list of chapters. At first I hardly considered anything other than chronological chapters, and most of the main divisions of the text suggested themselves. The resultant list contained twelve periods:

I   Prehistory
II   Ancient Greece
III   Ancient Rome to AD 330
IV   Birth of Europe, *c.* AD 330–800
V   Medieval World, *c.* 750–1270
VI   Christendom in Crisis, *c.* 1250–1493
VII   Renaissance and Reformation, *c.* 1400–1600
VIII   Absolutism and Enlightenment, *c.* 1550–1789
IX   French Revolution, 1789–1815
X   Nineteenth Century, 1815–1914

XI   World Wars, 1914–45
XII   Europe Divided and Undivided, 1945–1991[7]

Obviously, since the quantity of information increases as history progresses, the time covered by each chapter decreases accordingly. Chapter I covered some five million years, Chapter III, 1100 years, and Chapter X, thirty-one years. The shortening focus and accelerating tempo promised to present the reader with a satisfying zoom effect.

The internal organisation of the chapters posed innumerable puzzles. Both chronological and thematic sections had somehow to be accommodated. All peoples and all states had to be covered in each period. In the early chapters a special difficulty arose from the fact that Greece, Rome and the post-Roman world had entered the historical record early, leaving all manner of sources, whilst the rest of Europe was still in a pre-historic, pre-literary and pre-Christian phase. In the last chapters the need to give fuller attention to sophisticated ideological issues threatened to run out of control.

Nonetheless, the principal drawback with writing a historical narrative over vast expanses of time and space derives from the superfluity of abstractions and the scarcity of individual men and women. The historian is talking of trends and changes, of the rise and fall of states, of the migration of peoples from A to B, and of the spread and evolution of religions. There is precious little room for small-scale events, for 'history with a human face'. I was rescued, I think, by my hobby of photography. My Pentax SLR camera had several interchangeable lenses, and I was familiar with the principle that the focus and magnification of images could be varied to match the characteristics of the subject. Using a wide-angle lens, one can capture an entire cathedral. Using a telephoto lens, one can pick out a single gargoyle high up on the tower, or one pane of a stained-glass window. I decided that some equivalent literary devices were called for. Such was the origin of what I came to call snapshots and capsules.

The snapshot was to be an essay which would describe a very limited, symbolic event in close-up and be placed at the end of each chapter. It would halt the breakneck pace of the main narrative and bring the reader face to face with historical figures and with a real-life situation. The event was to be selected partly on the criterion of intrinsic interest and partly by suitability as a bridge between chapters. For example, the siege of Syracuse in 212 BC was chosen partly because it made a rattling good tale and partly because the death of the Greek philosopher Archimedes at the hands of a brutal Roman soldier made for a perfect transition between the chapter on ancient Greece and the subsequent chapter on ancient Rome. Since there were twelve chapters, twelve snapshots were needed:

- The eruption of Thera, 1628 BC: about environment and history
- The siege of Syracuse, 212 BC: Roman conquest of the Greek world
- The founding of Constantinople, AD 330: emergence of Byzantium
- Pope Stephen crosses the Alps, AD 753?: rise of northern Europe
- The Low Countries, 1262: from submergence to prominence
- The end of the world in Moscow, 1493: a view from the east
- Bernini completes St Peter's, 1667: history and architecture
- The première of *Don Giovanni*, Prague, 1787
- Napoleon at Fontainebleau, 1814: 'farewell' to the emperor
- Lights going out all over Europe, London, 1914: the onset of war
- The Nuremberg tribunal, 1946: the incomplete conclusion of the Second World War
- Summertown, 14 February 1992: the historian as part of the history

In line with my belief that the 'historian forms part of the history', the final snapshot shows the author at his desk in Oxford writing the final pages.[8]

The capsules in contrast were to be much shorter thumbnail sketches, and were designed to cater for the multitude of very specific topics that otherwise would never find a place in a general history. Each was to begin in exactly the same way with a precise sentence about some event that had occurred on a particular day at a particular place. Each could then be boxed and placed at an appropriate point in the main narrative. The reader would thereby be given the option either of examining the capsule as a self-standing item or of reading it in conjunction with the surrounding text. Post-publication feedback was to confirm that readers greatly appreciated the option.

The key operation of identifying suitable capsule topics proved a lengthy one. I had calculated that 300 was the maximum number of capsules that the text could stand, representing almost 20 per cent of the whole. But I took the precaution of preparing more than the maximum so that I could keep twenty or thirty in reserve. I started by drawing up a massive chart containing 300 boxes. Sixty vertical columns were headed by sixty categories of information ranging from 'Music', 'Philosophy' and 'Poetry' to 'The Senses', 'The Sciences' and 'The Social Sciences'. Five horizontal layers were reserved for five historical periods – Prehistoric, Ancient, Medieval, Early Modern and Modern. Five times sixty made 300. Each capsule was to be identified by its own brand name.

The next stage was to establish a working list by perming the informational categories both against historical periods and against the additional factor of geographical location. To this end, I worked for three months in 1992 in the Wiener Library at Harvard University, whose computerised catalogue possessed a unique 'multiple word search' facility that could sort the titles both of books and of scientific articles. It was an extraordinary experience. Day by day, I fed in groups of three search words – one for subject, one for period and one for location – and trawled through the resulting mass of reading lists. For example, when I found that I was short both on candidates for the medieval gender slot, and on items from the Nordic world, I typed in 'women', 'medieval' and 'Iceland', and was served up an article on 'breast-feeding techniques as recorded in fifteenth-century Reykjavik'. I could then decide whether to adopt that article as the basis for a capsule. (In the event, I decided against it.) Bit by bit the chart filled up. Some spaces were crossed off effortlessly from my own knowledge, others caused prolonged distress. I was particularly relieved when I found a solution for the space reserved for the history of smell. Entitled VIOLETS, it started with Napoleon's request to Josephine not to take a bath for three weeks before their meetings. I was also specially pleased with my discoveries in the history of food, which included SAMPHIRE, dealing with Neolithic recipes, and BRIE, which recounted the story of how Camembert was invented by a wandering monk of Meaux.[9]

Eventually, all that remained was to write it all up. The task took me a year – an average of one capsule per working day. I would write in the morning and head off to Bodleian Library in the afternoon to read up on the next day's subject. Amazingly, it all fitted together. When I came to the end, I had several things to regret, but I never regretted the decision to organise *Europe: A History* on the three-fold structure of chapter, snapshot and capsule.

Some unnecessary difficulties arose in the final product due to somewhat deficient indications of how the capsules worked and where they were located. An excellent Capsule Map was placed on the endpapers of the book, but it ought to have carried a reference to the List of Capsules in Appendix 1 on pages 1202–3. For the sake of inconvenienced readers, I am happy to republish that appendix here:

ABKHAZIA	BATAVIA	CATACOMBI	DASA
ADELANTE	BATT-IOI	CAUCASIA	DEMOS
AGOBARD	BAUME	CEDRA	DESSEIN
ALCHEMIA	BENZ	CHASSE	DEVIATO
ALCORFRIBAS	BERNADETTE	CHASTITY	DIABOLOS
ALPI	BIBLIA	CHERNOBYL	DING
ALTMARKT	BLACK ATHENA	CHERSONESOS	DIRHAM
ANGELUS	BLARNEY	CHOUAN	DOLLAR
ANNALES	B.N.R.	CODPIECE	DONHOFF
ANNO DOMINI	BOGEY	COMBRAY	DOUAUMONT
APOCALYPSE	BOGUMIL	COMENIUS	$E = MC^2$
AQUILA	BOUBOULINA	COMPOSTELA	ECO
AQUINCUM	BOXER	COMPUTIO	EESTI
ARCHIMEDES	BRIE	CONCLAVE	EGNATIA
ARICIA	BRITO	CONDOM	EIRIK
ATHLETOS	BUCZACZ	CORSICA	EL CID
ATHOS	BUDA	CONSPIRO	ELDLUFT
AUG	C14	CORVINA	ELECTRON
AUSCHWITZ	CABALA	COWARD	ELEMENTA
BALETTO	CADMUS	CRAVATE	ELSASS
BAMBINI	CANTATA	CRUX	EMU
BARBAROS	CANTUS	CSABA	EPIC
BARD	CAP-AG	DANNEBROG	EPIDEMIA
BASERRIA	CARITAS	DANUBIUS	EPIGRAPH

EROS	GROSSENMEER	LEPER	MURANO
ETRUSCHERIA	GROTEMARKT	LESBIA	MUSIKE
EULENBURG	GUERRILLA	LETTLAND	NEZ
EULER	GUILLOTIN	LEX	NIBELUNG
FAMINE	HANSA	LIETUVA	NIKOPOLIS
FARAON	HARVEST	LILI	NOBEL
FAROE	HATRED	LLANFAIR	NOMEN
FATIMA	HEJNAL	LLOYD'S	NOMISMA
FAUSTUS	HEPTANESOS	LOOT	NORGE
FEMME	HERMANN	LUDI	NOSTRADAMUS
FIESTA	HEXEN	LUGDUNUM	NOVGOROD
FLAGELLATIO	HOLISM	LYCZAKOW	NOYADES
FLAMENCO	HOSSBACH	MADONNA	OEDIPUS
FLORA	HYSTERIA	MAGIC	OMPHALOS
FOLLY	IKON	MAKEDON	OPERA
FREUDE	ILLYRIA	MALET	ORANGE
FUTHARK	ILLYRICUM	MARKET	OXFAM
GAGAUZ	IMPRESSION	MARSTON	PALAEO
GAT-HUNTER	INDEX	MASON	PANTA
GATTOPARDO	INFANTA	MASSILIA	PAPESSA
GAUCHE	INQUISITO	MATRIMONIO	PAPYRUS
GENES	IONA	MAUVE	PARNASSE
GENOCIDE	JACQUARD	MENOCCHI	PASQUA
GENUG	JEANS	MERCANTE	PETROGRAD
GESANG	KALEVALA	METRYKA	PFALZ
GGANTIJA	KATYŃ	MEZQUITA	PHILIBEG
GHETTO	KEELHAUL	MICROBE	PHOTO
GONCALVEZ	KHAZARIA	MIR	PICARO
GOOSE STEP	KONAMYA	MISSA	PLOVUM
GOTHA	KONOPIŠTE	MOARTE	POGROM
GOTHIC	KRAL	MOLDOVA	POTEMKIN
GOTTHARD	LANGEMARCK	MONKEY	PRADO
GRECO	LAUSSEL	MONTAILLOU	PRESS
GRILLENSTEIN	LEONARDO	MORES	PROPAGANDA

PROSTIBULA	SINGULARIS	SYROP	USOK
PUGACHEV	SLAVKOV	SZLACHTA	USERY
QUAKE	SLESVIG	TABARD	UTOPIA
RELAXATIO	SMOLENSK	TAIZÉ	VALTELLINA
RENTES	SOCIALIS	TAMMUZ	VENDANGE
RESPONSA	SONATA	TAXIS	VENDÉMIAIRE
REVERENTIA	SOUND	TEICHOS	VINO
ROMANY	SOVKINO	TEMPUS	VIOLETS
ROUGE	SPASIT'EL	TEREM	VLAD
RUFINUS	SPARTICUS	TOLLUND	VORKUTA
RUS'	SPICE-OX	TONE	WASTELAND
SAMOS	STATE	TOR	WIENER WELT
SAMPHIRE	STRAD	TORMENTA	XATIVAH
SANITAS	STRASSBURG	TOUR	ZADRUGA
SARAJEVO	SUND	TRISTAN	ZEUS
SCHOLASTIKOS	SUSANIN	TRONOS	
SHAMAN	SYLLABUS	TSCHERNOWITZ	
SHQIPERIA	SYPHILUS	UKRAINA	

Oddly enough, when the operation was already complete, the total number of capsules turned out to be 301 not 300.[10]

Some readers were to criticise the names of the capsules which they judged obscure and unhelpful. Others were full of praise. I can only say the naming system followed no plan or principle. It arose from the need to provide each capsule with a computer file name, and to this end I often wrote down the first thing in my head. As a result, the mixture of names was rather wonderful to behold. Many of them, like BARD, SONATA or USERY, are perfectly straightforward. Many, like BLARNEY, GGANTIJA or VORKUTA, are nothing more than place names. Many others, like ADELANTE or DANNE-BROG or MOARTE, use foreign-language forms relevant to the item concerned. But a few, admittedly, like CAP-AG or GAT-HUNTER, are distinctly odd or misleading. At some point, however, the decision was taken to leave the names as they were. Despite minor problems, the overall effect was both intriguing and, as a reflection of Europe's diverse and chaotic cultural heritage, educative.

*

Aim 5 was to convey something of the flavour of Europe's past and not to rely on the presentation of bare facts. As I had realised when designing the snapshots, the sort of crisp, efficient prose style required to expound large masses of historical information is in severe danger of growing tedious. In my view, it can only be sustained over a thousand pages and more (a) if the author, in true Gibbonian fashion, knows how to enliven it with wit, irony, paradox and metaphor; (b) if it is broken up into digestible chunks; and (c) if it is embellished by a variety of pictures, diagrams, maps, lists, musical items and literary extracts. It stands to reason that the impact of the embellishments will be greatly enhanced by being authentic historical items directly connected with the events in question.

Pictorial illustrations, for example, are not just a frivolous extra. Chosen with care, they can be a genuine source of historical insight. For this reason, an original mural of the legend of Europa from Pompeii[11] provides an ideal companion to Ovid's poem on the same subject. Generally speaking, historical paintings from the relevant period make a more harmonious and authentic impression than photographs from a different period.

Diagrams, too, can convey something more than mere factual information; graphs and tables of historical statistics often have less charm. But the extraordinary science of phenology, as publicised by Emanuel le Roy Ladurie, absolutely reeks of old village records and of medieval wine harvests. Following the charts which trace the vacillating data of the first grape-picking in each year of particular Burgundian vineyards one feels the shifting rhythms of medieval peasant life and learns about historical climate change almost as a bonus.[12]

Clear, simple maps are an essential aid to many forms of historical exposition; they often convey more at one glance than ten pages of prose. Yet historical cartography tells one still more. It shows how people in the past thought about geography and about their own place in the world. The magnificent print by Sebastian Müntzer which presents the map of sixteenth-century Europe in the guise of a woman[13] provided the inspiration for my own experiment with maps of Europe whose axis had been turned 90 degrees.

Those maps, which placed Portugal at the top, the Mediterranean on the left and Scandinavia on the right, provoked undisguised outrage among a small number of readers and reviewers.[14] Yet there was method in the madness. The purpose was to challenge conventional conceptions of Europe's geography, and to show that the familiar perspectives do not possess any absolute rights. The protestors belonged in large part to the last-ditch defenders of 'Western civilisation', who have no intention of permitting any elasticity of thought.

Lists are fascinating; historical lists are especially fascinating. No text-book could conceivably contain the names of all 301 popes and antipopes, for instance, or describe fifty-two Holy Roman emperors. Yet a simple list will flood the mind with authentic names and authentic sequences. Nothing could be more evocative.

History is full of music, and in this sense a silent history book is unfaithful to the past. No doubt the day will come when one opens a book on the Renaissance and the sound of a lute will float mysteriously from a microchip implanted in the binding. In the meantime, musical scores can serve the same purpose. To my mind, any account of the Reformation can only be enriched by the notes of Luther's 'Feste Burg' or of Tallis's Canon.[15]

I have written elsewhere of the historian's use of literary extracts (see pages 184–6). For the purists, it can be controversial, but on balance the advantages outweigh the disadvantages. An apposite poem can provoke the same authentic reverberations that emanate from a good song or hymn. In *Europe: A History* I was also at pains to illustrate the diversity of Europe's cultures by quoting a diverse selection of poetry in the original languages. The monolinguistic historical discourse which some editors insist on is as false as history shorn of melody.

In my enthusiasm, I probably overplayed my hand in this regard. I prepared so many embellishments to the text that they overflowed, and *Europe: A History* was published with no less than 106 appendices. Yet the appendices were not entirely out of place. They constitute a tidy historical compendium brimming both with information and with that elusive quality: historical colour. What other survey of European history can claim to feed its readers with Sarmatian symbols, with thirty-four variant designs of the Christian cross, and with three different runic alphabets?[16]

The sensation of writing an unexpected best-seller is rather like that of riding a roller coaster blindfold. One feels the exhilaration, and hears the cheers and screams, but the dips and twists come as surprises. After a time, one simply wants it to stop.

The official launch was held at Chatham House on 10 October 1996. The speakers were Timothy Garton Ash, my colleague from Oxford, and John Simpson, the BBC's political correspondent. Tim spoke pithily and precisely and John more effusively, but both were very kind. It was a time for celebration, not for lengthy discussion. I passed the evening in a daze, hardly believing that we had really reached the finishing tape. Nine years had passed since I had taken the first steps of the marathon.

Publicists say, 'No publicity is bad publicity,' but for anyone who is the unaccustomed subject of media attention, the advantages are not so certain. It is delightful to meet distinguished editors over breakfast at the Meridian Piccadilly or at the Langham Hilton. And it's great fun to appear on the BBC's *Start the Week* with Melvyn Bragg and on *Weekly Planet* with Jon Snow. One had to chuckle when a chauffeur-driven limousine first pulled up at the front gate to whisk one round a dozen London bookstores for impromptu signings. And the chuckle inevitably grew into a smile when the management of Hatchards and Waterstone's and Dillons enthusiastically announced that the book had been outselling its rivals that week by thirty or forty to one.

The downside, however, can be tiresome. Many journalists are not interested in 'Book Sells Well'; they want the author to come a cropper. At the first hint of controversy, they appear on the phone or on the door-step, full of the phoney bonhomie that is required to extract details of a 'scholars' war' which no one was actually fighting. And they adore egg-on-face. The *Sunday Times* specialist on intellectual affairs, who burst in during my lunchtime, could not begin to consider the book before he had first reported the 'mayonnaise on chin' of the 'flustered professor'. My rather banal observation to the effect that no political state, including the United Kingdom, can be eternal evoked a massive headline: 'Funeral Director to the Nation'. And that's only the quality press!

Pictures editors are no better. They're not there to choose the best pictures which their photographers provide. They're out to find the most graphic illustration of the most sensational aspect of the accompanying piece. Hence, Valerie Grove's interview in *The Times*, which had a lot to say about my childhood and education, was illustrated by a flattering but wonderfully misleading portrait by Denzil McPhalance, which showed me sitting on the steps of All Souls Langham Place looking thirty years younger than I really am. Similarly, to reinforce the funeral director image, the *Sunday Times* chose a suitably demonic portrait complete with beetling brows and curling lip. Earlier, I had fought tooth and nail with my publishers' design department to resist the glum-looking picture of an exhausted author that duly appeared on the jacket. The image was taken by one reviewer as proof of the author's 'self-indulgence'. (The photographer, Mike Harkins, had produced a score of alternatives, each emitting a different mood, for the publishers to choose from.)

Europe: A History was shortlisted for three major literary prizes. For the most lucrative of these, the NCR Award, it was the runaway favourite. William Hill, the bookmakers, fixed the odds at 3–1. The award ceremony was held in the dazzling ballroom of the Dorchester Hotel. I arrived by chauffeured limousine with my wife amidst the flashes of press cameras. We were accompanied by two other ladies, radiant in full evening regalia. One was representing OUP, which, as a staid academic publisher, was not used to the celebrity limelight; Amy White was representing the publicity department. Only a few months before she had been the tea girl. They were all excited. They all looked magnificent. None of us had been near a big prize before. We didn't win.[17]

Reviewers come in numerous categories. One group, often the most gushing in their praise, show few signs of actually having read the book. A second group absorb enough of the introduction and of passages relating to their own speciality to pass resounding judgements. A third group, in a distinct minority, follow careful reading with balanced comments. And then there's the Worshipful Company of Whingers, Carpers and Nit-pickers, whose sole aim in life is to find fault. Generally speaking, I was fortunate. Of thirty major reviews, at least twenty-five were positively, embarrassingly glowing. Three or four might be counted ambiguous or tepid. Only one, Theodore Rabb in the *New York Times*, awarded the book a decisive thumbs down.

By far the most thorough review appeared in the *New York Review of Books*. It was penned by an old friend, a fellow worker in the Central European vineyard, and it is hardly fitting for me to pass comment on his comments. Suffice it to say that it contained a couple of harsh judgements and a mass of positive ones. But it was mainly characterised by a long and systematic presentation of the issues, for which I was truly grateful.[18]

No reviewer who had read the blurb could have missed my intention of writing a history of all Europe, east as well as west. Most readers clearly approve. But a hard core of self-styled 'Western intellectuals' cling desperately to the old convention of ignoring or denigrating the East. A recent review in the *Spectator* headed 'The Face and the Backside of Europe' exemplifies the problem. The face of this Europe is resolutely turned to the west and no less a philosopher than Nikita Khrushchev is invoked to proclaim that it is better to peruse the human face than other less attractive parts of the anatomy. The sort of thinking that underlay both Chamberlain's appeasement and the Nazis' policy of *Lebensraum* is apparently still alive.

Yet even the well-wishers can miss the point. Too many imagined that east and west were being equated. There was no such equation. There is just the contention that almost all the main trends of European history have an east European component, and that all components must find their place.

Prior to the 'funeral director' interview, very few English reviewers noticed that *Europe: A History* contains an important British strand. A Welsh reviewer saw the passage on the Machynlleth Parliament of 1404; a Scotsman saw the Declaration of Arbroath; an Irish professor picked up the references to Blarney and to Bloomsday. But the great majority of English readers are mentally unprepared to see themselves as part of the European story. I am reminded of the moment in 1997 when I was sitting on the platform in the Examination Schools in Oxford, waiting to present the special faculty lecture. As he introduced me, the Regius Professor explained to the audience that the lecture was intended as a makeweight for the annual Fords Lectures in British History, and that it was devoted to 'continental European history'. My text was obviously out of bounds; it began with a comparison between Poland and Ireland.

I suspect that a history of all-Europe is likely to encounter far more resistance from the last-ditch defenders of 'Western civilisation' in the USA than from any group of British readers. American academia is far more politicised than its British counterpart; and 'Western civilisation' already provides one of the established battlegrounds between traditionalists and liberals. In my view, 'Western civilisation' is a highly artificial, not to say pernicious intellectual construct (see pages 46–60). On the other hand, I am not sure that a satisfactory alternative can be found in modish multi-culturalism. Perhaps my American publishers should adopt the slogan, 'Western civilisation out, European history in'.

One of my aims was to emphasise the role of lesser nations and ethnic minorities as distinct from the great powers. In this vein, I made a special attempt to integrate the history of Jews and Judaism at every stage, and I was pleased to learn that those efforts were publicly welcomed by the chairman of Israel's International Center for University Teaching of Jewish Civilisation. The chief carper of the *New York Times*, in contrast, raised so many complaints and insinuations on this score that he let loose the hounds of the press on a false scent. I leave it to my readers to decide. Using the index, they should start with the early discussion of the Judaeo-Christian tradition, which ends with an affirmation of the permanent presence of the Jewish strand throughout European history, graphically illustrated on page 200 by a beautiful Hebrew quotation; and they should read on to the capsule called RESPONSA, which examines the extraordinary religious discipline of Jews during the Holocaust and the remarkable series of moral decisions taken by rabbis in the condemned ghettos *in extremis*.[19] Nonetheless, one can't fail to notice how hard it is for historians to debate these matters in a level-headed manner. When a reviewer in the *Times Literary Supplement* was looking for a sting, he couldn't refrain from claiming that 'outrage' would be caused by the alleged likening of opponents of Holocaust denial with advocates of the fatwa against Salman Rushdie. That was a very wild shot. The only outrageous thing was to talk of outrage at a comparison that was never made.

Similar unnecessary friction was caused by comments on a capsule called NOYADES, which dealt with the delicate subject of the technology of death. A comparison was made between the reasons for the use of submersible drowning chambers by French Republicans during the suppression of the Vendée rising of 1793–4 and the use of gas chambers by German Nazis during the Holocaust of 1941–5. It was all about the inhumanity of man to man. But some people don't accept comparisons, and in the subsequent brouhaha the wretched historian was inevitably accused of approving the ghastly attitudes and practices that he was merely describing.[20]

The chief carper raised the important issue of factual accuracy. He did so, however, in a manner that hardly imbues the criticism with credibility. Ignoring the signpost sentence in the preface, which points to the 'level of precision appropriate to different genres of history' – and which in my view should be the starting-point of debate – he laid out a handful of dead nits and tried to conclude that the entire research had 'gone to waste': in other words, that the book was worthless.

Of course, history is not fiction. Every genuine mistake causes a prick of remorse. I blush to think that *hwl* came out as *hwll*; that Don Ottavio was turned into a baritone; and that Valetta's Grand Harbour was degraded to a mere bay. On the other hand, if one looks for a minute at the chief carper's accusations, one finds that they are nearly all either trivial or unsubstantiated or completely off target. Dr Bronowski was indeed Jacob not Joseph, but he was a biologist not a historian. Hannibal is *not* assigned to the wrong century. He is correctly presented as a soldier of the third century BC who died in exile in the following century. It is unfortunate that the regnal dates of Henry VIII and his children were somehow misplaced by one year, but it is not as grave an offence as that of the chief carper, who thinks that the Tudors were *British* monarchs. Even if the faults were as frequent as the chief carper suggests, the body of the text would still be 98–99 per cent accurate. There was nothing which a revised edition would not easily correct.

Far more important, to my way of thinking, are the natural consequences of writing broad historical panoramas. The unusually high degree of selectivity and compression, the unavoidable generalisations and the reliance on secondary sources necessarily result in a cruder factual texture than that which a narrow monograph or a scientific article can achieve. The problem was tackled in part by adding the detailed snapshots at the end of each chapter and by scattering a wide selection of very specific boxed capsules throughout the text. With two or three exceptions, the great majority of reviewers applauded the exercise. One loses in precision but one gains in breadth of vision and comparison. Even so, I was conscious of engaging in something akin to a form of historical Impressionism – I called it *pointilliste* – and I half-expected that the academic pedants would dislike it. I talked of constructing an illusion of the un-attainable past and that is not what they wish to hear.

Actually, it would be more appropriate if I were to feel embarrassed for having unintentionally maltreated some of my colleagues. I certainly felt sorry for Professor John Roberts, the late warden of Merton College, who seems to have come off worse from a collision that neither of us intended. When I was first commissioned by OUP to write *Europe: A History*, I made an appointment to meet Dr Roberts, who, as the author of a 'history of the world', was well placed to give advice on the pitfalls of large-scale projects.[21] I found him surprisingly unforthcoming, and I suppose that he ought to have told me about the rival work on which he must already have embarked. Nonetheless, he was perfectly entitled to keep the information to himself, and I'm sure he would not have complained of the coming competition. Even so, we all know that comparisons are invidious, and that few of them are likely to give equal praise to two different and complemen-tary studies of the same subject. Reviewers prefer blood and glory. Some of them, including prominent commentators, clearly opted for Roberts's *History of Europe*.[22] But most did not. And the 'war of the bookshops' was very one-sided. Norman Stone, in the *Guardian*, said it all: 'It was a great misfortune for J.M. Roberts,' he opined, 'that his frigate put to sea at the same time as Norman Davies's battleship.'

In the meantime, the roller coaster rushed on. Continental reviewers went to work. One of them, Professor Peter Alter, penned an appreciative piece entitled '*Warum auch Grossbritannien ein Teil Europas ist*' (Why Great Britain as well is part of Europe). *Europe: A History* was not written as a contribution to the contemporary political debate, but it is not going to escape that destiny.

The author's involvement with a successful book does not cease when it has been printed, published, promoted and put into the bookshops. The British hardback edition was but the first of many rounds. In the case of *Europe: A History*, three further editions were published in the English language. And, as soon as it hit the Number 1 spot in the best-seller list, a flood of enquiries about foreign translations flowed in.

The British paperback edition arrived twelve months after the hardback. Thanks to a complicated contractual arrangement, it was not published by OUP but by Random House. But that's only half the story for I found myself in the middle of major company mergers. My original contract had been signed with Reed International, the paper conglomerate, which had planned to publish the paperback through its subsidiary, Octopus Books, whilst sub-licensing the hardback rights to OUP. But Reed International was broken up before I had finished writing. The Octopus branch of the business was bought by Random House. I thereby gained another publisher, Will Sulkin, under whose guidance the paperback edition of *Europe* became a great success.[23]

The Polish edition, published by Znak in Cracow, followed next. Beautifully translated by the formidable Professor Elżbieta Tabakowska, who is fully awake to wit, irony, paradox and metaphor, it defied all the gloomy predictions about it being too big and heavy to be popular. Within a short time, it had shot to Number 1 in the Polish ratings. Yet the best part of the experience for me was to read the fascinating book which Professor Tabakowska wrote herself 'on the problems of translating Norman Davies'.[24]

Next came the American hardback published by OUP in New York. I have known the firm – which is now separate from OUP in Oxford – for many years, and everything went well. The most interesting aspect, though, arose from that one hostile review in the *New York Times*. My editors said that no book can survive a bad review in the *Times*. 'The bookstores will drop it.' 'The US Library Association won't touch it.' It simply wasn't true. *Europe* sailed on with barely a hiccup.

By the time HarperCollins brought out the American paperback edition in 1998[25] negotiations were well advanced for more foreign translations. The Japanese won the race, producing a fine four-volume set. The Italian publishers Bruno Mondadori came up with a boxed, two-volume set. And in Kiev the Ukrainian firm of Odnovy brought out a massive blockbuster that in 2000 was due to be voted 'Book of the Millennium'. Which was all very satisfying. From then on, more than a score of contracts were signed, and every year brought its crop of new translations. At the time of writing, a Chinese edition is awaited from Beijing, an Arabic edition from Riyadh, and a Portuguese edition from Brasilia.[26]

Oddly enough, the two countries which might have been expected to show the keenest interest in a history of Europe have proved to be the

EUROPE EAST AND WEST

least enthusiastic. One is France. Despite the intervention of Jacques Delors, who heard me talk about *Europe: A History* at a conference in Athens, no French publisher has risen to the bait. The other is Germany. There, the company which bought the rights announced that they could not proceed without a subsidy. They told me that the German book market was depressed. As I dared to tell one of their executives, if the Lithuanians can afford to publish it, one would hope that the Germans could some day follow suit.

I began by saying that the task of writing *Europe: A History* was impossible. That judgement still stands, even though something has obviously been written. The task was impossible in the sense that all attempts to reconstruct the past are ultimately impossible. Historians simply do not have the means to comprehend the near-infinite complexities of their subject matter. We are never going to be able to see through the glass except darkly. All that can be done is to raise public awareness, to add a little to the limited store of prevailing knowledge and, above all, to arouse the readers' enthusiasm.

On several occasions I have been asked what I think the ultimate impact of the book will be. The stock answer would be to say that it is hardly for the author to judge. I can only guess, and hope. But I do hope that *Europe: A History* will play its part in strengthening European identity, both in the minds of Europeans and in the eyes of non-Europeans. By presenting a pan-European view of the past, it could assist in the promotion of pan-European views in the future. By discrediting the old equation of Europe with Western Europe, it may help to foster European unity, and by appearing in bookshops and libraries in local languages in countries as far apart as China and Brazil it could conceivably do a little to improve Europe's tarnished image around the world. I believe strongly that the old closed circle of dominant European cultures can no longer speak for Europe as a whole. Just as national consciousness was being built in the nineteenth and early twentieth centuries, a new, less truculent and less divisive European consciousness is slowly coming to life. And, as the once-dominant European image becomes more familiar in a more fallible but more credible form, one may tentatively anticipate a more realistic understanding of global humanity.

V

NOT FOREVER ENGLAND: A EUROPEAN HISTORY OF BRITAIN[1]

THE launch of *The Isles: A History* took place one evening in November 1999 in the hall of the Royal Geographical Society in Kensington. The main speaker was the late Hugo Young, senior columnist of the *Guardian*, biographer of Mrs Thatcher and chief ideologue of the pro-European camp of British political opinion.[2] It was a dark and stormy night. Hugo arrived late, having been delayed on his return from distant parts, and he left early, since he wasn't feeling well. But he stayed long enough to deliver a passionate speech about British attitudes, about the obstacles to a better understanding of European affairs and about the book. Transfixed by his performance, I made no notes – which I regret. All that stuck in my mind were two comments. One was, 'This book's time has come.' The other was, 'This is the first European history of Britain.' (The latter had already been used in a pre-publication review by the BBC's chief political correspondent, Andrew Marr.)

I ran into Hugo Young once or twice more before his tragically early death, but we never had the opportunity to talk at length. So I was left with nagging thoughts regarding what exactly it was that gave the book its European credentials. I hope that my memory is not at fault, but I don't recall that I set out with a clear plan of writing a 'European history' of this country. It's true that I had planted a British strand in my previous book, *Europe: A History*; and that, as a result, I decided to plant a European strand in *The Isles*, by prefacing each chapter with an essay outlining the state of affairs on the continent in the period in question. But this idea was more connected with giving a wider context to insular affairs rather than with interpreting them in any particular way. My main concern at the time was to mount an offensive against Anglocentrism in history writing. I wanted to show once and for all that the entrenched English tradition sorely diminished Britain's past, that there was far more to be said than most English historians dreamt of.

This Anglocentrism is worth examining closely. It used to pass under the heading of 'Our Island Story', to borrow the phrase of H.E. Marshal and of Arthur Bryant, and is very much the product of England's imperial expansion. One would be tempted to call it the 'English Ideology', if the term had not already been pre-empted for more specific purposes in the Reformation period. It may best be regarded, therefore, as a collection of assertions that are endlessly repeated until most people (in England) accept them to be true:

1. England is an island.
2. England is ruled by the queen of England (formerly by the kings of England).
3. England is the name of the country in which we live.
4. England is also the name for the family of nations and peoples over which England rules.
5. 'English' and 'British' are virtually synonymous terms.
6. English history and British history are one and the same thing.
7. The English people and their magnificent traditions have been the model for all others in the family, and hence are the only ones that count.
8. The English people are native to these shores, and their traditions have grown continuously in their native soil since the days of King Alfred and beyond.
9. The English heritage has little or nothing to do with the continent of Europe. We and our ways are completely separate.
10. England is a tolerant country, and has always given refuge to unfortunate foreigners. But, thanks to its unconquered isolation, foreigners and foreign ways have played no significant role since the Norman Conquest of 1066.

I am fairly confident that all the above contentions could be substantiated by chapter and verse, but they are so common and so ubiquitous they no longer have to be spelled out and have become the unwritten assumptions of popular English thinking about the past. (I have never seen them written down in this form.)

The first question is: are they true?

1. In actual fact, England is not an island; it is roughly half an island, just as Haiti forms part of Hispaniola and Brunei forms part of Borneo. The island is called Great Britain and it is divided between Scotland, England and Wales.

2. England is *not* ruled by a queen of England, because there has been no queen of England since Queen Anne became queen of Great Britain in 1707. Queen Elizabeth II is the eleventh British monarch in the line of the Hanoverian succession beginning from the same date. By rights, she should not be counted 'Elizabeth II' because Elizabeth I (Elizabeth Tudor) was the queen of different realms – of England and Wales, and of Ireland. Logically, if the present queen's son, Prince Charles, were to succeed to the British throne, he should be given the title of Charles I, since he would be the first Charles to have reigned as king of Great Britain and Northern Ireland. One may be sure, however, that he intends to take the title of Charles III. The English tradition has precedence, and does not respect logic.

3. It all depends on who 'we' are, and what is meant by 'our country'. All the inhabitants of England are subjects of the British monarch and citizens of the United Kingdom of Great Britain and Northern Ireland. (Please check with the cover of your passports.) The accepted shorthand name for the United Kingdom is either 'the UK' or 'Britain' but not 'England'.

None of the citizens of the UK who are not English and who live in Scotland, Wales or Northern Ireland would ever make the mistake of calling their home country England.

4. England used to be the popular collective name for all the peoples both of the British Isles and of the British empire. But this inaccurate convention has ceased to be current for the last fifty or sixty years.

5. The adjective 'English' refers to England. 'British' refers either to the island of Great Britain or to the state of Britain, i.e. the UK. In other

words, they have quite straightforward meanings, and are not synonymous. For example, there is an English football team, which represents the Football Association of England and an English cricket team representing the MCC. There is no British football team and no British cricket team because there is no such thing as a British FA or a British equivalent of the MCC. However, there *is* an all-Union rugby team called the British Lions, which draws on players from England, Scotland, Ireland and Wales. Supporters of English teams should wave the English flag, the Cross of St George, and not the British flag, the Union Jack.

6. English history is the history of England. Strictly speaking, it came to an end in 1707, when, like Scotland, England ceased to be a sovereign state, but it may also be seen to be a constituent part of British history, in that England since 1707 has been one of several constituent parts of the United Kingdom.

In so far as England was once the collective name in popular parlance for the whole of the empire, 'English history' could once be used to include all the peoples and all the territorial possessions within the empire. Nowadays, however, 'British history' has been almost universally adopted as the correct term for this purpose. At all events, English history and British history are by no means the same thing.

7. England and the English people have been the dominant element in the British Isles for many centuries. As far as modern history is concerned, their traditions and their interests should undoubtedly be given pride of place. Yet there is no good reason to use English dominance to suppress or minimise the traditions and the interests of the non-English, especially in the pre-Union period.

8. Good Heavens! The English are no more natives of these isles than the Vikings or the Normans were. The ancestors whom they acknowledge, the assorted Germanic tribes commonly called Anglo-Saxons, were migrants from the continent in the period following the downfall of Roman Britain. The ancestors they don't always acknowledge, the ex-Romano-Britons with whom the Anglo-Saxons mixed and intermarried, were the descendants of Celtic tribes whose origins are lost in the mists of prehistory. Those 'ancient Britons' are the only true natives of Great Britain. They are the direct forebears of the modern Welsh nation. King Alfred was king of Wessex. He never unified

England, let alone Great Britain or the isles as a whole. He was not British.

9. The English heritage, like the British heritage, of which it forms part, is an amalgam of many elements, most of them continental. For a start, one may list the Celtic, the Roman, the Anglo-Saxon, Danish, Norman, Plantagenet, Welsh, Irish, Scottish and Hanoverian elements.

10. For much of modern history, England was an extremely intolerant country, especially on religious grounds. Jews were totally excluded from 1290 to 1654. Protestant refugees, like the Huguenots, were welcomed, whilst Catholic refugees would only have come here at their peril. Mass immigration by the Catholic Irish in the nineteenth century caused great friction. Nonetheless foreigners and foreign imports have exerted enormous influence. The Reformation, which cut England off from most of its neighbours, was itself a continental import. Foreign trade forged permanent contacts abroad. The monarchy, a central institution for centuries, has rarely been staffed by purely English monarchs. Between the eleventh and early fifteenth centuries, no kings of England were ethnically English; and between 1552 and 1952, only three out of eighteen English or British reigning monarchs had two English-born parents, and each of those three was a woman.[3] There are countries in the world, like Japan, which *did* seal themselves off from the outside world, but England was never one of them.

The second question is: do these matters get properly explained in the main works of reference and in authoritative textbooks? The answer has to be, 'No', or, 'Not very often'. Students are more likely to meet confusion than clarity. Most British libraries and library catalogues are structured on the false assumption that English history and British history form one single subject while Welsh history, Irish history and Scottish history belong to separate compartments. The Oxford University On-Line Libraries Catalogue (OLIS) is a good case in point. Similarly, the introduction to the *Oxford History of Britain* (1999) contains the following convoluted muddle. 'A basic premise of this book,' it explains eccentrically, 'is that it deals with the history of Great Britain, two partitioned, poly-cultural islands, and not merely with England.'[4] One suspects that the mix-ups are being disseminated by the very works that should be disentangling them.

The third question is: does it matter? In my experience, most English people do *not* think it matters. The typical reaction from someone challenged for talking about their 'English passport' or the 'queen of England' is, 'For God's sake, stop quibbling!' or, 'Of course, we all know that!' I respectfully beg to differ. I don't think that everyone does know. And it *does* matter. For one, it is very demeaning for non-English people to find themselves excluded. For another, it is extremely divisive. It may be in the interests of English nationalism for confusion to be sown, for minorities to be excluded or humiliated and for the language of English dominance to be perpetuated, but the community of Britain can never be entirely healthy or harmonious unless and until all its members, great and small, are afforded equal respect.

Which is something to be felt in the bones. To begin with, reading the reviews of *The Isles*, I could not fathom whether I had succeeded or failed. The first hint of success came from an old friend, Alistair Moffat, who told me, 'You know, at every single turn, you write exactly the opposite of what they expect.' I was flattered. On the lips of a canny Scot, 'they' could only mean one thing: the Sassenachs!

What I did not fully realise at the time is that the offensive against Anglocentrism had a great deal to do with European affairs. Yet, having had some time to reflect, I can now propose that the issue should be discussed under three headings: the European setting of British history, the European components of Englishness, and Britain-in-Europe.

The European Setting of British History

One of the most frequent misconceptions to be encountered lies in the notion of English and later of British insularity. The English lived on an island surrounded by sea, therefore they were cut off from the continent. Or as the English would say, the continent was cut off from England. Nothing could be further from the truth. At any stage of history prior to the Railway Age, communication by sea was much quicker and more effective than communication by land. Given a fair wind, a sailing ship could cross from Dover to Calais or from Calais to Dover in two or three hours. In two or three hours a lumbering horse-drawn coach could not have made it from Dover to Hythe or from Calais to Dunkerque. One of the wonders of the age of the horse was Dick Turpin's legendary non-stop ride from London to York. Before dropping dead, Black Bess covered 187 miles in twenty-four hours – an average of 7.8 mph. A fast sloop in full sail running before a westerly gale would probably make twice the speed for days on end. English pilgrims journeying to Rome walked for three months. In three months an ocean-going merchantman could cruise in leisurely fashion through the Straits of Gibraltar to Italy, and come all the way back. (The record for sailing round the world single-handed stands at seventy-two days.) And ships carried heavy loads. They brought men, money, news, goods, trends and ideas, as well as soldiers, guns and disease. They made England unusually accessible to foreign influences. They gave her a head start in the race which built up the preconditions of the Industrial Revolution and of socio-economic modernisation. Geography, therefore, did not insulate England from the outside world. On the contrary, it pushed it into the forefront of the mainstream.

The one institution capable of curtailing England's close relations with the continent was the Royal Navy. If the sea encouraged the sinews of cultural and commercial intercourse, it equally opened the way for foreign invaders. Hence, from the early sixteenth century onwards, the Tudors determined to maintain a standing naval force strong enough to repel all would-be boarders. They did so in an era when the Reformation was spreading distrust between the Protestant states of northern Europe and the Catholic powers of Poland, Germany, France and Spain. Here was the source of the real problem. Religion became entangled with security; religious prejudices dominated politics; and paranoia set in for a very long season. Clearly, the devil could be hiding in the hold of any Spanish ship!

Even so, paranoia is easy to exaggerate, and England was never completely isolated. English ships continued to trade with Scandinavia, with the Low Countries, with Germany. Prior to the Act of Union, to confound the English independent Scotland cultivated its continental links, especially with France and the Baltic. Ireland never severed its ancient links with Iberia. The Dutch fleet roared into the Medway in June 1667 and stole the Royal Navy's flagship. And the French and Spanish never had too much trouble putting landing parties ashore in Ireland and Wales.

In short, England was not Japan. Continental affairs, which had provided the background to developments in the isles from the earliest times, continued to do so, even if subdued during the centuries of Britain's imperial 'splendid isolation'. This point was driven home by the essays that precede each of the main chapters of *The Isles: A History*. The prelude to Chapter I, which started with the story of Cheddar Man, revealed that the isles had not yet been formed in the ninth millennium BC. For 99.9 per cent of prehistory, the land that was to become Britain was a continental peninsula. The prelude to Chapter II, which introduced Celtic Britain partly through the microcosm of the port at Din Albion (Hengistbury Head), showed that the Sleeve (not yet the English Channel) had been a highway of unity between two related segments of the Celtic world. Chapter III, which opened with the Arch of Claudius in Rome, where the conquest of 'the greater Isle' was celebrated, showed that Britannia was but one more province of Rome's empire. And so, the structure proceeded:

Chapter IV   Hengist and Horsa: the continental origins of the English
Chapter V   Norse sagas: the isles overrun by Scandinavian invaders
Chapter VI   Angleterre: a part of France d'Outremer
Chapter VII   The Homage of Amiens: French prelude to 'The Englished Isles'
Chapter VIII James VI and I: king of two isles and three kingdoms
Chapter IX   Darien: a Scottish disaster precedes the British empire
Chapter X   Delhi Durbar: starting point of the post-imperial isles[5]

Examples of this kind are endless. A little comparative history would help to emphasise that almost all the institutions which English historians like to portray as unique actually have continental counterparts. Take the Anglican Church – a state-sponsored Protestant monopoly. What could be more English? Well, the Church of Sweden, or at a later date the State Church of Prussia. Or take the English parliament – a two-chambered legislature, enshrining the principle of popular liberties to balance the monarch's prerogatives. The kingdom of Poland had fostered something very similar in the sixteenth century, and it came up with statutes equivalent to Habeas Corpus and to 'no taxation without representation' long before

Westminster did. So, too, did the estates of Aragon. Or take the British empire based on overseas colonies. Actually, the English were laggards in this respect, starting the best part of a century behind the Portuguese and the Spaniards. And the Royal Navy? It did not overtake the navy of the United Provinces until the late seventeenth century, and only after some mammoth engagements. And the Bank of England? That, too, was preceded by the Bank of Amsterdam. And the English monarchy transformed into a constitutional British monarchy? Yet again, one of its chief architects, William of Orange, who sponsored the Bill of Rights, was a Dutchman. And constitutional monarchies were hardly an insular monopoly. One could probably put the high-medieval Holy Roman Empire into the same category.

Of course, England was not made just by imitating continental models. It came up with a very original mix of its own – as all countries did. But it was not so original that it defies all comparisons.

The European Components of Englishness

No one suggests that England was a vehicle assembled from a pile of European spare parts. All one needs to demonstrate is that many things which the English consider to be unique belong equally to other discourses. Was he Canute, king of England, or was he really St Cnud, king of Denmark? Evidently, he was both. The different perceptions derive from the different viewpoints of the beholders. As they say, *Punkt widzenia zależy od punktu siedzenia* – One's angle of sighting depends on one's place of seating.

Roman Britain

The English are very fond of Roman Britain. They speak and write of it with awe. They start most of their national history books with the landings of Julius Caesar in 55–54 BC as if it were the beginning of their own story. And they gush with enthusiasm over Roman roads and hypercaust heating and Hadrian's Wall. They think of the Romans as their own predecessors, civilised and imperial, born to rule, and they empathise with the governors who had to cope with the barbarians pouring over the wall. What could be more congenial, in the most literal sense, than Rudyard Kipling, bard of the British empire, musing with nostalgia about the emotions of a Roman centurion:

Legate, I had the news last night – my cohort ordered home
By ship to Portus Itius and thence by road to Rome.
I've watched the companies aboard, the arms are stored below:
Now let another take my sword. Command me not to go!

I've served in Britain for forty years, From Vectis to the Wall.
I have none other home than this, nor any life at all.
[. . .]

Legate, I come to you in tears – My cohort ordered home!
I've served in Britain forty years. What should I do in Rome?
Here is my heart, my soul, my mind – the only life I know.
I cannot leave it all behind. Command me not to go![6]

Well, there's the imperialist talking. He was thinking of the story of the Romans as if it was part of the history of England. Very few of the enthusiasts pause to reflect on the fact that it was the English, or rather the Germanic ancestors of the English, who smashed up the civilisation of Britannia and, by one means or another, eradicated the greater part of Romano-British culture.

The people the English call the Welsh – from an Anglo-Saxon word for 'foreigner' – remember Roman Britain in a very different way. From the Welsh point of view, Britannia was a happy blend of Latin and Celtic cultures which took its name from the Celtic *Prydain*. In its later phase, it was also a land where Christianity was starting to flourish. Its downfall was an unmitigated disaster from which the natives would never recover. It opened the gates to hordes of primitive, pagan, illiterate marauders who in the end grabbed the jackpot. In Welsh eyes, pride can be taken from the centuries-long rearguard action mounted both in the former Britannia or in the 'Old North', in the British kingdom of Strathclyde. Whether King Arthur was a British war leader from the south 'before England', or, as now seems equally probable, from the north, 'before Scotland', is a moot point.[7] But the Welsh still sing songs about the fourth-century Machsen, whose legions marched under the standard of the Red Dragon, and their name for England is *Lloegr*, the 'lost land'; they rightly see themselves as the only true Britons, and they are the only group in modern Britain whose forebears could boast of being *civites Romani*.

The Danelaw

The Danes and the Vikings have invariably had a bad press in England. They are viewed as hordes of primitive, pagan, illiterate marauders who grabbed a large slice of what was the rightful property of the English nation. These were the ultimate Dark Age terrorists whose depredations threatened to overturn the stability of civilised Europe. Eric Blood-Axe, king of York, was reputedly the last pagan ruler in the isles. We were only saved from the likes of him by the patriotic heroics of Alfred, Aethelred and in the last battle before the Norman Conquest, Harold Godwinson.

Or were we? The Danes did not pack up and go home. Having settled a very large tract of eastern England between the Thames and the Humber in the ninth century, they stayed on. Because of their initial illiteracy they left few records, and they have been easily dismissed as a passing phase of little significance. They were converted to Christianity by Anglo-Saxon missions who also taught them to speak Old English and to forget their previous culture. Yet their impact cannot have been so slight. They were still in place in the eleventh century, when Hereward the Wake offered stiff resistance to the incoming Normans. Thereafter, they disappear from view, merging imperceptibly into the general population. Nonetheless, they must have supplied a leaven in the overall cultural and ethnic mix, especially in the eastern counties. If one asks why Middle English, when it finally resurfaced in the fourteenth century, was so markedly different from its antecedent, Old English, the explanation must surely have something to do with the long fermentation of Anglo-Saxon, Danish and Norman French.

Similarly, in the political sphere the Danes and the Vikings quickly sank out of sight. Yet the very English image of the final phase of Anglo-Saxon history may be something of an illusion. In 1066 the fate of the kingdom of England hung on the outcome of a three-cornered contest. Harold Godwinson held the throne. Harald III Hardrada, king of Norway, landed in the north. And Guillaume Le Bâtard, duke of Normandy, landed in the south. The first was leader of a court party with Danish roots. The second was the latest of the pagan Viking monarchs. The third was the great-grandson of Vikings: French by language, Viking by temperament and heritage. Whoever won the contest, it was certain that in one way or another the Vikings were going to take their belated revenge.

And then there is the small matter of the striking similarity between the lifestyle of the Vikings and that of the original Anglo-Saxons. Both lived from piracy and sea-raiding. If one group is to be condemned as Dark Age terrorists, so should the other. But that is not how English history works. Droves of English historians have succeeded in identifying the Anglo-Saxons with Us, and the Vikings with Them.

The Norman Conquest

As far as I know, no one has ever described William the Conqueror as a true-born Englishman. Like all the kings of England for the next 300 years, he could not speak a word of English. He made a clean break with the past in many spheres, introducing a new legal system, a new administration and a new francophone ruling class. Yet he has not attracted the opprobrium which English public opinion usually reserves for intruding foreigners. One reason, no doubt, lay in the fact that a large part of that ruling class, even when later anglicised, did not forget to whom they owed their lands and their fortunes.

The most interesting aspect of Norman history, however, concerns who those Normans thought they were. For overseas ventures were their speciality. The Conqueror's entourage were well aware that they were the beneficiaries of the overseas venture of Red Rollo, who had taken over Normandy in 911. And they must have watched with interest as Robert and Roger Guiscard, their compatriots, sailed to Sicily in 1057 to found a kingdom whose independence was to last as long as England's. British observers in later times were to look back at the Normans and see a hardy band of conquerors who made England their permanent home, but the assumption is slightly dubious. Many Norman families not only maintained their lands in Normandy, but cultivated their Norman roots. For them, England must have felt like a temporary abode: a home from home, an outpost for further adventuring. They were a restless crowd. They moved into the Welsh borders, and subdued a huge sliver of territory from Chester to Chepstow. They moved into Scotland, where a group of francophone clans like the Stewarts, the Bruces and the Bailliols displaced the preceding Gaelic elite. And in 1169 they crossed the sea to Ireland where they launched yet another long-lasting venture. One is tempted to say that Viking blood was still coursing in their veins.

Many centuries later, when Norman England had passed away and Norman energies had been finally dispersed, the English themselves took to overseas ventures. They went first to Virginia, then to Ulster, and in due course to India, Australia and Africa. Together with the Scots, and for a time with the Irish, they built the vastest empire in world history. Yet wherever they went, they didn't mix terribly well. Unlike some other European colonists, they didn't intermarry very enthusiastically with the natives, and in many places from New England to New Zealand they founded self-sufficient, English-speaking communities that stayed apart. Even in India, where the British were a tiny minority, the British sahib would sit under his sunshade on the hills of Simla, reading *The Times*, dreaming of his distant home and pondering his next imperial assignment. One wonders if that was not a very Norman attitude.

The Reformation

The Protestant Reformation in the sixteenth century split one half of Europe into two unequal parts. It did not affect the Orthodox Churches in the east, and it did not win out in the southern parts of Western Europe. But in the countries of north-west and northern Europe, from Scotland to Finland, it gave rise to a mass of differentiated and not always compatible Churches and denominations, whose lowest common denominator was their rejection of the authority of the Roman pope. Many of these new Protestant Churches established a monopoly in the states where they were established. In Germany, the home of Martin Luther, where political power was already fragmented into hundreds of tiny statelets, the principle of *cuius regio, eius religio* determined that every princeling could settle religious matters within his own territory. Similar arrangements were made in the cantons of Switzerland, the home of John Calvin. In some of the bigger countries, like Poland, Hungary and France, no clear result was obtained. France and Germany were the scene of the most appalling religious wars. The newly formed Commonwealth of Poland-Lithuania was the one European state which in 1572 formally and successfully passed a statute of religious peace.

England's place in all this was characterised by an extreme form of Erastianism, where the link between Church and state turned religious dissent into treason. The Elizabethan settlement with its Act of (compulsory) Uniformity of 1559, which is often praised by Anglican sympathisers for its judicious sense of balance, did not ensure religious stability in the long term. The exclusion of Roman Catholics led in 1605 to the Gunpowder Plot which, as an act of religious terrorism, would have rivalled St Bartholomew's Eve. Its exclusion of Calvinist puritans or nonconformists was at least partly responsible for the Civil War of 1642–6. And, from the Popish Plot of the 1670s to the Gordon Riots of 1780, religious bigotry played a prominent role in English life.

Protestant politics supplied the key factor in the construction of the United Kingdom. When the English decided to join with Scotland in 1707 they could only do so by guaranteeing the unchanged independence of the Presbyterian Church of Scotland. By this, they deprived the United Kingdom of the chance of forming a state Church. When they decided on a union with Ireland in 1801, they could only do so by promising Catholic Emancipation – a commitment that for three decades was observed in the breach. No one should have been surprised, for by that time anti-Catholicism had become a foundation stone of English, Scottish and British identity.

The Protestant establishment in Britain systematically shunned all close connections with Catholic Europe for centuries. But they did recognise communion with most other Protestant faiths and with Christian Orthodoxy. In consequence, the international marriage market for British princes and princesses was strictly defined from the outset. The favourite destinations for outgoing brides were Prussia and Russia. Among the preferred springboards for incoming spouses were Denmark, Greece,

Holland and a large number of obscure German statelets like Hanover, Saxe-Coburg-Gotha and Teck.

The House of Hanover/Saxe-Coburg-Gotha/Mountbatten-Windsor

Georg Ludwig, elector of Hanover (1660–1727) was a middle-ranking German prince. He had never been to England. He had no close British relatives. Indeed, like William the Conqueror, he couldn't speak a word of English. In short, he was the ideal candidate to be crowned as the first king of the United Kingdom. He had unbeatable qualifications: he was a Protestant, he was not British. And there were fifty-one other candidates with a better hereditary claim to succeed. In consequence, he would be entirely dependent on the Whig lords in London, who were pulling the strings. He was appointed by act of parliament. And, if necessary, he could be removed by act of parliament. Such were the inauspicious beginnings of the British monarchy, and of a royal family that would still be sitting on the British throne 300 years later.[8]

In the eighteenth century the Hanoverians stood at the summit of a system where the little direct power that they had been given dwindled further, but as symbols and figureheads they were key players in the creation of the new British nation. The powerless monarchy proved a powerful instrument in the craft of national image-building. They offended no vested interests, appealed to the English and Lowland Scots alike, and as commanders-in-chief presided over all the glorious victories of the Royal Navy. Above all, anointed by divine will of their Protestant God, they symbolised the propriety of the government's anti-Catholic ideology and of the nation's wars against France and Spain:

> When Britain first at heav'n's command,
> Arose from out the azure main,
> This was the charter, the charter of the land,
> And guardian angels sang this strain:
> 'Rule, Britannia! Britannia rule the waves:
> Britons never will be slaves.'

The nations not so blest as thee,
Shall in their turns to tyrants fall;
While thou shalt flourish great and free,
The dread and envy of them all.[9]

In the nineteenth century the monarchy recovered from the treason of
the American colonies and the scandal of a royal divorce to become the
focus of Britain's imperial pride. Queen Victoria, who reigned for sixty-
four years, was empress of India as well as the British queen. Her subjects
lived through the last period when they could claim to be leaders of the
world. They had the men; they had the guns; they had the money, too.

Throughout those two centuries, though, the royal family had clung
tenaciously to their Germanity. Every single prince of Wales, as heir to the
throne, had been given a German bride imported from Germany, and
behind the scenes German was the mother tongue of all royal children.
At one point Queen Victoria had to be asked not to talk in German to the
Prince Consort in cabinet, because her ministers could not follow the
conversation. This tradition still prevailed in the early twentieth century.
George V, son of a German mother, was husband to a German queen and
cousin to the German kaiser.

A major crisis erupted in 1914, therefore, when Britain found itself at
war with Germany. The royal family, which had adopted Prince Albert's
surname of Saxe-Coburg-Gotha after the male Hanoverian line failed,
change its name again to Windsor. The kaiser is said to have thereupon
uttered his only known joke: he said that he'd been to the theatre for a
performance of 'The Merry Wives of Saxe-Coburg-Gotha'.

A similar stratagem had to be put in place after the Second World War,
when the Princess Elizabeth (Windsor), first in line to the throne, became
engaged to Philip (Mountbatten), prince of Greece and Denmark. It was
decided the pair should be Mountbatten-Windsor. Yet Prince Philip
was not really a Mountbatten; his mother was a Battenberg, and his father
was a Schleswig-Holstein-Sonderburg-Glücksburg. He had quietly adopted
the surname of his uncle, Admiral Mountbatten, so as not to suffer the
fate of his great-uncle, Admiral von Battenberg, who, being a German
citizen as well as first lord of the British Admiralty, had been summarily
dismissed. Fortunately, since Prince Philip speaks near-perfect English – his

third language – no one but the most observant of observers would ever know.

I once pursued an entertaining correspondence with Prince Philip on this matter. Having visited his seventy-fifth-birthday exhibition at Windsor, where it was impossible to discover his family name, I had written to ask him, very politely, what it was. It then became abundantly clear that the captain of the Coldstream Guards penning the replies either did not know the answer or was under orders not to reveal it. At first, he gave me 'Prince of Denmark and Greece'. Then he gave me Mountbatten, wrongly described as the prince's mother's surname. But to the end he would not let the right answer fall from his pen.[10]

Britain-in-Europe

The United Kingdom entered the European Community on 1 January 1973 in the company of Ireland and Denmark. The prime minister of the day, Edward Heath, knew perfectly well that the Treaty of Rome, which he had signed, committed all signatories to 'ever closer union' but, fearing dissident voices in his Conservative Party, chose in his public addresses to stress the economic advantages and to downplay the political commitment. The impression was created that Britain had joined nothing more than an updated version of the European Free Trade Area, which had just folded. The Labour Party was also seriously divided on the issue, and when it won the general election the following year, the result was a split cabinet and irresistible demands for a referendum. In this way, the British voting public took part in 1975 in the only referendum ever staged to determine whether a member state should actually leave the community. The pro-Europeans won, and the question has never been posed again.

Nonetheless, the chaotic episode of 1973–5 revealed how deeply divided the British public was. The divisions ran down the middle both of the Conservative and Labour Parties, and they did not go away. In the 1980s the government of the deeply Eurosceptical Margaret Thatcher did not kick against the traces partly because she succeeded in negotiating a hefty financial rebate and partly because her chief foreign policy advisers, like Geoffrey Howe, were committed Europeans. In the 1990s Mrs

Thatcher's successor, John Major, signed the Treaty of Maastricht, but only at the price of unending rows with his colleagues.

British attitudes to the European Movement, however, cannot be understood solely in terms of government and party policy. Other key factors became apparent at a later stage. For example, as so-called devolution came over the horizon, people realised that Scotland and Wales were markedly more Europhile than England. Mrs Thatcher had deeply offended the Scots and the Welsh on a number of occasions, and their natural reaction was to seek a counterweight in Brussels to centralised rule from London. Apart from that, Scottish and Welsh nationalism was on the rise, and national movements on the 'Celtic fringe' were bound to be impressed by the startling success of the Republic of Ireland. Ireland, in fact, had become the model to follow. It had left the UK in 1922, left the British Commonwealth in 1945, and, since joining the European Community, had prospered mightily. At the turn of the century its GDP per capita exceeded that of the UK for the first time in history, and it was full of confidence. So, everyone could see that a small ex-British state wholeheartedly committed to the European project could hold its own. If Ireland could do it, some day Scotland and Wales might do the same.

In 1997 the incoming New Labour government of Tony Blair gave urgent priority to devolution, and the granting of autonomy to a Scottish Parliament and a Welsh Assembly did much to hold back the nationalist tide. But other shifts were afoot. The Conservative and Unionist Party (to give its full name) lost all its seats in Scotland and Wales. So, since it did not compete in Northern Ireland, it became a purely English party. At the same time, the Scottish and Welsh branches of the Labour Party partly recovered from the nationalist challenge in their home constituencies, whilst exerting a powerful influence on New Labour. Tony Blair's circle had first been assembled by his late predecessor, John Smith, whose Scotto-Brit colleagues – i.e. Scots like Gordon Brown, Robin Cook, Donald Dewar and Lord Irvine, who opposed the break-up of the United Kingdom – moved into the British cabinet in force.

Indeed, the European issue was polarising British opinion. The Europhile interest, which was fully supportive of British membership of the EU and hoped to push the union forward, was concentrated in Scotland and Wales, in the business and social-moderate wings of the

Conservative Party, in the New Labour group of the Labour Party, and among Britain's third party, the Liberal Democrats. The Eurosceptic or Europhobe interest, in contrast, was almost exclusively English. It drew its support mainly from the right wing of the Conservatives and to a lesser degree from the ranks of left-wing 'old' Labour. It had become the rallying point of English nationalism, of prediluvian types who didn't recognise the difference between English and British, who thought 'our traditions' and 'our culture' and 'our sovereignty' were in mortal danger, and who secretly longed for the days when the English could tell the 'lesser breeds' what to do. The lesser breeds included the Scots and the Welsh and the 'wogs beyond Calais'.

It takes no genius to see that the Eurosceptic cause is based on a collection of absurdities. It is simply not true that the EU is a centralised 'superstate' or that it is aiming to be one in the future. It is simply not true that 'we are ruled from Brussels'. The EU Commission is the servant of the executive Council of Ministers, in whose decisions Britain has an equal voice to all other members. It is also not true that the separate identity of member states is under threat, even though a new European identity is being formed. Multiple identities are the norm in humankind, and there is no obstacle whatsoever to someone being a good European, a loyal British citizen and an English patriot all at the same time. The only obstacle lies in the exclusive/nationalist and xenophobic mentality which views 'Englishness' as incompatible with any other form of belonging.

As I now see it, my own contribution to this particular debate was made in the two last chapters of *The Isles*, where I presented a systematic exposé of the rise and fall of 'the pillars of Britishness'. And I can remember being surprised at the very clear-cut pattern that emerged. In Chapter IX, 'The Imperial Isles', which covered the period 1707–c.1900, I started out by examining the rise of six pillars – the Royal Navy, the British army, the empire, the Protestant ascendancy, the Westminster parliament and the constitutional monarchy. I soon realised that six was too few, and the chapter swelled to embrace twelve more including the aristocracy, the civil service, manufacturing industry, the Sterling Area, demographic expansion, standardised English, race, sport, law, weights and measures, ethos and the semi-detached stance to Europe. The material presented gave rise to a picture where every one of the pillars was going from strength to strength. In Chapter X, in contrast, 'The Post-Imperial Isles Since *c.*1900', an analysis based on the same eighteen pillars produced exactly the opposite – namely, a picture of almost universal disintegration. All the traditional pillars of Britishness were either in serious decline or, as with the empire itself, had already crumbled. The inevitable conclusion arose that the institutions and values on which the British state was founded had decayed much further than outward appearances may suggest. Writing before the effects of devolution on Scotland and Wales could be assessed, I risked the prediction that the United Kingdom might not reach its tercentenary in 2007. I pointed out that the UK had begun to break up in 1922, when the Irish Free State was formed. And Ireland's dramatic success as a sovereign member of the European Union supplies the model to which the non-English countries within the British state can aspire. In other words, Britain's destiny is pretty uncertain. Forty years ago the American statesman Dean Acheson stated prophetically that Britain had lost an empire but had not yet found a role. Since then, the inability to fix on a clear role either as a major power or as a wholehearted and leading member of the European Union has continued to characterise – and to plague – our predicament.

Yet rational arguments, in a sense, are beside the point. English nationalists, like nationalists the world over, operate on their passions, their convictions, their nostalgia for the 'good old days' that probably never existed. They are suckers for every myth going, starting with the oft-repeated nonsense about 'a thousand years of British parliamentary history'. Above all, they dislike 'foreigners': they are xenophobic. And, since membership of the European Movement demands partnership, international solidarity, shared sovereignty and reconciliation with former enemies, they don't want anything to do with it.

All of which should illuminate the problem from which I started. English nationalism and Europeanism now constitute the two central poles of British politics. So, as Hugo Young must have instantly realised, an all-out offensive against Anglocentrism in history is bound to operate in the pro-European interest. For Anglocentrism is one of the hallmarks of the English nationalist approach both to history and to current affairs. And the European Movement by its very nature is the sworn enemy of all nationalisms – French, German … Welsh, Scottish, Irish … Polish, Russian, Estonian, Albanian … or English. All nations have their patriots – men and women who love their country without deriding others. All nations have a block of indifferents. And all nations have their nationalists – men and women of a truculent disposition who seethe with daily indignation at perceived insults and who sincerely believe that loving one's country necessarily involves not loving the rest.

Nationalism, after all, had given the spur which set the post-war European Movement in motion. A group of European politicians who had seen the ravages of two world wars and the resultant catastrophe of Europe came together during and immediately after the war to discuss ways of running our continent more sensibly. They were all men, and all from Europe's many borderlands, where cultures and interests have had to be reconciled. Robert Schuman was from Lorraine, and would not have known whether he was a Frenchman or a German. Alcide de Gasperi came from South Tyrol, where the Austrian and the Italian spheres coincide. Paul Spaak came from Belgium, a country of two rival ethnicities. Konrad Adenauer, sometime lord mayor of Cologne, was a Rhinelander from the banks of a Swiss and Franco-German river. Joseph Retinger, 'the grey eminence of Europe', was a Pole from Cracow, where Polish and Austrian history overlaps. Prince Bernhard of the Netherlands was a German who had joined the Dutch royal family. These people knew instinctively that unrestrained sovereign states fired by nationalism were a menace so they looked for ways of binding Europe's sovereign states into a common enterprise.

Britain can be proud of many people of the same temper. Winston Churchill, who was the guest speaker at the Hague Conference, was half British and half American, and one of the more attractive sides of his imperialism lay in a willingness to see different races and cultures merging into one great family. The Scotto-Brits are another case in point. So, too, are the many advocates and practitioners of multiculturalism. The inner politics of all the so-called nationalist parties like Plaid Cymru or the SNP centres on the conflict between the 'true' nationalists, who burn down English holiday homes in Wales or call for the expulsion of all English intruders from Scotland, and the moderate independentists, who may be dubbed nationalists by their enemies for demanding the sovereignty of

their country but who also regard membership of the EU and good relations with England as crucial. Indeed, when one looks closely, it is
extremely difficult to find an English family that does not have close
connections with Ireland, Scotland or Wales, or with other countries
further afield. In a markedly mongrel population, thoroughbreds are a
rarity, and not all the thoroughbreds care much about it. Generally
speaking, if human beings are not embittered by wars and disputes, if they
are not seduced by nationalist propaganda, they are more interested in
cooperation and getting along with their neighbours than in waving a flag
or shouting insults.

So what, after all that, do those English nationalists believe in? They
are people who hold that long-suffering England, despite possessing more
than 80 per cent of the UK population, is being wildly exploited by
ungrateful Scots, thieving Welsh and wayward Irish and by unstoppable
tides of sponging immigrants. They are those who think that 'British is
best' because Britain is supposedly England. They are those who believe
in a false doctrine of England's eternal history, clinging to the absurdity
that England was forever English in the past and will remain so until the
end of time. One can see them every day. If they don't support the blus-
tering type of Tories, they vote for the National Front or for the BNP. Not
only do they chant 'Inglunt, Inglunt' at football matches, they also run off
after the match to thump a foreigner. And they tell us that they can't stand
being betrayed by our unpatriotic politicians or being dictated to by the
petty despots of the Brussels bureaucracy.

Yet if European identity is growing, if we are all growing this new crust
of Europeanness, it is only a matter of time before Europe gives birth to
its own form of nationalism. European nationalists, one assumes, will hate
everything American, despise the Chinese and the Indians, and fear Islam.
The European Movement will then have another fight on its hands.

Yet it would be wrong to end on a sour note. One of the truly redeeming
graces of the English is that they can laugh at themselves. Even the English
of the imperial era could see the amusing absurdities of their condition.
The following immortal lines were composed in 1930 on the long road
from Hong Kong to Saigon.

It's such a surprise for the Eastern eyes to see,
That though the English are effete, they're quite impervious to heat.
When the white man rides, every native hides in glee,
Because the simple creature's hoping he'll impale his solar topee on
    a tree.
It seems such a shame when the English claim the earth,
That they give rise to such hilarity and mirth.
[...]

The toughest Burmese bandit can never understand it.
In Rangoon the heat of noon is just what the natives shun.
They put their Scotch or Rye down, and lie down.
In a jungle town where the sun beats down to the rage of man and
    beast
The English garb of the English sahib merely gets a bit more creased.
In Bangkok at twelve o'clock they foam at the mouth and run,
But mad dogs and Englishmen go out in the midday sun.
[...]

The smallest Malay rabbit deplores this stupid habit.
In Hong Kong they strike a gong and fire off a noonday gun.
To reprimand each inmate who's in late.
In the mangrove swamps where the python romps
There is peace from twelve to two.
Even caribous lie around and snooze, for there's nothing else to do.
In Bengal to move at all is seldom if ever done,
But mad dogs and Englishmen go out in the midday sun.[11]

VI

SICUT LILIUM:
HISTORY AT MAGDALEN COLLEGE[1]

IT was exactly forty years after arriving at Magdalen College as a gentleman commoner that Edward Gibbon wrote the part of his *Memoirs* which describes his brief career at Oxford. His chapter on the subject contains a number of notorious comments that have since become so commonplace that they need not in the main be repeated here. Gibbon's views of Oxford, like his judgement on 'the manufactures of the monks of Magdalen' may best be passed over, as he put it, 'with a silent blush'. Suffice it to say that, as always, Gibbon's remarks were prefaced by a perfect lead sentence. 'A traveller who visits Oxford or Cambridge', he wrote, 'is surprised and edified by the apparent order and tranquillity that prevail in the English seats of learning.' After the word 'apparent', one knows exactly what is coming.

However, some passages are simply too good to avoid. Gibbon had reached Oxford at the age of fifteen in 1752. It was a year marked by his conversion to Roman Catholicism, by a long vacation that saw England's adoption of the Gregorian Calendar and the loss of eleven days, and by a general election. On this last subject, Gibbon waxed specially eloquent:

> As a gentleman commoner I was admitted to the society of the fellows and I fondly expected that some questions of literature would be the amusing and instructive topics of their discourse. [But]Their conversation stagnated in a round of college business, Tory politics,

personal stories and private scandal: their dull and deep potations excused the brisk intemperance of youth, and their constitutional toasts were not expressive of the most lively loyalty for the House of Hanover. A General Election was now approaching: the great Oxfordshire contest already blazed with all the malevolence of party-zeal. Magdalen College was devoutly attached to the old interest: and the names of Wenman and Dashwood were more frequently pronounced that those of Cicero and Chrysostom.[2]

Like many others, I had never been to Oxford before coming up for the dreaded scholarship interview, and I can still recall the trepidation with which I made my first timid tour of the cloisters, first gazed in wonder at the Tower, the Grove and the deer. I can remember puzzling in vain over the college's coat of arms and its motto of *Sicut lilium*, which I long took wrongly to refer to 'Consider the lilies how they grow'. In fact, *Sicut lilium* is taken from the Vulgate text of the Song of Songs, and has altogether more interesting associations:

> Sicut lilium inter spinas
> sic amica inter filias;
> sicut malus inter ligna silvarum
> sic dilectus meus inter filios.[3]

> Like the lily among thorns
> is my dearest among the maidens;
> like an apple tree among the trees of the forest
> so is my beloved among young men.

At all events, it was 1957. The president of the college was the art historian T.S.R. Boase, a man of the generation which had fought in the First World War; the senior historian who interviewed me with others, Kenneth Bruce McFarlane. On the way home to Lancashire, my anxious parents waited at Manchester Piccadilly Station, where the neat little white envelope was opened to reveal the news that I had won something called an Open Exhibition in Modern Subjects (history and geography). My father said something scathing along the lines of, 'And what is an exhibitioner supposed to exhibit?' After that I passed a final agreeable and examless term at school steadily reading my way into Gibbon on the orders of my history master who approved of the Magdalen connection. On the last day, anticipating the holidays, the school assembly roared out the old school song:

> Forty years on, when afar and asunder
> Parted are those who are singing today,
> When we look back and forgetfully wonder
> What we were like in our work and our play.[4]

At the time, forty years on was unimaginable.

I trust, therefore, that a few sentimental recollections are not entirely out of place. For it is remarkable how the choices and accidents of our early days map out the paths which we subsequently follow. In my case, in the era of National Service, I had expected to join the Royal Navy and to apply for the navy's intensive Russian course, which an older schoolmate had recently finished. As luck would have it, since I was still only seventeen, the navy would not take me, and the senior tutor at Magdalen advised me to disappear for a year. So I did two things. Firstly, being deeply ensconced in Gibbon, I decided to see Constantinople for myself. The next summer, with three school friends, I drove an old US army jeep right across Soviet-occupied Europe, saw the Theodosian Walls at sunset, crossed the Bosporus, climbed Mount Olympus, strolled through unspoiled Sarajevo and formed an abiding passion for Eastern Europe. Secondly, after earning some money as a teacher in a primary school, I decided to spend the rest of the year at the University of Grenoble, dividing my time between French classes and student excursions.

One such excursion, to Lake Geneva on a sunny weekend in May 1958, was especially memorable. The main destination, I think, was Ferney-le-Voltaire, but what I remember most was a piece of football history. Sitting in a Swiss café, watching a tiny black-and-white TV screen, I watched Nat Lofthouse score the winning goal for Bolton Wanderers in the FA Cup Final – by bundling both the ball and the Manchester United goalkeeper into the back of the net. The next day we were in Lausanne. Walking through the old town that overlooks the lake with its stupendous views to the distant snows of Mont Blanc, I suddenly heard the French guide talking nasally of a famous writer called 'Édouard Zhibbon' (to rhyme with 'bonbon'). Who was this 'Zhibbon'? I thought. Only then did the penny drop. This was the town where Gibbon had studied as a youth, and where also, on a similarly balmy day in May 1787, he had penned the final lines of *Decline and Fall of the Roman Empire*.

Rereading Gibbon's *Memoirs*, one is struck by two unusual aspects about his formative years in Lausanne. One is his bewildering academic precocity, the other his total immersion in French culture.

At the age of sixteen, Gibbon already possessed mastery of Latin and a confident command of ancient Greek. He now launched into a systematic reading schedule, which would take him author by author through every single major work of the classical repertoire. After an extensive examination of Cicero, he started on the historians, before working his way methodically through *all* the poets, *all* the orators and *all* the philosophers. What is more, he supplemented his basic reading by studying all the leading commentaries on each major author, by writing up abstracts in French of every book he read, and in due course by corresponding in Latin about his studies with senior scholars in France, Switzerland and Germany. This was the self-imposed schedule of a teenager who had no Nintendo, no computer games and no CD-Rom. When his father recalled him to England after 'four years, ten months and fifty days' he had very nearly completed the task. By his own admission, he would have completed it if he hadn't been diverted by a series of forays into modern authors – namely, Grotius, Pfuffendorf, Locke, Montesquieu, De Crouzas, Bayle, Pascal, the Abbé de la Blêterie's *Life of Julian* and Giannoni's *Civil History of Naples*. When one realises that today many faculties of modern history in British universities have dropped the compulsory language test because the average student can't cope with foreign texts, one begins to gauge the measure of Gibbon's prowess.

Not that he was complacent about his achievements. In order to improve his style, he devised a method which, he says, he 'would recommend to the imitation of students':

I chose some classic writer ... the most approved for purity and elegance of style. I translated, for example, an epistle of Cicero into

French, and, after throwing it aside till the words and phrases were obliterated from my memory, I retranslated my French into Latin . . . and then compared each sentence of my imperfect version with the ease, the grace, the propriety of the Roman orator. A similar experiment was made on . . . the *Revolutions* of Vertot. I turned [the French] into Latin, then after a suitable interval . . . turned it again into my own French . . . By degrees I was less ashamed . . . and I persevered till I had acquired a knowledge of both idioms and the command at least of a correct style.[5]

Being somewhat less proficient in Greek, and angry with the mechanical methods of his early schoolmaster, he took still more radical measures. 'In the nineteenth year of my age,' he announced blandly, 'I determined to eradicate the defect.' In effect he relearned Greek from scratch, using French textbooks and a French tutor, painstakingly working through the alphabet, the grammar and the pronunciation, 'according to the French fashion' and French terminology. If anyone thinks they were badly taught at school, they'll know what to do.

During his first stay in Lausanne the young Gibbon lived in the household of Monsieur Pavillard, a Calvinist minister, into whose religion he would duly be received. His only complaints related to the meagre diet, to the pastor's wife whom he characterised as ugly, dirty, proud, ill-tempered and covetous, and above all to his 'ignorance of the language'. He had once studied French grammar and could 'imperfectly understand the easy prose of a familiar subject'. But, 'suddenly cast on a foreign land', he found himself 'deprived of speech and hearing'. So he had to improve himself.

In the Pays de Vaud the French language is used with less imperfection than in most of the distant provinces of France . . . and if I was at first disheartened by the apparent slowness, in a few months I was astonished by the rapidity of my progress. My pronunciation was formed by the constant repetition of the same sounds: the variety of words and idioms, the rules of grammar and distinctions of genders were impressed on my memory; ease and freedom were obtained by practice, correctness and elegance by labour.

'As soon as I was able to converse with the natives, I began to feel some satisfaction in their company, awkward timidity was polished and emboldened, and I frequented for the first time assemblies of men and women', being 'received with kindness and indulgence in the best families of Lausanne'. He added, like a true scholar, 'My unfitness to bodily exercise reconciled me to a sedentary life, and the horse, the favourite of my countrymen, never contributed to the pleasures of my youth.' The effects of this regime were profound. 'Before I was recalled home,' he relates, 'French, in which I spontaneously thought, was more familiar than English to my ear, my mouth and my pen.' Gibbon's Swiss education, he says, 'discovered the statue in the block of marble'. But it also generated 'a serious and irreparable mischief in the eyes of his countrymen'. 'I had ceased,' he wrote, '*I had ceased to be an Englishman.*'⁶ Britain's greatest historian, one of the supreme masters of English style, was a thoroughgoing European.

This happy blend of Englishness and continentality, so prominent in Gibbon's life and work, is perhaps the most abiding characteristic of the history-making and the history-makers at Magdalen College.

The college itself is unambiguously English. This is not due to its magnificent Gothic architecture – Gothic, after all, being an international style – but more to the circumstances of its foundation and its connections over the centuries. Between the initial creation of Magdalen Hall in 1448 and the death of the founder in 1486, Magdalen came into being in the decades when England was shedding its age-old continental obsessions and establishing a more self-sufficient and insular place in the world. The legal foundation of the college in 1458 coincided with the terminal actions of the Hundred Years War. Thereafter the college buildings began to take shape on the site of the old Jews' Burial Ground and the former St John's Hospital. The founder, William Waynflete, bishop of Winchester and chancellor of England (1395–1486), never went abroad and never possessed any properties or office beyond the Channel. In this regard, his career reflected the shift in England's condition, contrasting sharply with that of his predecessor at Winchester, the great Cardinal Beaufort (died 1447), who had been educated in Aachen, had attended the Council of Constance, had fought in the Bohemian crusades, and had crowned Henry

VI king of France at St Denis. As Henry VI's later chancellor, Bishop Waynflete became embroiled in the domestic conflict between the Houses of Lancaster and York. Yet by the time he died in 1486, his foundation in Oxford on the banks of the Cherwell was prospering; the Wars of the Roses were over; and Tudor England was setting sail on a new, non-continental course. In the next reign, Thomas Wolsey, sometime fellow and bursar of Magdalen College, assumed a prominent position in the counsels of Henry VIII.[7]

This same period witnessed profound changes on the continent. The foundation of Magdalen College in 1458 coincided with the year when the Ottoman Turks, having conquered Constantinople, finally stormed the Acropolis in Athens. After overthrowing the last remnant of the Roman empire, Islam had taken control of the most precious symbol of ancient Greece. As Greek scholars fled to the west, the movement now known as the Renaissance accelerated. It was to affect all of Europe's universities, including Oxford, where Magdalen was one of the centres of the new learning. The relative position of theology declined, and the study of classical civilisation advanced by leaps and bounds. Magdalen was one of the seminal institutions which trained the generation of classicists who staffed the new grammar schools all over England.

In Central Europe 1458 also saw an important milestone in the march towards the Reformation. The election in Bohemia of a native Hussite king, Jiří z Podiebrady, marked something more than the success of the local Utraquist party. It briefly marked the creation of a national, non-Catholic Church and state in the heart of Catholic Europe – a precedent for the path which England itself was destined to follow. For in many essential respects, Hussitism too was a pioneering branch of the Protestant Reformation before the Protestant label had been invented. In its intellectual and theological roots, it owed no small debt to the Oxford scholar John Wycliffe and his Lollard followers. One of Waynflete's first actions as chancellor in 1457 was to participate in the trial of Reginald Peacocke, bishop of Chichester, who was condemned for doubting the Church's infallible authority in the struggle with the Lollards.

It is impossible to overemphasise the impact of Protestantism on this country's development, nor of England's growing isolation from its Catholic continental neighbours. Opposition to, and rivalry with, the Catholic powers was to form a cornerstone of the English world view. Yet one tends to forget that it was only in the late fifteenth century that the most powerful of those Catholic powers were being established. When the young William Waynflete had been a scholar at Oxford in the 1420s, possibly at New College, the kingdom of France had been reduced to ruins. Most of the north and west from Calais to Bordeaux and beyond belonged to the kings of England. The English realm stretched to the Pyrenees. Paris itself was in English hands. Much of the east, from Amiens to Dijon, was absorbed by the brilliant, breakaway duchy of Burgundy. Yet, when Waynflete died, France was resurgent and reunited, rapidly setting course for its modern supremacy. The English plague had been dispelled, the Burgundian inheritance divided between the Valois and the Habsburgs.

Similar changes were afoot in the Iberian peninsula. In 1458 there was no such thing as a kingdom of Spain. But Ferdinand of Aragon and Isabella of Castille were only years from the political marriage which laid the foundations of Spanish greatness. As joint masters of Iberia, they would soon complete the conquest of the last remaining Muslim state, the emirate of Granada, and would commission Columbus to sail west for 'the Indies'. It was during the siege of Granada that Henry VII sent Magdalen's second president, Richard Mayew, to Ferdinand and Isabella's court to open negotiations for the betrothal of their daughter, Catherine of Aragon.

Once the Hundred Years War was lost, the Protestant Reformation imposed and the Catholic powers established, England's position was radically transformed. Possessing no army of significance, England could only play a marginal role in continental conflicts. But by concentrating her resources on a navy which grew to become the most powerful in the world, she became impregnable. She could turn her mind to forging a dominant not to say dominating stance in the British Isles, to strengthening the sinews of trade, and in time to creating a vast overseas empire.

As a pillar of England's educational establishment and the constant object of royal manipulations, Magdalen College played a part in all these developments. In the sixteenth century the college survived the Reformation with several abrupt changes of president and a few violent moments. John Foxe (1516–87), who was to gain fame as the author of the ferociously Protestant *Book of Martyrs* (1559), was student, lecturer and fellow at Magdalen during the decade prior to his resignation *ex honesta causa* in 1545. He is said to have protested against the enforced celibacy of fellows and their obligation to take holy orders. A period of tutoring in aristocratic houses followed, and a decade of foreign exile in Basle and Strasbourg. By 1559, when he returned to England, the Latin edition of his martyrology was ready. The English edition finally appeared in 1563 as the *Actes and Monuments of these latter and perilous Dayes ... commonly known as The Book of Martyrs*. It was to prove the mainstay of the Protestant English doctrine of 'the elect nation', a bulwark of English nationalism for centuries to come.

Foxe, however, had not been a lone dissident at Magdalen. In 1547, on the death of Henry VIII, the Eucharistic host was desecrated and the Mass interrupted in the college chapel by one of the more fanatical Protestant fellows. Yet after Elizabeth's accession, a long succession of devotedly Anglican divines set the tone of academic life. In the seventeenth century the college was firmly attached to the High Church and to the royalist cause. During the Civil War, when Oxford was the king's capital, Magdalen Grove was the main depot of the royal artillery. The college president, John Oliver, had been Archbishop Laud's personal chaplain. But once again, as during the Reformation, political conflict was reflected in the president's removal and subsequent restoration. In the reign of James II the college caused such displeasure that the king forcibly 'intruded' his appointed president and fellows, but to no ultimate avail. In the eighteenth century, as Gibbon noted, it was still a den of opposition to the ruling Whigs. In the nineteenth the college as expected was sympathetic to the Tractarian movement, the president being one of the few heads of Oxford houses not to condemn Newman's *Tract 90*. Over the years, the epithets applied to the college varied from 'loyal but troublesome' to 'stubborn and turbulent'. During the confrontation with James II, the college was said to have resembled Milton's Pandaemonium.[8]

Throughout Magdalen's first four centuries, of course, history was not taught as a formal discipline. Yet this does not mean that Magdalen's intellectual life was devoid either of a historical or of a European dimension. There was a long line of fellows who made their name as historians of the classical world as epigraphists or archaeologists, or as antiquaries.

The Rape of Europa by Rubens, 1628–9: Zeus in the guise of a bull takes his prize to the west.

Europa and the bull, Apulian vase painting, fourth century BC.

Magdalen College, *c*. 1928.

Edward Gibbon (1737–94):
the historian content.

The Venerable Bede (673–735):
the historian imagined.

Pierre de Ronsard (1524–85):
the poet crowned.

William Blake (1757–1827):
'O rose, thou art sick!'

Juliusz Słowacki (1809–49):
'Europe is a nymph'.

The Black Madonna of Częstochowa.

The Crucifixion:
Greek icon painting,
sixteenth century.

Johann Wolfgang von Goethe (1749–1832):
'God's is the east! God's is the west!'

Rudyard Kipling (1865–1936):
'East is East, and West is West'.

Plato and Aristotle in *The School of Athens* by Raphael, 1508–11.

Llanfair PG, the Welsh railway station with the world's longest place name, 1935.

Dante Alighieri (1265–1321)
in *Hell, Purgatory and Paradise*
by Domenico Michelino, 1465.

Vladimir Mayakovsky (1893–1930):
'Poetry is like mining radium'.

Botany Bay, eastern Australia, *c*. 1800.

Fort Ross, California, 1828.

King Władysław Jagiellon at the battle of Grunwald, 1410, by J. Matejko:
the forces of Poland-Lithuania defeat the western crusaders.

The reception of August the Strong, King of Poland and Elector of Saxony,
in the Berlin Palace, 1728.

Above all, one can see how the college served as a secure and tranquil English base from which its scholars could sally forth to the continent, to pursue their studies abroad, often at considerable length, and return home laden as often as not with a refined knowledge of continental affairs. One finds a recurring interest in the geographical foundations of history, in landscape and ethnography, and in the historical dimension of other disciplines. The outlook was anything but insular.

Several Magdalen alumni of the sixteenth century made singular contributions to historical research. John Foxe was a historian of a sort, though often criticised for his cavalier treatment of evidence. From the purely academic point of view his edition of the Anglo-Saxon Gospels probably ranks higher than his martyrology. William Camden (1551–1623), the antiquary, after whom the later Camden Society is named, was in large degree the founder of modern documentary compilations; and Thomas Bodley (1545–1613) re-founded the library where so many generations of Oxford scholars have worked.

So the earliest figure to qualify fully both as Magdalen scholar and as historian was Peter Heylyn (c. 1599–1662). Born in Burford of Welsh descent, he came to Magdalen as a demy in 1615, and seems to have lost his fellowship in the 1630s through contracting a clandestine marriage. But he was back in Oxford during the Civil Wars in the 1640s and '50s, one of the most prolific apologists of the royalist and anti-Puritan cause. He was only a young man when he published *Microcosmos: or a little description of the great world* (1621), a work that rapidly ran into eight editions. When the first edition was presented to Heylyn's patron, the prince of Wales (the future Charles I), the prince objected to a sentence stating, 'France is the greater and more famous Kingdom than England.' Heylyn pleaded a misprint, claiming 'was' had inadvertently been changed to 'is'. Notwithstanding, the sentence was excised. Another sentence might be taken as the founding manifesto of historical geography. 'Historie without geographie,' Heylyn wrote, 'like a dead Carcasse hath no life and motion at all ... geographie with historie hath life and motion, but at randome and unstable.' Much of his other writing had a historical flavour. In 1641 he published what the Oxford University Press would now call a companion to English history, which was immensely popular. Later on, he published an introduction to historical method with the charming title of *Examen historicum: or a discovery and examination of the mistakes, falsities and defects in some modern histories* ... He wrote much on religious history, including an account of the Reformation and a biography of Archbishop Laud, and his survey of France, written from personal knowledge, became a standard work.[9]

George Hickes (1642–1715) entered Magdalen as a servitor-undergraduate at the Restoration, a couple of years before Heylyn's death. He rose to become a doughty High Church divine and dean of Worcester. After the Glorious Revolution of 1688–9, he became a non juror pursued by the authorities, and the titular bishop of Thetford appointed by the exiled James II to preserve the 'true episcopal' succession. Crucially for posterity, he spent his long years of disfavour studying Old Germanic linguistics as 'a poor scholar' unsupported by the college foundation. His *Institutiones grammaticae Anglo-Saxonicae et Moeso-Gothicae* (1689) and above all his multi-volume *Linguarum veterum septemtrionalium thesaurus grammatico-criticus et archaeologicus* (1703–5) are seen as the founding works of Anglo-Saxon studies.[10]

Joseph Addison – poet, playwright and satirist – after whom the college's Addison Walk is named, was a senior demy at Magdalen in 1687, and fellow from 1693 to 1711. He spent the best part of five years abroad, in France, Italy, Switzerland, Germany and the Netherlands, at the height of the War of the Spanish Succession. In the length of his continental studies, he matched Gibbon. He lived on the income from a grant made by William of Orange, following his well-judged *Address to King William* (1695), and he returned to the college on the eve of the Battle of Blenheim. His ode to Marlborough's victory betrays a fine sense of a historic occasion:

> Marlborough's exploits appear divinely bright,
> And proudly shine in their own native light;
> Rais'd of themselves, their genuine charms they bost,
> And those who paint them truest, paint them most.

Clearly, 'shine' and 'divine' were two of Addison's favourite words. And one always wonders whether his most famous poem was not conceived whilst walking round the college:

The spacious firmament on high
With all the blue ethereal sky
And Spangled heavens, a shining frame
Their great Original proclaim.

[...]
While all the stars that round her burn
And all the planets in their turn
Confirm the tidings as they roll,
And spread the truth from pole to pole.

What though in solemn silence all
Move round the dark, terrestrial ball?
What though no real voice nor sound
Amid the radiant orbs be found?
In reason's ear they all rejoice
And utter forth a glorious voice,
Forever singing as they shine,
'The hand that made us is divine.'[11]

Richard Chandler (1738–1810) was born in the year that Magdalen's classical New Buildings were constructed, and was just too young to have met Gibbon. Yet he, like Addison, was a hardened traveller, especially in Italy and the Ottoman empire, which he toured under the auspices of the Society of Dilettanti. His expert knowledge of Greek and Latin inscriptions enabled him to do for classical epigraphy what Hickes had done for Germanic studies. After cataloguing the Ashmolean's classical marbles, he published his *Ionian Antiquities* (1769), his *Inscriptiones Antiquae* (1774), several learned travel books, and a *History of Ilium or Troy* (1802). He is best remembered in college annals for his posthumous life of the founder. 'Bishop Waynflete,' wrote Chandler, 'was humane and benevolent to an uncommon degree: As a bishop, he was a kind father revered by his children. As a founder, he was magnificent and munificent ... The prudence, fidelity, and innocence which preserved him when tossed about ... during the long and mighty tempest of the civil war was justly a subject of wonder.'[12]

Dr Martin Joseph Routh (1755–1854) lived for ninety-nine years from the mid-Georgian era to the mid-Victorian. Elected a fellow in 1775, he was Magdalen's president for over six decades. An eighteenth-century man preserved in aspic, he was still acting and talking like Dr Johnson on the eve of the Crimean War. He lavished immense time and patience on two scholarly works – a five-volume edition of early patristics, and an enlarged, annotated edition of Bishop Burnet's *History of his Own Times*, which appeared, appropriately, more than a century after the original publication. When asked why he spent so much time on Bishop Burnet, whom he patently disliked, he replied, 'A good question, Sir! Because I know the man to be a liar and am determined to prove him so.'[13] The only thing in Magdalen to live longer than Dr Routh was the huge plane tree planted to celebrate Nelson's victory at Aboukir Bay in the seventh year of Routh's presidency. The original seedling failed to take root, but the replacement planted in 1801 is still going strong today.

After Routh, Charles Reade (1814–84) was one of Magdalen's longest-serving fellows. In practice, he passed most of his time in London, where he worked as a dramatist and theatre manager. Yet he was also both a formidable scholar and a very popular novelist, inventor of the genre of 'matter-of-fact romance'. His historical novel *The Cloister and the Hearth* (1861) is one of the monuments of Victorian literature, and is notable for the extremely copious and detailed historical research which under-pinned the vivid, late-medieval love story set in the Netherlands, France and Italy.[14]

In 1854, the year that Routh died, the parliamentary Oxford Act began the long process of reforming the university by permitting colleges to amend their statutes. Henceforth, there was a Regius Professor of modern history, Halford Vaughan, who, unlike many of his predecessors, presented regular lectures, and a combined School of Law and Modern History. But there was no Board of Studies or Faculty Board, and a nascent Tutors' Association was battling to bring order to the chaotic state of teaching and examining. Magdalen apparently participated in intercollegiate history studies, but it is not possible to identify the college's first official history tutors with any certainty. The Reverend Frederick Bulley, fellow of Magdalen, is listed in the university calendar for 1851–5 as 'Tutor, Lecturer in Jurisprudence and Modern History', but does not seem to have continued in that capacity after he succeeded Routh as Magdalen's president. Sidney James Owen of Christ Church, who took his MA in 1853, only appears on Magdalen's list of tutors from 1867. His main interest lay in pre-British Indian History. But tutoring did not have the same kudos as academic scholarship, and tutors were not necessarily fellows. For some time yet, Magdalen's most distinguished historians were still highly independent figures who taught students intermittently and spent very long intervals abroad. One of these was a distinguished Alpinist; another a distinguished orientalist.

The Reverend William Augustus Brevoort Coolidge (1850–1926), an American and a mountaineer in the style of Whymper, and David George Hogarth FBA (1862–1927), a wandering scholar in the footsteps of Chandler and C.M. Doughty, had much in common. Both were intrepid travellers, one in the high Alps, the other in Anatolia and the Levant; and both were 'hands-on' historians, who wrote with verve about the remote places they explored. Coolidge started a long publishing career with *A History of the Swiss Confederation* (1887), Hogarth with *Modern and Ancient Roads in Eastern Asia Minor* (1893). Both were fellows of Magdalen for decades. Coolidge's summer residences in Grindelwald got longer and longer until eventually he never came back.[15] He completed 1750 major Alpine ascents. Hogarth became keeper of the Ashmolean and, in 1915–18, a prominent intelligence officer.

The range of Hogarth's interests is especially impressive. His lifelong fascination lay with the Hittites, but he also worked with Arthur Evans at Knossos, directed the British School in Athens, served as a war correspondent for *The Times* in Crete, and headed the Royal Geographical Society. Oddly enough, he only ever travelled once to the country, Arabia, on which he wrote most. However, he is probably best remembered as the don who spotted and recruited one of the great 'history-makers' of the day – T.E. Lawrence, otherwise Lawrence of Arabia (1888–1935). Hogarth recognised the potential after Lawrence undertook a lone trek round Syria and Turkey in order to complete an undergraduate dissertation on Crusader castles. So in 1911 he arranged for Magdalen to award the young graduate a 'Senior Demyship for Travel', then sent him off for three years with Leonard Woolley to excavate the ancient Hittite site of Carcemish on the Euphrates. (It was more than a fortunate accident that

Carcemish lay very close to the strategic railway bridge over the Euphrates which German engineers were building for the *Baghdadbahn* and which greatly interested British intelligence at the time.) After the outbreak of war, Woolley and Lawrence conducted a survey of the Negev Desert. But in 1915, when 'Commander Hogarth RNVR' was appointed director of the Arab Bureau in Cairo, he called in Lawrence once again, and sent him off on the mission to Prince Faisal that would transform the history of the Middle East.[16]

Nonetheless, the man who perhaps did most to establish history as a major subject in the college, and indeed the university, was Charles Robert Leslie Fletcher (1857–1934), an Etonian who had rowed in the Magdalen boat and is described in the *Dictionary of National Biography* as 'a fierce Protestant Anglican'. This no doubt explains his earliest book, *Gustavus Adolphus and the Struggle of Protestantism for Existence* (1890). He was also described as 'a red-hot free trader' and 'an anti-feminist opposed to women having degrees'. As tutor in modern history from 1883 to 1906, he set up Magdalen's undergraduate library, and managed it 'with a rod of iron'. Together with the likes of A.L. Smith of Balliol and A.H. Johnson of All Souls, he was an active reformer of the history faculty, and remained a dutiful delegate to the university press. After resigning his tutorship, he published on a wide variety of subjects. The narrative of his *History of England* (1911) was interspersed with evocative poems by Rudyard Kipling and with dramatic illustrations, including one of Prince Rupert riding over Magdalen Bridge in full colour. It became a popular patriotic textbook throughout the country. In the words of the preface: 'This book is written for all boys and girls who are interested in the story of Great Britain and its Empire'. In reality, Great Britain meant England, and the non-English element of the story was ignored. The boys and girls were told nothing, for example, about the Act of Union with Scotland. As for the Irish, they had never recovered from the failure of the Romans to conquer the whole of the British Isles: 'So Ireland never went to school, and has been a spoilt child ever since'. On the outbreak of war, Fletcher contributed to the volume composed in record time by a team of Oxford history tutors entitled *Why We Are at War*. He was already engaged on his *Introductory History of England* (1904–23), which eventually ran into five volumes. Among many other varied titles, he wrote a popular local guidebook to Oxford, a memoir of D.G. Hogarth and a lively sketch of *Mr Gladstone at Oxford*.[17]

Reginald Lane Poole (1857–1939), a lifelong fellow from his election in 1881, belonged to the same generation. He was a solid documentary historian, serving as university lecturer in diplomatic. His labours at the archival coalface produced works on the medieval English exchequer and the papal chancery, which were followed by his son's authorship of the third volume of the *Oxford History of England*. But Reginald was not always content. He belonged to the body of university lecturers whom the new Regius Professor, Sir Charles Firth, was urging to give more attention to the professional standards of their offerings. In his inaugural address Firth had demanded that Oxford lectures reflect the latest findings of academic research. In 1907 Poole wrote a formal letter of complaint to the history faculty pointing out that the lecture course which had taken him months to prepare was only attended by two or three students. *Plus ça change . . .*

Fletcher was succeeded as Magdalen's history tutor by Charles Grant Robertson (1869–1949), a lifelong fellow of All Souls. Born in India, Robertson had a strong interest in historical geography, and it was during his fifteen years at Magdalen that he published his two well-known atlases, as well as two distinguished studies of Prussian history and a collection of English constitutional documents.[18] He left the college in 1920 to take up the vice-chancellorship of Birmingham University, where he continued to produce a stream of books, including a popular textbook of modern European history.[19] Sir Isaiah Berlin, who remembered him well, wrote about him: 'He was a very noted, dry, somewhat pedantic lecturer in the style of ". . . exit Cavour, enter Bismarck . . .". He taught the Prince of Wales (Edward VIII), not very successfully, and kept repeating "Remember the Bourbons, Your Royal Highness, remember the Bourbons", this did little good as the Prince had probably never heard of the Bourbons.'[20] Those fruitless royal tutorials took place in Magdalen in 1912–14.

Magdalen's condition during the First World War, like that of all Oxford colleges, is most eloquently summed up by the memorial placed at the entrance to the cloisters. The memorial carries the names of 208 members of the college who gave their lives in 1914–18 'For God and Country'. It represents a loss equivalent to almost half the number of all the Magdalen men active in the university in 1914. It is now accompanied by a tablet to the memory of a German scholar, Ernst (Maria Richard) Stadler – 'POET, SCHOLAR, SOLDIER' – who had taken a BLitt at Magdalen in 1912 and was killed at the first battle of Ypres in 1914: 'MENSCH, WERDE WESENTLICH'.

By the inter-war period history at Magdalen was fully operational. There were three or four tutors at any one time – each covering the ancient, medieval, early modern and modern periods. E. Murray Wrong (fellow, 1914–28) taught medieval English and European history, whilst S.G. Lee was the early modernist. The young Kenneth Bruce McFarlane was elected in 1928, A.J.P. Taylor in 1938. Even so, as in pre-war days, there was much important thinking and writing about history beyond the immediate circle of history tutors. Tom Boase, for example, wrote a study of Pope Boniface VIII, and another of St Francis before taking up the editorship of the *Oxford History of English Art*.[21] A strong historical dimension prevailed in the work of several fellows formally allocated to other disciplines. Of these, C.S. Lewis was an English tutor famed for his religious enquiries and children's stories; another, J.M. Thompson, was a theologian turned French expert; and a third, R.G. Collingwood, an archaeologist turned philosopher.

Little can now be added to the numerous accounts of the multifaceted talents of C.S. 'Jack' Lewis (1898–1963), a fellow of Magdalen from 1925 and the central figure in the film *Shadowlands* (1993). Lewis's presence contributed greatly to the intellectual cross-fertilisation so evident in the college of that era. Many of his books, like those of his colleague, J.R.R. Tolkien, contained a strong historical flavour.[22]

Nor can one do more than gasp at the astonishingly productive career of the labour historian, G.D.H. Cole (1889–1959). Cole started off as a prize fellow at Magdalen from 1912 to 1922. Apart from his numerous editions of English poetical classics, the greater part of his writings on economic, socialist and trade union matters possessed a historical dimension. At 251, the number of items under his name on Bodley's OLIS listing far surpasses even that of A.J.P. Taylor.[23]

The Reverend James Matthew Thompson (1878–1956) was an

Oxonian through and through. Educated at the Dragon School, Christ Church and Cuddesdon Theological College, he was appointed a fellow of Magdalen in 1904, and soon afterwards, as an enthusiastic modernist theologian, dean of divinity. But the bishop of Oxford withdrew his licence to preach, and by other accounts the Great War had damaged his Christian faith. At all events, by the early 1920s he had switched to modern European history. He was to write widely on French Revolutionary and Napoleonic studies, and he published a pioneering textbook of European historical geography.[24]

Thompson's lectures at Magdalen in 1921–4 were published as *Lectures on Foreign History 1494–1789*. They had an enormous influence far beyond Oxford. Directed at first-year students, they aimed to arouse their critical sense. 'You don't study history to learn historical facts, but to acquire historical judgement,' he told them. 'It is not learning which makes a historian but discernment. Historical truth ... is hardly ever attainable ... But historical truthfulness is within the reach of all.'

That opening lecture then took the audience on an imaginary tour of Europe at the turn of the fifteenth and sixteenth centuries. Quite naturally, the tour began not just in Oxford, but in Magdalen itself:

> This college was not in a very good state at this time. At a visitation in 1507, 'it appeared that many of the Fellows kept dogs, one of them also having a ferret, and that they made frequent poaching expeditions ... The use of Latin in conversation, enjoined by the Statutes, had been set aside. (I'm afraid it still is.) There were several factions in the College, and several members were in the habit of wearing arms.' Nor was that all. The Vice-President of the College was accused (among other crimes) of dabbling in black magic: he had, it was said, 'baptised a cat', as a means of discovering treasure. He afterwards became a bishop.[25]

Some points of emphasis were redolent of inter-war attitudes. Thompson, like Fletcher, was unashamedly patriotic. When talking of this country, Thompson did not hesitate to say, 'England in 1494 is already 400 years ahead of the rest of Europe.' When he reached Eastern Europe, he preferred no comment. 'We might extend our imaginary tour beyond Germany ...' he mused. 'But I doubt whether we should find much to add to the picture ... It will be better to stop here.' That is how most historians felt until very recently.

Thompson's *Lectures* affected my own career in a very special way. A revised edition published in 1956 reached my school library just in time for my A levels, and I drew up a set of essay plans based on the topics that attracted me. One of them, based on the concluding section of Thompson's Lecture Number 20, 'Enlightened Despotism', summarised the partitions of Poland. I was soon to realise that the partitions were the only event in Polish history that any British history examiner had ever heard of. And so that one essay plan stood me in good stead for years. Still, Thompson had grasped the essence. He called the partitions 'the classic crime of the eighteenth century'. And after the partitions, he concluded, 'Poland became a cradle of music and revolution.' Not bad at all.[26]

Robin George Collingwood (1889–1943) is probably best remembered these days as a specialist in Roman Britain and the co-author of the first volume of the *Oxford History of England*. Indeed, he had numerous distinguished publications to his name in that field. Yet his interests were far broader. As he explained in his candid *Autobiography* (1939), 'My life's work ... has been ... an attempt to bring about a rapprochement between philosophy and history.' In this endeavour, he was something of a lone wolf among the Oxford philosophers of his day. (He bluntly described Cook Wilson's central doctrine of 'Knowing makes no difference to what is known' as 'meaningless'.) Even so, he participated in the life both of the historians and of the group dubbed The Magdalen Metaphysicals. His pen was rarely idle. A dozen titles began in 1913 with a translation of Benedetto Croce's study of the eighteenth-century Italian historical philosopher Vico, followed later by an edition of Croce's own autobiography. The central concern was always, as in the title of his published lectures from the 1920s, *The Idea of History*. When appointed to the Waynflete Chair of Metaphysical Philosophy in 1935, Collingwood chose as the theme of his inaugural lecture 'The Historical Imagination'.[27]

Collingwood's exposé of the nature and vital function of the historical imagination over sixty years ago is a model of lucidity. It was written in a mood of ill-disguised dismay at a tendency among his colleagues to discuss problems of knowledge without any reference to history whatsoever. It can equally be reread today as a forceful reminder that the supposedly scientific school of history writing and the dry-as-dust documentary school have severe limitations. Collingwood started from basic principles. 'The imagination,' he began, 'that blind but indispensable faculty without which, as Kant has shown, we could never perceive the world around us, is indispensable in the same way to history.' Or again:

> In history, just as there are no authorities, so there are properly speaking no data ... The web of imaginative construction is something far more solid and powerful than we have hitherto realised ... It actually serves as the touchstone by which we decide whether alleged facts are genuine ... For any source may be tainted, any writer prejudiced, any inscription misread ...

Collingwood even drew a parallel between history writing and fiction:

> Both history and the novel are the product of an autonomous or self-authorizing activity; and in both cases this activity is the *a priori* imagination. As works of the imagination, the historian's work and the novelist's work do not differ. Where they do differ is that the historian's picture is meant to be true.

There can be little doubt, of course, that Collingwood was a man of small tact and large resentments. A meticulous scholar who was never happier than at a Romano-British dig, he boiled with anger at what he regarded to be the political betrayals of his day. His opinion of the First World War was summed up as 'a war of unprecedented ferocity closed by a peace-settlement of unprecedented folly'. The leaders of the victorious Allies were 'a mob of imbeciles'. Fascism was 'capitalist socialism', and the British government's faint-hearted policy during the Spanish Civil War and at Munich made it 'a partisan of Fascist dictatorship'. His autobiography, published on the eve of the Second World War, ends with these harsh words:

I know now that the minute philosophers of my youth, for all their profession of a purely scientific detachment from practical affairs, were the propagandists of a coming Fascism. I know that Fascism means the end of clear thinking and the triumph of irrationalism . . . Henceforth, I shall fight in the daylight.

One needs no great historical imagination to guess how that sort of frank opinion went down in Oxford's senior common rooms.

Still, the era when Magdalen's academic brilliance in history combined most effectively with tutorial excellence was yet to come. The 'Formidable Four' of McFarlane, Taylor, Stoye and Leyser came together in 1948, and stayed together for twenty years. The two senior men, McFarlane and Taylor, both of pre-war vintage, were said not to see exactly eye to eye. Indeed, since they were located as far apart as possible in a very spacious college – the one in Longwall Quad and the other at Holywell Ford – they would rarely have seen each other at all. But their respective medieval and modern fields did not overlap, and their acolytes did not form warring factions (or carry arms). They were both in their idiosyncratic ways inspiring.

As I remember, McFarlane's tutorial technique relied heavily on long dramatic silences, on penetrating glances from the winged-back chair dispatched unnervingly between the essay reader and the prowling cats, and on quiet but devastating interventions, such as, 'Where exactly did you find that idea?' or, 'You shouldn't believe everything you read in books.' Tutorials with Taylor, in contrast, were enlivened by his phenomenal memory, by telephone calls from the *Sunday Express* and by his frequent habit of leaning over the fireplace, of lifting a lump of coal in the tongs, and holding it suspended over the flames whilst the essay reader, transfixed by the performance, desperately tried to reach the end of the paragraph. In my recollection, meetings with Taylor could also be coloured by his romantic attachment to Manchester and to Lancashire, where he had worked as Namier's assistant, and whose highways and byways he knew intimately from years of rambling. Though the son of a very wealthy family, in his heart he would have loved to belong to the Lancashire working class. It goes without saying that he was a very paradoxical man, whose passion for left-wing causes like CND was matched by his unbounded admiration for various right-wing phenomena like Lord Beaverbrook and, one suspects, the British empire itself. Consciously the champion of all underdogs and troublemakers, his intellectual career was spent poring over power politics. Yet he was as indulgent to his pupils as he was, so we heard, peevish with his peers.[28]

The undoubted success of that team was due not just to their individual skills but to the sheer variety of their interests. Their charges knew that they were in the hands of leading professionals with the broadest experience and expertise. During my own time in college, Taylor, who had just presented his Ford Lectures on English history, was writing *The Origins of the Second World War*, probably the most controversial history book of the decade. He was Oxford's only historian to contribute major volumes both to the *Oxford History of Modern Europe* and to the *Oxford History of England*. John Stoye, always the friendliest and most reassuring of tutors, who pulled me through English Constitutional Documents II, was preparing his *Siege of Vienna*, the first of several riveting books on European history. In due course, I would always recommend his *Europe Unfolding, 1648–88* as a rare example of a textbook which put the affairs of Central and Eastern Europe at the beginning and not as an afterthought at the end.[29] As for Karl Leyser, then a bachelor fellow of the old type, he was the living embodiment of Anglo-continental relations. That most unmistakable sight of a diminutive German-Jewish refugee bounding purposefully across the lawns dressed in the regimental kilt of the Black Watch was a history lesson in itself. His interests in continental medieval history, notably in Carolingian and Ottonian Germany, were the perfect foil for McFarlane's expertise in medieval England, where his researches into bastard feudalism provided one of the concepts we all had to master. Surely, at Magdalen at least, Firth's ideal of Oxford history being a *Fons Scientarium* was now being realised.

One should equally pay tribute to the backup team. Supplementary medieval tutorials with Alan Bennett at Exeter were worthy of one of the deadpan sketches that would make him famous in *Beyond the Fringe*. Students like myself who chose 'The Age of Dante' for a special subject were rewarded with one of the college's classicists, Colin Hardie, who was no less an authority in Dante studies than he was in Classics.[30]

Of course, the real test of any college lies in the quality of the graduates which it rears. On this score, the post-war Magdalen history school has sent out several cohorts of distinguished historians both into the profession and into the world at large. In my own generation, the most prominent name is probably that of Keith Robbins, historian and administrator, and former senior vice chancellor of the University of Wales. What does seem unusual, however, is that Magdalen graduates have virtually cornered the market in the recent wave of monster narrative histories, each covering huge panoramas of time and space. With only a very few exceptions, all these popular best-sellers have been written by Magdalen men. One only need mention Paul Johnson's acclaimed *History of the Jews* and *Birth of the Modern*; John Roberts's elegant *History of the World* and *The History of Europe*; Felipe Fernandez-Armesto's amazing *Millennium*; my own *Europe: A History*; and the colossal compilations of Sir Martin Gilbert, biographer of Churchill and without doubt the most prolific historian of our generation.[31] I doubt that this is due to pure coincidence. All these Magdalen authors appear to possess an unusually broad vision that answers Collingwood's call to the historical imagination, a firm sense of the interplay of history and geography in the vein that runs from Heylyn to Hogarth and Thompson, a strong attachment to the Gibbonian legacy of large-scale history as fine literature, and a dose of courage, or perhaps of foolhardiness, reminiscent of Taylor. One suspects the workings of a tradition.

In conclusion, one has to say there is something about the grandeur of Magdalen's physical presence and its eccentric location beyond the Eastgate and city walls which gives the college an air of unusual self-sufficiency and independence. Magdalen may be part of Oxford University, but it is not dependent on it. This fact may have proved especially congenial to the blithe, independent spirits who found refuge within its Longwall but who also sallied forth to all points of the globe. The state of affairs seems particularly fitting for the incomparable 'AJP' who, whilst being the best-known historian in contemporary Britain, the original 'teledon' with an audience of millions, took inordinate pride in being the finest non-professor of which the Oxford faculty ever boasted.

Equally, it may be worth reflecting on the overall thrust of Magdalen's historian-scholars. On several occasions, they gave the impression of being narrow-minded 'Little Englanders'. Gibbon complained of the fellows' Tory politics. Dr Routh was better known for his long years than for his broad vision. The 'muscular Christian' C.R.L. Fletcher was preoccupied with England and its empire. And even J.M. Thompson had his moments of patriotic parochiality. Yet over the decades and the centuries it is astonishing to see how widely the historical interests of the college were spread. If anything, continental and transcontinental concerns outweighed the national. George Hickes placed the Anglo-Saxons firmly in their Germanic context. Joseph Addison had strong links with the Netherlands, just as Peter Heylyn had with France or Richard Chandler with Greece. The Reverend Coolidge devoted both his physical and his intellectual energies to Switzerland. And Dr Hogarth was the leading Arabist of his day. Even Fletcher was much exercised by the Thirty Years War. As for the stars of the early twentieth century – Robertson, J.M. Thompson and R.G. Collingwood – they were all prominent Europeanists.

Nor can one accuse the Magdalen school of confining its gaze to Western Europe. A.J.P. Taylor's favourite country was Hungary. One could meet him regularly at Bartók concerts. Like Stoye and Leyser, he was very conscious of Central and East Central Europe, and his first published work dealt with Italy. Yet the model before all their eyes was surely that of their great predecessor Edward Gibbon – the Englishman so steeped in continental culture that he once claimed to have stopped being English. Gibbon, having first immersed himself in French culture, devoted his career and his masterwork to Byzantium, to the eastern Roman empire. In the eternal tug of war between east and west in European history, the greatest of England's historians was no less an easterner than a westerner. *Floreat Magdalena.*

VII

EUROPE OVERSEAS AND OVERLAND[1]

1788 was the year when King George III went mad and when he founded a colony in Australia. I hope that you noted the word 'and'. George III was not mad *because* he set up a colony in Australia. He was declared mad because he addressed an oak tree in Windsor Great Park as the king of Prussia. It just so happened in the same year that the First Fleet, which had sailed from Portsmouth on 13 May 1787, dropped anchor in Sydney Cove on 24 January 1788.

It also happened that 1788 saw the first meeting of the US Congress. This is not irrelevant to the story. Britain was losing thirteen old colonies at the very time that it gained a new one. Look out now for the word 'because'. The British decided to create a new colony in Australia because, among other things, they had just lost their colonies in North America. If the Americans had not won their independence, there is every probability that the First Fleet would have set sail with its cargo of convicts not for the South Seas but, as in preceding decades, for the Deep South.

The history of transportation is a grim one. Australia supplies only one chapter in a very long book that spans many centuries and many continents, and the British were only one of many transporting agencies. Botany Bay might not come off too badly if compared with one or two of its counterparts, such as the French penal colony on Devil's Island in Guiana. Even so, the British record is not very pretty. The best estimate is that some 160,000 convicts were forcibly shipped to Australia during the eight decades when the scheme was operating. They had to endure a sea voyage of many months, a life of abuse and bondage whilst their sentence lasted and, when it ended, no provision for their return. Up to one third of them were Irish people who had been sentenced for so-called political crimes, often minor acts of courageous insolence against English officials.[2] It is no surprise that the survivors turned out to be one of the hardiest breeds on earth – inured to the terrors of the wilderness, to the torments of heat and drought and, not least, to the tedium of cricket.

The British record in Canada was no prettier. In the same period that saw Australia founded, the Highlands of Scotland were being mercilessly harried. For eighty years after the last Jacobite rising of 1745, the Gaelic clans were forbidden to wear their national dress, to speak their native tongue in public or to organise any form of assembly. In the terrible Clearances, which were organised both for political and for economic reasons, whole counties were denuded of their native population; the land was taken over by English lords or Lowland loyalists and handed over to sheep. The human livestock, the lifeblood of the clans, was shipped off to Nova Scotia or to Newfoundland. Even today, there are more people who speak Gaelic in Canada than in their homeland in Scotland. And that Highland home, once inhabited by the clans, became as wild and empty as anything you can find in the wild and woolly hills of South Australia.[3]

And then there was the Irish Famine. By the 1840s, when the convict scheme was still operating, Ireland was an integral part of the United Kingdom. Irish MPs sat at Westminster, and the Irish Catholics, in theory, were fully emancipated. But this did not prevent one of the greatest preventable disasters of European history. When the potato crop was blighted in the years following 1846, the staple food of the Irish people was cut off. Aid and assistance was so slow in coming that by the end of the decade a million Irish had died and a million had fled. This was not Ethiopia or central Asia; it was a constituent country of the richest and most powerful state of the age. Most of the Irish who perished expired within a couple of hundred miles of the heart of England, whose well-stocked fields and farms were untouched. Most of those who fled were forced to take ship to America, often in conditions that were worse than those of the spartan but well-prepared convict ships bound for the Antipodes. Here was transportation through hunger. Even today, at the end of the twentieth century, Ireland has far fewer inhabitants than she had at the start of the nineteenth.[4]

Of course, 'Europe overseas' can never be reduced to the history of convict policy or of flight from hunger. One could equally talk of the Pilgrim Fathers, who sailed overseas in search of religious freedom, of English East Indiamen, who sailed in search of trade, of English pirates-cum-admirals like Francis Drake, who sailed for booty, of the English poor, who sailed for a job or a plot of land or the hope of feeding their children, of English orphans and adoptees, and of the great discoverers like James Cook, who 'went to sea to see what they could see'.[5]

Nor is there any reason to limit the subject of Europe overseas to the British or the English experience. The British Isles were but one starting-point among many. One could equally talk of Spanish conquistadores, of Portuguese navigators, of Dutch spice merchants, of French colonists, of Italian Jesuits, in due course of Belgian and German imperialists or Protestant and Catholic missionaries, of everything from the South Sea Bubble to the Society for the Propagation of Christian Knowledge. The common denominator is that they sailed. They took ship from Europe, and landed somewhere far away, overseas. The story always starts in a European port – Chatham, Le Havre, Antwerp, Amsterdam or Hamburg – and it always ends on some distant lonely shore.

Just imagine, however, that they didn't sail, but that they walked: that they travelled not overseas, but overland. There's another magnificent Australian label – *The Overlanders*, one of the great films of my schooldays.[6]

If my geographical information is correct, to reach Australia from London one flies some 15,000 miles. If my historical information is correct, there were quite a few European overlanders who travelled similar distances – mainly on foot. And, if my mental arithmetic is accurate, to walk for 15,000 miles at a regular pace of fifteen miles per day – half the pace of a Roman legion – would require a non-stop march of exactly 1000 days – two years, nine months. Yet who but an athlete without luggage could keep going for nearly three years without a break? To walk at the same rate non-stop for half that distance, say 7500 miles, would take 500 days, or one year, four months and two weeks. For a convict column of men, women and children, 7500 miles meant a march of three, four or five years. There were lots who did it, and lots who didn't make the end of the road.

Adelaide was founded in December 1836, a few months before the accession of Queen Victoria. In that same year a little-known event took place in central Siberia. It was the Lake Baykal Rising, or, in the language of Russian monarchists, the Baykal Mutiny. Baykal is the deepest lake in the world, containing more water than all the lakes of Europe put together. It lies roughly halfway between the western fringe of Siberia in the Urals and the easternmost coast of Siberia on the Bering Strait. At the time, a large group of convicts, many thousands strong, was supposed to be settling down to its Siberian servitude. Instead, they took on the tsar's soldiers, won some of them over, then fought a series of pitched battles until they were all destroyed, disarmed or dispersed. The insurrectionaries (or mutineers) were Poles, men who had dared to take up arms against the tsar in the Russo–Polish War five years earlier. At that stage, they were between 5000 and 6000 miles from home. Of those who survived, many were to be taken still further to the east, to still more remote penal settlements on Sakhalin and in Kamchatka – the counterparts of Norfolk Island. Those who returned to Poland from there, and some did, would have tramped a total distance equivalent to an overland trek from Australia to Europe.[7]

These may be the byways of European history, but are not unimportant for being little known. By my reckoning, there were seven great Polish risings against Russian rule between the Great Northern War in the early eighteenth century and the Second World War in the twentieth. Each round of the contest saw a fresh generation of Polish prisoners setting out on the endless trail to Siberia. Nobody knows exactly how many made the terrible journey. The total numbers easily surpass the sort of figures mentioned about British convicts sent to Australia. There were certainly far more Poles sent to Siberia over the years than, say, Bolsheviks, of whom of course we hear much more.

A little more about the rising of 1830–1 which preceded the affair on Lake Baykal may not be amiss. At the Congress of Vienna, the historic independence of Poland had not been restored. Instead, the powers chose to set up a dependent kingdom of Poland of which the tsar of Russia was *ex officio* king. They also provided the kingdom with an extremely liberal constitution, guaranteed by international treaty. But when the tsar ignored the constitution and his Polish subjects rebelled, none of the powers was prepared to intervene. In the war of 1831 between the tsar's Polish army and the tsar's Russian army, the odds were pretty even. But in the end numbers told. Warsaw, the Polish capital, was stormed; the constitution was arbitrarily suspended; and a population similar to that of present-day Australia was placed under military rule. The rebels were dealt with in a series of military tribunals which handed down verdicts without representation or appeal. All landowners who had supported the insurrection were declared confiscate. All office holders who had failed to support the tsar were dismissed. All patriots who had volunteered to fight for their country were classed as traitors. The commonest sentence was deportation to Siberia. Some 80,000 Poles were convicted, and those sent to Siberia had to walk. No transport was provided. As yet there were no railways. One of their leaders, Prince Roman Sanguszko, who happened to be a relative of the tsar, was singled out for special punishment. Nicholas I personally ordered that he walk to Siberia in leg irons. And he made it. But it took rather a long time. He was probably still on the road when Adelaide was being founded.[8]

One of the honoured rituals of that journey was observed whilst passing the post on the ridge of the Urals which marked the boundary between Europe and Asia. As from the reign of Catherine the Great, the geography of Europe had been officially extended far from its ancient position on the River Don, and a huge wooden boundary post was erected on the main trail to mark the new divide. As the line of convicts shuffled past, roped or chained together, each would scoop up a handful of European earth and cast it onto an ever growing mound. 'Earth to earth' was an integral part of the funeral rite. It was common knowledge that few of those who left Europe in that way would ever return.

Thirty years after the war of 1831, in January 1863, the next generation of Poles rose in rebellion against continuing tsarist oppression. This time, since they had lost both their kingdom and their army, they resorted to guerrilla warfare. They held out for fifteen months, but the outcome was much the same. The tsar, Alexander II, revoked all the concessions which he had tentatively introduced, and he never restored the constitution for which the Poles had been fighting. (For some reason, he is known to history as a liberal tsar.) After the leading rebels had been hanged in public before the Warsaw Citadel, the tribunals began. Tens of thousands more were condemned to deportation. By now, there was a paved road, built by convicts from the previous rising. It could carry the convoys of prisoners crammed into black-painted carriages. But it only went as far as Moscow. From there on, they had to walk. By 1875, as the tsarist encyclopaedia records, the principal city of central Siberia, Irkutsk, some 3500 miles from Warsaw, was almost three quarters Roman Catholic. And there was no passage home at the end of their sentences. When Lenin arrived in eastern Siberia towards the end of the century, in so-called free exile, he lived in the cabin of a former Polish political prisoner of the 1863 generation – they were, he said, the happiest, most carefree days of his life.[9]

The Poles, of course, were not alone. They probably made up the largest contingent of tsarist political exiles, just as the Irish formed the largest political contingent in Australia, but they were far outnumbered by the great mass of non-politicals. Of the millions forcibly dispatched on the long trail to Siberia, by far the largest category of convicts were ordinary Russian and Ukrainian peasants: serfs condemned to oblivion for something or nothing by the whim of their landlord or by some petty local magistrate.

Now, the scene shifts again: to northern California. About 150 miles north of San Francisco, on the magnificent, lonely, rocky Pacific coast, stands an old wooden fort, called Fort Ross. When I visited it in the mid-1980s, it was flying the flag of tsarist Russia even though the USSR was still in existence. For Fort Ross – more properly Fort Ru – was built by Russian pioneers in 1812, the year that Napoleon occupied Moscow. Yes, the Russians were in California before the Americans were. They came down from Alaska to see if they could grow corn. They persevered for three decades, and when they failed, they left. That was in 1845, only four years before the gold rush.[10] Can you imagine? The Russians could have kept Alaska, the USA's largest state; and they could have laid claim to California, its richest state. But they didn't. It's rather as if Captain Phillip when he landed in Botany Bay in January 1788 had found an abandoned Russian fort a few miles up the coast in Queensland, only those first European colonists had mysteriously gone away.

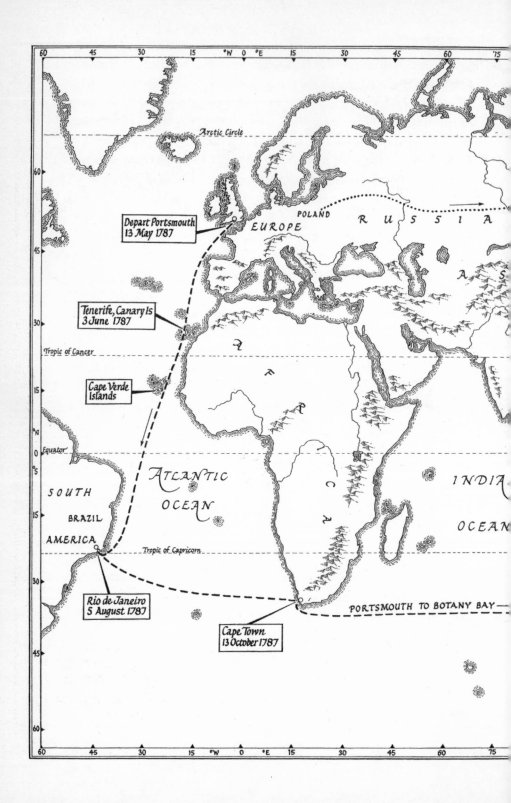

Arctic Circle

POLAND

EUROPE

RUSSIA

A S

Depart Portsmouth
13 May 1787

Tenerife, Canary Is
3 June 1787

Tropic of Cancer

A

F

Cape Verde
Islands

R

°N

Equator

°S

ATLANTIC

OCEAN

SOUTH

C

BRAZIL

AMERICA

Tropic of Capricorn

A

Rio de Janeiro
5 August 1787

INDIA

OCEAN

Cape Town
13 October 1787

PORTSMOUTH TO BOTANY BAY

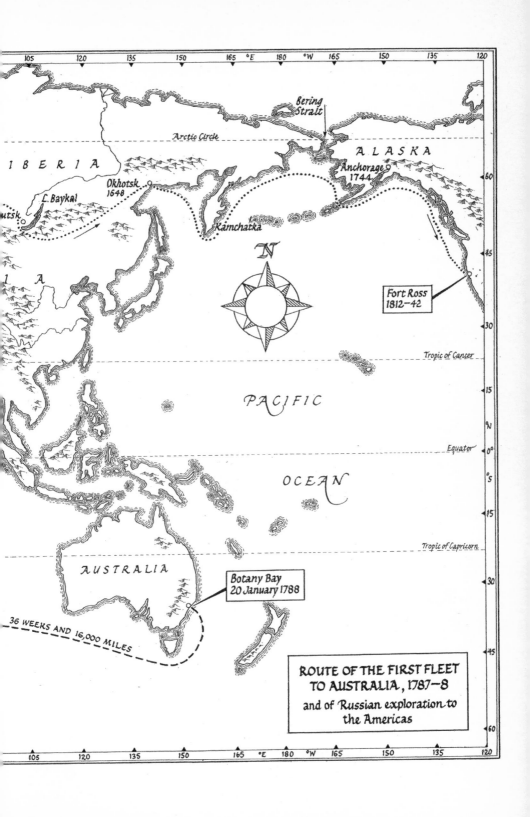

105 120 135 150 165 °E 180 °W 165 150 135 120

Bering
Strait

Arctic Circle

ALASKA

SIBERIA

Anchorage
1744

Okhotsk
1648

L. Baykal

...utsk

Kamchatka

Fort Ross
1812–42

N

Tropic of Cancer

PACIFIC

N

Equator

S

OCEAN

Tropic of Capricorn

AUSTRALIA

Botany Bay
20 January 1788

36 WEEKS AND 16,000 MILES

ROUTE OF THE FIRST FLEET
TO AUSTRALIA, 1787–8
and of Russian exploration to
the Americas

105 120 135 150 165 °E 180 °W 165 150 135 120

It is hard to comprehend just how far those Russians had come to reach California. Only time of travel really counts. Australia's First Fleet, which called both at Rio de Janeiro and at Cape Town on the way, covered some 15,000 miles. But they did it in eight and a half months. Yet those Russians heading for Fort Ross had no such ocean-going ships. They had no major shipyards on the Pacific, so all they could build were some small sloops in which they edged down America's Pacific coast on the freezing Alaska current. To get to Alaska, they had first to edge round the coast on either side of the Bering Strait from their outpost on Kamchatka – again, over many weeks. And to reach Kamchatka, they had to sail up from Okhotsk or Magadan on the mainland – another lengthy voyage. In other words, Fort Ross was almost as far away in time from Russia's Far East as Botany Bay was from Cape Town. On top of that, the overland track from Okhotsk to Moscow stretched out for perhaps another two years' march. It brings home the meaning of the Russian term for distant provinces. They used to call them *gluchoe provintsii* or 'deaf provinces', lands beyond communication. One presumes that the men at Fort Ross, who arrived there as Napoleon was approaching Moscow, would have been lucky to hear of the event before the battle of Waterloo nearly three years later.

One should not exaggerate. Not everyone had to walk across Siberia. Tsarist officials and imperial couriers could travel in light horse-drawn carriages which in certain conditions moved at what in those days was lightning speed. The best season was winter, when the rivers and lakes froze hard and great ice roads came into use over long stretches of water and forest. Once the terrible Siberian snowstorms had abated, a relay of sturdy two-horse sleighs could wing its way across the ice at 15 or even 50 mph, ten times the speed of a trudging convict. In good weather, the only inhibitor was the short daylight hours. Just as the defeated Napoleon raced back to Paris across the ice and snow of western Russia and Poland, so the news of his defeat would have sped eastwards at perhaps a thousand miles a month, arriving on the Pacific coast in the summer of 1813. From there it would have had to await a packet boat to Alaska, and from Alaska, at the end of the spring thaw of 1814, for a sloop to California. So yes, in terms of travelling time, the garrison at Fort Ross was much further from home than the British garrison in New South Wales. And their reply, sending congratulations to the tsar, was unlikely to have arrived in St Petersburg before Napoleon would have been settling in on St Helena.

But then again, what and where was *home*? A historian who checked the roll of the Russian garrison at Fort Ross found that a significant proportion of the men – between a quarter and a third – were not Russians at all but Poles.[11] These would have been men deported from Poland to Siberia at the end of yet another Polish rising: the one in 1794 headed by Tadeusz Kościuszko. After serving their sentence, and with no ticket back to Poland, many stayed on to take a leading part in the exploration and surveying of Siberia and Alaska. For a long time those Polish exiles formed the only educated elite that Siberia possessed.

Exploration? Kozzy-usko? Those words may well ring a bell in Australian heads. Many people may be puzzled to know why the highest mountain in Australia has an unpronounceable Polish name. The answer is that one of the many patriots who went west (instead of east) after the 1830 rising, Pawel Strzelecki, found his way to England, where he was employed as a military surveyor. His work took him to Australia, where he undertook what several of his comrades were already doing in Siberia – exploring and drawing maps. Here in South Australia, there is a Strzelecki Desert.[12] In eastern Siberia they have a breed of wild horses called Przewalski's after one of the pioneers who travelled through and surveyed the region.[13]

Here, with apologies, comes a personal anecdote. I learned to ski many years ago in Andorra of all places, in the Pyrenees. The instructress of the beginners' class happened to be a young Australian woman who told us that she had learned to ski on the slopes of Mount 'Kozzy-usko'. She was relentless. Every time one of us fell down, she raced over, poked the fallen body with her ski stick, and screamed, 'Get up, and stay up.' I was the most frequent faller in the group, so I was most frequently on the receiving end of her stick and her tongue. Eventually, I could take no more. When she raced over again to berate me, as I lay off piste in the middle of a snowdrift, I decided to get in first.

'It's easy,' I said.

'Of course it's easy. Get up!'

'No, it's easy to say Kościuszko properly, instead of "Kozzy-usko".'

'What?'

'You think that skiing is easy; some of us think other things easy. I shall stop falling over if you stop saying "Kozzy-usko". So repeat after me: "COSH – CHEW – SHKO".'

And she did it. It was a deal. Before the day was over, I had learned to stay on my skis and she had learned to pronounce the name of her country's highest mountain. Twenty years later, when we went to see the Snowy Mountains and stayed in Jinderbine, we noticed that the Australian park authorities had been correcting the spelling on all the signs pointing to 'Mount Kościuszko'. I have often wondered if my former ski teacher was somehow responsible.

Australia grew up within the British empire; Siberia formed a large slice of the Russian empire. A comparison of the empire-building of the two imperial peoples, English and Russian, may not be out of place. In each case, there were three stages. In the first stage the imperial power creates a national base by uniting all the local principalities. In England this was temporarily achieved by the kings of Wessex in the tenth century, and at the second attempt by the Normans. In Russia it was achieved by the grand dukes of Moscow, who finally knocked out Moscow's chief rival Novgorod in 1475. (How different history would have been if Mercia had knocked out Wessex, or if democratic Novgorod had knocked out autocratic Moscow!) In the second stage the imperial power expands its national base by taking over and absorbing all the adjacent countries to form a new multinational state. England did this by conquering Wales, Scotland and Ireland, from which was forged a new English-dominated 'British nation'. Russia did it by taking over Ukraine, Belarus, the Baltic states and parts of Poland to form a much larger, multinational tsarist empire. The third stage is for the imperial power to set off from its initial home base, and then to pick off country after country in various continents of the globe. The English did this overseas; the Russians did it overland. London ended up by ruling about one quarter of the earth's surface, Moscow about one fifth. England's first overseas colony was Virginia, settled in 1606; Moscow's first foreign overland colony was the Tartar khanate of Kazan, conquered in 1552. Nearly half a millennium later London only has five or six tiny dependencies left – the Falklands, Gibraltar and a few more. Moscow, though it recently lost fourteen out of fifteen republics of the former USSR, still has a bigger concern. The Russian Federation is a country of seventy nationalities including Tartars, Ingush and Chechens.

And so to Siberia. *Sybyr* is a Tatar word meaning 'The Sleeping Land'. It was the name of a tiny principality which Cossacks in Muscovite service first encountered when they crossed the Urals in 1581. The name then grew and grew in pace with Russian conquests, until it was used for the territory which stretches all the way from the Urals to the Pacific. Precise definitions vary, but Siberia is, in effect, Russia-in-Asia.[14]

Siberia, even by Australian standards, is rather large. It contains 4.95 million square miles. It is not far short of the size of Australia and the USA put together. One of its rivers alone, the Ob, drains an area of 1.31 million square miles and at 3380 miles is longer than the trip from Adelaide to Darwin and back. Its present population, 35 million, is very largely concentrated in a string of modern cities along the southern rim or else in the Far East.

Siberia, however, wasn't empty. It wasn't *terra nulla*. Like Australia, it had been inhabited since time immemorial by indigenous peoples – in Siberia's case by five or six very varied ethnic and linguistic groups. In the Urals live an assortment of Finno-Ugrians, one group of which, the Finns, migrated long ago to Scandinavia. At the other extremity, near the Bering Strait, live Inuits and Aleuts who are the kin of what used to be called North American Eskimos. In the far north, too, are the Samoyeds – literally 'cannibals' in Russian. South of Lake Baykal, the Buryats are Mongol pastoralists. The Yakuts and Tungus of the taiga are Altaic reindeer herders. One tribe, the Chukchi, did not submit to Russian rule until the 1930s. Massacres did take place. Unlike the aborigines of Australia, however, the native Siberians were not decimated. They were most usually co-opted as scouts and trappers. Even so, one wonders how long it can be before native Siberians, like the Chechens – who have been battling the might of Russia for 200 years – come up with the slogan, 'Your land is our land.'

The reasons for the European colonisation of Siberia closely resemble those which are familiar in Australia, though the priorities may have been somewhat different. Yermak the Cossack, an officer of Ivan the Terrible, was sent, like Captain Cook, on an official mission to see what he could see. One can envisage him and his successors climbing steadily over the endless ridges of forest and tundra much as Dutch and English navigators rode the endless swell of the oceans. They pushed on with such persistence, building forts as they went, that after sixty-seven years they finally saw the Pacific. That was in 1648, only a couple of years after Abel Tasman had completed his voyages to New Holland. They reached Kamchatka in 1699, Alaska in 1741, California, as mentioned, in 1812. Why did they go? Curiosity, dreams of loot and profit, military orders, transportation, escape from the intolerable – all were part of it. Not all those frontiersmen, however, were orderly explorers. Many were the landlubbing counterparts of William Dampier and his ilk – pirates and bandits. From the start, Siberia was largely a lawless land, a paradise for outlaws and for Russia's huge company of fugitive serfs. Ned Kelly, if he could have stood the winter cold, would have been in his element.

Siberia's untold natural resources were a constant magnet. The fur trade was the initial attraction, as in Canada. But then it was gold and diamonds, and timber that was floated down the great rivers. In the twentieth century, the world's largest reserves of coals were tapped. And then it was oil and natural gas. By the end of the USSR, 80 per cent of Soviet foreign currency earnings derived from Siberian exports. Siberian miners, bandits and lumberjacks were joined by religious exiles. Russian Old Believers took refuge there in the seventeenth century, as did Protestant sects and assorted Orthodox hermits and mystics. Siberia was the home of native shamanism, which had a way of permeating imported Christian practices. Rasputin started his dubious career as a Siberian mystic.

Not surprisingly, Siberian society suffered from a serious imbalance of the sexes – or to put it in a man's terms, from a serious shortage of women. The result seems to have been sex and violence on a continental scale.[15] If one looks at those columns of Polish exiles, for example, the men always heavily outnumbered the women. When they completed their sentences, as often as not they married local Russian women, if any were available, and founded families that in a couple of generations were thoroughly Russified. But being founded by Polish men, those families have kept their Polish surnames. One and a half, two centuries on in the age of the Internet, quite a few of those families are seeking out their Polish roots.

Land hunger in European Russia proved another powerful motor for settlement. Over one third of Siberia lies under unbroken permafrost and is totally unsuitable for agriculture. But a long thin strip on the border of the northern forest and the southern steppes has great potential for cereal growing; it's the counterpart of the Canadian prairie. Two huge agricultural campaigns were staged there. One, before the First World War, was inspired by the Stolypin reforms, and created a sturdy class of free Siberian peasants. This experiment was soon eradicated by the Bolsheviks, who could not forgive the Siberians' support for anti-Bolshevik forces during the Civil War, and who would not tolerate a free or prosperous peasantry. The second campaign, 'To the Virgin Lands', was launched by Khrushchev in the 1960s. This one came to grief through mismanagement, scientific bungling and the incurable ills of collective farming.

Industry came to Siberia to exploit the colossal energy reserves, both hydroelectricity and fossil fuels. Gigantic schemes, though, have not always been a gigantic success. The first great push took place during the five-year plans of the 1930s when the Kuznetsk Basin, the 'Kuzbas', was opened up. The second came with the Second World War, when whole towns and factories were evacuated from the European republics, like Ukraine, threatened by Nazi invasion. The fundamental obstacle lay in the diabolically inadequate infrastructure. To this day, the one and only railway to cross Siberia from end to end is the single-track Trans-Siberian built by the tsars between 1895 and 1905. There is still no all-weather, trans-Siberian link.

The tsar's great railway was built, among other things, for strategic purposes. By the late nineteenth century, the vast mass of Siberia was a critical geopolitical conflict zone. Russia has long had poor relations with Siberia's powerful Asian neighbours, China and Japan, both of whom dispute the historical treaties of demarcation. In the nineteenth century, especially in London, Russian Siberia and central Asia were seen as a threatening hinterland to British India. And in the twentieth century, it was still viewed as a possible base for further expansion. Now that the USSR has evaporated and the zone is no longer adequately policed, one wonders what may happen. The juxtaposition of the world's most populous nation in China and the world's least populous territory is bound to have consequences.

Here is a paradox which Australians will grasp instinctively. Siberia has simultaneously been a land of chains and a land of hope and freedom. Exactly because free Siberians lived in the unmentionable shadow of the camps and the convicts, they have valued their liberty more keenly than others. Siberia is the only part of Russia that, prior to Stalinist collectivisation, never knew serfdom. Yet the convict story has to be finished. If the penal colonies of the tsarist period held their tens of thousands, the camps of the Soviet Gulag consumed their millions. Whilst tsarist Siberia held a handful of notorious convict settlements – most notoriously on the island of Sakhalin, which Chekhov wrote about – Soviet Siberia became an archipelago of pain and death on an unequalled scale.

This is a subject where many Western scholars follow the nefarious Sovietological tradition which always refused to call a spade a spade. Talking of the history of deportation to Siberia, a recent encyclopaedia of 'Russia' edited by a bevy of distinguished Oxford professors uses the wonderful euphemism 'state-sponsored migration' employing 'both coercion and incentives'.[16] Only the other week, an American editor of a prominent historical journal asked me to withdraw the word 'camps' in relation to the Soviet Gulag, because it might remind his readers of Nazi practices. I had to remind him that Gulag stands for *Gosudarstvenniy Lagier* or state-camp system and is a close parallel to the German *Konzentrationslager*. Any doubters should be confronted with the information that the gateway to the vast Siberian collection camp at Magaden was adorned with the inscription, ' Через труд' – 'back home through work'. *Arbeit macht frei*, as over the gateway to Auschwitz I, makes a very passable translation. And Auschwitz came nearly twenty years later.

Of course, a distinction has to be made between concentration camps on the one hand, whether Nazi or Soviet, and on the other the special category of death camps or death factories, such as Treblinka or Sobibór, which the Nazis constructed for the perpetration of the Final Solution. To my knowledge, only one author – an Israeli – uses the term 'death camp' in relation to Soviet installations, and then only to a small number of locations where unprotected prisoners were made to clean nuclear installations in the sure knowledge that they would die from radiation.[17]

Decent historians, however, must not mince words. In the Stalinist decades, more people died in the Gulag than from Nazi persecution. People sent to the 'Great White Bear', as the saying went, could enjoy an average life expectancy of one winter. The normal sentences of eight, twelve, twenty or twenty-five years' hard labour, therefore, were a criminal fiction. Soviet officials knew full well that most convicts would never serve even a fraction of their terms. And the Gulag was not the worst of it. Historians are now looking at NKVD random killings by quota, the terror-famine in Ukraine, and the mass shootings of the pre-war Great Terror.[18]

The scale of these operations, taken as a whole, beggars belief. Solzhenitsyn, who was himself a Siberian *zek*, talks of 66 million victims. He may be too high, but the English historian Robert Conquest, who has borne the brunt of battling with Stalinist apologists who still talk of thousands, is not far behind. And he is widely fêted nowadays in Russia itself. But such statistics are virtually incomprehensible. Mention was made earlier of 160,000, the total number of Australian transportees, the population of a small city. Talking of tsarist deportations from Poland, a comparison with the total number of Poles sent to Siberia in the nineteenth century suggests that they may have reached the same level. But that's a drop in the Stalinist ocean. In 1939–41, when the USSR occupied eastern Poland and Stalin's NKVD started deporting Polish citizens to Siberia and Kazakhstan by railway convoy, there are several well-documented occasions when more than 160,000 people were deported in *one single day*.[19] That gives food for thought: all the convicts in Australian history deported to Siberia at one go.

This terrible episode ends with another fascinating footnote from the history of walking. In 1941 the Poles became the only group ever to receive a collective amnesty from exile and the Gulag. After Hitler's attack on the USSR, Stalin needed a Polish army. Hundreds of thousands of Polish deportees were released. No transport was provided. So they walked. Most tried to walk across Russia to Uzbekistan, where the army of General Anders was forming – twice the journey of Burke and Wills. But several hundred made it from north-east Siberia to India, crossing Mongolia, Tibet and the Himalayas on the way. An account of this ordeal, which many reviewers thought to be a fabrication, was published in Britain in the 1950s as *The Long Walk*.[20] British officials in Delhi could not believe their eyes. Yet in essence it was accurate.

The factor of duration is not without significance. The history of transportation to Australia began in 1787 and ended in 1868. The history of transportation to Siberia, which began in the early seventeenth century, hopefully ended in 1991. 1991 is not that long ago. And by Siberian standards it is not a long time for the survivors to find their way home.

It would be wrong to leave the impression that academic cant is somehow the preserve of the Sovietologists. It is not. I rather liked the view of a recent edition of the *Encyclopaedia Britannica* on the huge Irish contingent among the convicts bound for Australia. 'The Irish,' it states, 'became offenders through socio-political unrest.' *Socio-political unrest.* 'Socio' stands for state-sponsored hunger, and 'political' means normal human patriotism. How wonderfully similar are those Irish to the Poles: both nations are mainly Catholics; both used to live off potatoes; and both have a penchant for the 'hard stuff'. As you all know, 'whiskey', meaning 'little water' in the Gaelic, is an almost exact rendering of the Slavonic *wódka*. Oh yes, and both nations have a terrible weakness for socio-political unrest.

One of my constant preoccupations when commenting on European history has been to counteract the inveterate 'Westernism' of most western scholars. They write about Europe as if only the west counts. Eastern Europe is ignored and derided by turns.

Yet, whenever one examines the great themes of the subject, the conventional western angle can usually be matched with a less conventional eastern angle. There was a Roman empire in the west, but there was a longer-lived eastern Roman empire in Byzantium. There was a *Völkerwanderung* of the Germanic tribes, but there was a parallel *Völkerwanderung* of the Slavs. There is a Catholic, Latin Christendom in the west and Orthodox Greek Christendom in the east. The Italian Renaissance radiated to France and England, and also to Poland and Hungary. There was one sort of Enlightenment in the west, and another sort in the east. The history of Europe overseas is very largely a western phenomenon. But the history of Europe overland is very much the matching eastern phenomenon.

Several historians have already seen this parallel. In his wonderfully evocative work *The Fatal Shore* Robert Hughes saw it. At more than one point Hughes talks of Botany Bay as the precursor of the Gulag.[21] Of course, he's right. But I doubt if it's the best way of putting it. At the time the First Fleet dropped anchor, the penal colonies of Siberia were already well established. Siberia was the precursor of Botany Bay. Apart from that, one must keep a sense of proportion. Horrific though the old British convict system was, it does not top the scale of global horrors. Neither imperial British nor imperial Russian penal policies can be remotely equated either in scale or depravity with the Gulag archipelago or indeed with the Nazi Holocaust.

Finally, if penal colonies are a phenomenon of the past, one has to think of the future. Two hundred years on, Australia is moving towards complete independence, debating whether to sever the last link with that Germano-British monarchy which set up the colony in the first place. Canada may follow suit. But Siberia is still an integral part of the Russian republic. What will come of that?

Judging by the Antipodean precedent, three things may be suggested. One, the lot of the indigenous peoples has to be addressed; Russian democracy cannot withstand another Chechnya. Two, the devolution of dependencies is a natural adjunct to democracy at the centre. One of the reasons why the British empire was able to fall apart so gracefully was the readiness to grant self-governing dominion status at an early stage. London reached that point with Canada in 1867 and with Australia in 1901. Moscow has not yet taken its first step in that direction. Thirdly, all children grow up and separate their adult lives from that of their parents. But independence does not mean rejection. Relatives are always relatives. Australia will always be related to Britain through their common history. A future independent Siberia would never entirely break the bonds with Russia.

For, though the world constantly changes, a historical legacy invariably remains. In 1788, apart from the founding of Australia and the first meeting of the US Congress, the Parliament of the Commonwealth of Poland-Lithuania assembled for the penultimate time. It was to pass the first state constitution of its kind in Europe. The empress of Russia, Catherine the Great, was so furious at this outbreak of democracy that she sent an army into Poland. The constitution was crushed. The Polish parliament, surrounded by Russian guns, acquiesced. So the Polish democrats rebelled. Led by Tadeusz Kościuszko, a veteran of the American War of Independence, they fought yet another war against the odds. When Kościuszko fell, he is said to have cried 'Finis Poloniae' – Poland is finished. But it wasn't. Warsaw was stormed; thousands of civilians were massacred; the king of

Poland abdicated; the Polish commonwealth was declared extinct; and Kościuszko's defeat inspired all the other subsequent Polish catastrophes. Yet Poland has somehow survived. So, too, has Kościuszko's reputation. His name is forever associated with that wonderful Polish sentiment, 'Victory is to be defeated but not to surrender.'[22] It is inevitably linked with a low point of Polish history, but it provides a most fitting label both for the high point of Australian geography and for faith in a better future.

VIII

HISTORY, LANGUAGE AND LITERATURE: A JOURNEY INTO THE UNKNOWN

HISTORY and literature are twins born of the same mother, *humanitas*. Their lives are so intertwined that it is hard to imagine writing about the one without referring to the other. For literature forms a continuous strand that runs through and alongside all the other strands of the past, whether social, economic or political. By the same token, history is not just the background which moulds the life of writers and against which literary works are conceived and written. Directly or indirectly, it is an indispensable element of the final product. This strikes me as a truism so obvious that it hardly needs to be stated. But in view of the widespread belief that history deals with fact and literature with fiction, the indivisible nature of the two subjects perhaps needs to be restated.

One small exercise can be fruitful. If one takes the greatest poem, the greatest novel and the greatest drama in the European repertoire – and one could argue endlessly about the choice – the historical dimension in each of them is easily demonstrated. Dante's *Divina Commedia*, for example, describes an epic journey through hell, purgatory and paradise that never took place. It is not historical in the literal sense. So much is obvious. Yet the torrent of theological concepts, of philosophical comments, of references to classical literature, to people, places and events, real or imagined, indeed the very structure of the poem, adds up to an unparalleled exposition of the medieval world view. It provides a picture of the life and times of Dante's contemporaries that could not possibly be achieved by straightforward description and analysis. Apart

149

from that, the precision and melodies of Dante's language form an example of an astonishing intellectual vehicle, whereby the deepest verities of the human condition can be conveyed.

Similarly, Shakespeare's *King Lear* is set in a period of prehistoric Britain about which almost nothing is known for certain. So it is a fable, even though its full title is *The True Chronicle Historie of the life and death of King Lear and his three Daughters*. Yet its observations of people in power, and of individuals under threat of madness or despair, expressed again in matchless language, reveal timeless truths. In the age of monarchy, when Shakespeare was writing and when the divine right of kings was believed implicitly, Lear's problems must have seemed like a commentary on current affairs. And to a modern audience, 400 years on, they offer a lesson in the history of Stuart England as well as in politics and psychology.

Tolstoy's *War and Peace* may at first sight appear to be a simple historical novel set against the backcloth of Russia's wars with Napoleon. In reality, the backcloth is reworked with the same powerful imagination that fashions Bezuchov's fictional tale. The historical and the non-historical elements are inseparable. The novel is not the most reliable guide for military historians seeking to establish what exactly happened at Austerlitz, but it is an indispensable aid for any social or cultural historian who is trying to examine the impact of those wars on post-war society.

Naturally, few people start with Dante, Shakespeare or Tolstoy. Young readers begin with simpler things. In my case, it was an old edition of *The Tales of Robin Hood* based on the original ballads. And it conjured up a wonderful aura of the age of knights, monks and outlaws. Then came historical novels. I never acquired a keen taste for Jane Austen or even Charles Dickens, but I loved the genre of historical adventures. *With the Eagles*, which follows a lad who somehow attaches himself to a Roman legion marching round Britannia, was given to us at school. *The Children of the New Forest* provided a heady story of children fending for themselves during the English Civil War; *The Count of Monte Cristo*, which my father loved, and *The Three Musketeers* whisked me onto the continent for the first time. After that, it was the Hornblower stories and the Scarlet Pimpernel set in the Napoleonic Wars, *Kidnapped* and the *Black Arrow*, *The Cloister and the Hearth* and *The Prisoner of Zenda* . . . When

I was old enough to climb Pendle Hill on my own, I took to exploring local history with the help of Harrison Ainsworth or *Mist over Pendle*.

As far as I recall, however, though awake to the links between the historical and literary strands of the past, I never set out to gain a methodical acquaintance with European literature. My impression is that literature somehow pursued me; not that I pursued literature. My route led through a long-standing interest in languages, which in turn gave me the ability to read foreign works and in due course to enjoy the ability. Looking back, I can identify three key moments. One came early on, in the late 1940s, when my family drove off from Lancashire on our first post-war holiday to Wales. Somewhere on the road, probably in Denbigh, we stopped for a break and I noticed that the newspapers in the rack outside a shop were not written in English. My father, who was totally uninterested in his own father's Welsh origins, scolded me and said something like, 'That won't interest you.' So I was entranced. I was nine or ten years old. My first given name was Ivor. And I instinctively knew that I belonged. Despite my father's protests, I spent my precious pocket money on a Welsh newspaper, and I sat in the back of the car for hours, obstinately pretending to read it. Soon after, I asked for a Welsh–English dictionary, *Geiridur: Cymraeg– Saesneg, Saesneg–Cymraeg: gan T. Gwynn Jones D.Litt*, which I still possess. And on a subsequent trip to Anglesey, where we visited Llanfair PG,* I took a passionate interest in Welsh place names. Within a couple of years, I had bought myself George Borrow's *Wild Wales* and was revelling in the wonderful travels of that Victorian clergyman, who had learned the Welsh language and had walked the length and breadth of the valleys and the mountain villages. Borrow taught me that English is not the only culture in the world. And I took special pleasure in trying to read aloud his massive quotations of Welsh poetry which I could not decipher but which filled me with awe.

> Oer yw'r Eira ar Eryri – o'ryw
> Ar awyr i rewi:
> Oer yw'ria ar riw'r ri,
> A'r Eira oer yw' Ryri.

*Llanfairpwllgwyngyllgogerychwyrndrobwllllantysiliogogogoch.

O Ri' y' Ryri yw'r oera – o'r âr
Ar oror wir arwa;
O'r awyr a yr Eira,
O'i ryw i roi rew a'r ia.[1]

Cold is the snow on Snowdon's brow
It makes the air so chill . . .
From Snowdon's hill the breezes chill
Can freeze the very snow.

Such was 'the harangue' which Borrow 'uttered' on the summit of Y *Wyddfa*, adding when he noted the 'grinning scorn' of some passing English tourists, 'I am ashamed to say that I am an Englishman.'[2] Borrow's sense of outrage has stayed with me. In my list of deadly sins, there are few things worse than pouring scorn on other people's cultures through ignorance.

Around the time that I encountered Borrow, I also came across an unusual form of the French language. I had already started to learn French at school, and I belonged to a generation which was sent to church twice every Sunday and was expected to sit for forty-five or fifty minutes through incredibly tedious and verbose sermons. I was saved by a small black volume which someone had left in our family pew box long before. It was *La Sainte Bible*, published in a late-nineteenth-century Protestant edition, either in Grenoble or Geneva. Twice a week I would pore over its tiny print, comparing its stilted cadences with passages that I knew from the King James Bible and wrestling with its fondness for things like the past subjunctive. Bit by bit, as the booming sermons bounced off my lowered head, I made sense of it. At school I had benefited from the direct method as invented by an enterprising Bolton teacher called Emma Saxelby and from her textbook called *En route*. But it was the little black book in the pew box which taught me another important lesson. The funny foreign sounds and strange words that we practised in class were tiny cogs in a much bigger machine. They were steps leading to a much wider world still to be experienced. Somewhere out there were other intriguing countries with languages and literatures and histories of their own.

Heureux les pauvres en esprit, car le royaume des cieux est à eux:
Heureux ceux qui sont dans l'affliction, car ils seront consolés:
Heureux les débonnaires: car ils hériteront la terre.
Heureux ceux qui ont faim et soif de la justice, car ils seront raissaisiés:
Heureux les miséricordieux: car ils obtiendront la miséricorde.
Heureux ceux qui ont le coeur pur: car ils verront Dieu.
Heureux ceux qui procurent la paix, car ils seront appelés enfants de
    Dieu.
Heureux ceux qui sont persécutés pour la justice: car le royaume des
    cieux est à eux.
Vous serez heureux lorsqu'à cause de moi on vous dira des injures,
    qu'on vous persécutera, et qu'on dira faussement contre vous toute
    sorte de mal.
Rejouissez-vous alors, et tressaillez de joie, parce que votre récompense
    sera grande . . .[3]

Blessed are the poor in spirit: for theirs is the kingdom of heaven.
Blessed are they that mourn, for they shall be comforted.
Blessed are the meek, for they shall inherit the earth.
Blessed are they which do hunger and thirst after righteousness, for they
    shall be filled.
Blessed are the merciful: for they shall obtain mercy.
Blessed are the pure in heart, for they shall see God.
Blessed are the peacemakers, for they shall be called the children of
    God.
Blessed are they which are persecuted for righteousness's sake: for
    theirs is the kingdom of heaven.
Blessed are ye, when men shall revile you and persecute you, and say all
    manner of evil against you for my sake.
Rejoice and be exceeding glad: for great is your reward in heaven.

I'm not sure that I prefer 'Heureux les débonnaires' to 'Blessed are the meek'.

In the sixth form I made no special effort to study literature. I had dropped both English and Latin after O level, and the set books in the French A-level course were my only literary fare. I was focused on my main

choices of history and geography, and looked no further afield. Fortunately, to my abiding benefit, all pupils in my position were obliged to
follow a none-too-serious weekly 'extra', which turned out to be taken by
a young teacher called David Curnow. Mr Curnow was straight out of
Cambridge – tall, suave, cavalry twills and passionately devoted to English
poetry. (He would later became professor of English at the American
University of Beirut.) Every week he strolled into the classroom, silently
wrote a short poem on the blackboard, took up station lolling on a desk,
grinned, and waited for his sceptical audience to react. He won us over
effortlessly. The first of the poems to which he introduced us was by
William Blake:

> Ah, Sunflower, weary of time,
> Who countest the steps of the sun,
> Seeking after that sweet golden clime
> Where the traveller's journey is done;
>
> Where the youth, pined away with desire
> And the pale virgin shrouded in snow
> Arise from their graves and aspire
> Where my Sunflower wishes to go.[4]

For teenage boys, all pined away with desire, this was irresistible. I found
a biography of Blake in the town library, and read it without being told.
Week by week we read a chunk of Milton, a Shakespeare sonnet or extracts
from Wordsworth's *Prelude*. I was off and away for a lifetime.

School trips were an established feature in the Bolton School tradition, and in the Easter vacation of 1956 our year group embarked on a
dangerously radical experiment, a co-educational tour of Verona, Florence and Venice. The leader of the expedition was Miss Margaret
Higginson MA, sometime head of English at St Paul's, and the newly
appointed headmistress of the Girls' Division. Impressions rained down
on our impressionable heads during that tour, and some of them stuck.
One day, our group drove from Verona to the nearby shores of Lake
Garda. The aim was to visit the villa of Catullus at Sirmione, but since
we were met by a cloudburst, the visit was a washout. Yet one moment

remained with me. Cowering under umbrellas from the downpour, Miss Higginson told us about a book about to be published called *Poets in a Landscape*, which opened with a chapter on Catullus. For some reason, the title appealed, and in due course I sought it out. I was riveted. The author, Gilbert Highet, wrote in a marvellously terse style, placing each of the great Roman authors in a very precise place and time.

> He came from the north. He lived a brief, passionate, unhappy life. He wrote magnificent poetry. And he introduced a new word for 'kiss' into the European languages ... Whenever a Frenchman says *baiser*, whenever an Italian talks of *un bacio*, when a Spaniard says *besar* or a Portuguese *beijar*, they are using the word which this poet picked up and made into Latin to amuse his sweetheart. The woman was unworthy. The poet died. The word lives.[5]

Here was a wonderful guide for a teenager who was concentrating on history and geography but needed a little more creative stimulation. And Catullus was intriguing, too. He wrote the sort of intense, crystal-clear, word-perfect verse that defies thousands of would-be translators:

ODI ET AMO QUARE ID FACIAM FORTASSE REQUIRIS
NESCIO SED FIERI SENTIO ET EXCRUCIOR

I hate and I love. You ask, perhaps, how I do it.
I know not. But I feel the agonising pain.[6]

The trip to Italy had further unplanned spin-offs. One was a long-standing girlfriend; the other was a lifelong love of Italian. At the age of seventeen, I surprised my teachers by passing the scholarship exam at Magdalen College, Oxford, well ahead of schedule. It left me with several months at school free of all obligations. My enlightened history master, W.B. 'Bill' Brown, who had accompanied Miss Higginson on the earlier Italian jaunt, decided that apart from feeding me Gibbon, he was going to teach me Italian. I received personal tuition. I soaked up the language, which an existing knowledge of Latin and French greatly facilitated. My notebooks show that I was already reading Italian literature before I left school.

Sono i colori della terra natia
Sono i colori dell'anima mia!

C'è il verde, emblema di dolce speranza
onde il fior germogliò della costanza.

C'è il bianco, della fede, per tant'anni
temprata nelle prove i nelli affanni.

C'è il rosso della fiamma del mio cuore
che arde, brilla, consuma, e mai non muore

Petali bianchi e rossi, e verde stelo
Che non v'involga mai brina nè gelo!

Siete i colori della terra natia
siete i colori dell'anima mia.[7]

You are the colours of my native land:
and the colours of my soul!

There's the green, the emblem of gentle hope,
whence the flower germinates from constancy.

There's the white of faith, for so many years
tempered in trials and hardship.

There's the red of my heart's flame
which burns, shines, dims but never dies

White and red petals, and green stem,
never enveloped by frost or cold!

You are the colours of my native land.
You are the colours of my soul.

Such were the effortless beginnings of a long journey.

No one ever told me that Europe's oldest literature was probably written in Ireland. At least for many centuries it was not written down, but memorised and recited by generations of professional bards, perpetuating the Celtic oral tradition. I stumbled across it when researching *The Isles* and it was one of the last pieces of the overall jigsaw to fall into place. I was reading up on the Celtic revival in Ireland in the late nineteenth century, and was moved to look at some of the ancient texts which W.B. Yeats and others had discovered. At some point I found out that Robert Graves had published a translation of 'The Song of Amheirgin', whose origins may go back to 1268 BC:

I am a stag:	of seven tines,
I am a flood:	across a plain,
I am a wind:	on a deep lake,
I am a tear:	the Sun let fall,
I am a hawk:	above the cliff,
I am a thorn:	beneath the nail,
I am a wonder:	among the flowers
I am a wizard:	who but I sets the cool head aflame with smoke?

I am a spear:	that rears for blood
I am a salmon:	in a pool
I am a lure:	from paradise
I am a hill:	where poets walk
I am a boar:	ruthless and red
I am a breaker:	threatening doom
I am a tide:	that drags to death
I am an infant:	who but I peeps from the unhewn dolmen arch?
I am the womb:	of every holt,
I am the blaze:	on every hill,
I am the queen:	of every hive,
I am the shield:	for every head
I am the grave:	of every hope.[8]

My involvement with ancient Greek was still briefer. In the fourth or fifth form at school I was taken aside by the Classics master and invited to join the elite set that did Greek as well as Latin. I was given a primer, told to learn the alphabet, do the initial exercises, and to report for duty at the end of the holidays. But that's as far as it went. I shied at the first fence. It was a dead end, just like my vain attempts to play the violin. So, apart from the alphabet and one or two words, I had gained nothing except for a vague feeling that I had missed something good.

A better understanding arrived decades later when I began to prepare the sections on Greek philosophy and Greek literature for Chapter II of *Europe: A History*. I spent many happy weeks in the Classics reading room of the Bodleian, lingering on fascinating things like collections of epigrams or prophecies of the oracle at Delphi. I read Homer again in the Penguin translation, sorted out the great triad of tragedians and chuckled uncontrollably over Aristophanes. Eventually I wrote, 'It is no exaggeration to say that Greek letters form the launch-pad of the European humanist tradition.'

> Wonders are many on earth, and the greatest of these
> Is man, who rides the ocean . . .
> He is master of the ageless earth, to his own will bending
> The immortal mother of gods . . .
> He is lord of all living things . . .
> The use of language, the wind-swift motion of brain
> He learnt; found out the laws of living together
> In cities . . .
> There is nothing beyond his power . . .[9]

Ten years after that, another moment is worth recording. I was in Warsaw researching the rising of 1944, and I came across a series of books called *Nasze Termopile*. Each of the slim volumes in the series dealt with the battlegrounds and monuments connected with the rising in particular districts of the city. And after some delay I realised that *Termopile* was the Polish transliteration of Thermopylae. When I headed out to one of the most dramatic monuments, at Służewiec, I found that the verse inscribed on the boulder to 'those who chose to fight to the end' was inspired by the last message of Leonidas nearly three millennia before. The classical tradition was alive and well in Eastern Europe.

ὦ ξεῖν᾽, ἄγγειλον Λακεδαιμονίοις ὅτι τῇδε
κείμεθα τοῖς κείνων ῥήμασι πειθόμενοι.[10]

Tell them in Lakedaemon, passer-by.
That we kept the rules, resolved to die.

My own translation of the Polish verse on the monument gave me much satisfaction:

Traveller!
Lower your head; hold your step awhile.
Every grain of this earth is soaked with martyrs' blood.
This is [Służewiec], this is our Thermopylae.
Here lie those who chose to fight to the very end.

No funeral way conducted us to this spot.
No one received a wreath or salvo of honour;
Just a quick shot in the neck in [Mokotov] Jail
And a pony cart to carry us to this forsaken ground.
We marched with [Wolf] . . . with her name on our lips,
To conquer or to die, to the walls of the Old Town
To Narvik, to Tobruk and to Monte Cassino,
Only to end our soldiers' journey in this sand.[11]

The book ended with yet another invocation of Thermopylae:

For everyone who values the free world of today owes the Varsovians of 1944 a deep debt of gratitude. They set a worthy example of the old-fashioned values of patriotism, altruism, steadfastness, self-sacrifice, and duty. Like the Spartans of Leonidas at Thermopylae, magnificent in defeat, and like the Ghetto Fighters of 1943, they merit a similar, admiring epitaph:

Go, passer-by, and tell the world
That we perished in the cause,
Faithful to our orders.[12]

I was put to the study of Latin between the ages of eight and fourteen, and the effort should have produced better results. I clearly remember the very first lesson with Wing Commander Cunningham at Park Road School. As a wartime fighter pilot, he had immense prestige and held us spellbound. He wrote on the blackboard REX AMAT REGINAM and told us it meant 'The king loves the queen.' Then he wrote REGINAM AMAT REX, and asked the class to translate. The class roared out the wrong answer: 'The queen loves the king.' We had been completely brainwashed by the English concept of word order. Unfortunately later teachers were as poor as the wing commander was sharp, and I went through the routine mechanically, without enthusiasm. We were given a taste of the usual authors – Caesar, Tacitus, Livy – and I gained a good grade at O level, but I never really reached take-off, where I might have read Virgil without some effort – which is a matter of regret: 'Sunt lacrimae rerum et mentem mortalia tangunt' (There are tears shed for things, and mortality touches the mind).

Nonetheless, as an Oxford student, I belonged to a generation which still had to pass an exam in unseen Latin translation and to study a Latin text. The set text was the Venerable Bede's *Historia Ecclesiastica Gentis Anglorum*, which I wrote out by hand as a sort of penance. Everyone loves Bede with his clear narrative and ready explanations. Only later did I realise that our Oxford tutors were weaning us onto a very Anglocentric tradition. As an English monk and a loyal servant of Roman Christianity, Bede was not the best of guides to an age where the Celtic peoples and Celtic Christianity were still a force in the land. Even so, his prose was very straightforward and I wrote out the whole of his *Historia* in longhand, and I learned it with enjoyment:

Hic est impraesentiarum universae status Brittaniae, anno adventus Anglorum in Brittaniam circiter ducentesimo octogesimo quinto, Dominicae autem incarnationis anno septingentesimo tricesimo primo: in cuius regno perpetuo exultet terra, et congratulante in fide eius Brittania laetentur insulae multae, et confiteantur memoriae sanctitatis eius.[13]

This, then is the present state of all-Britain about two hundred and eighty-five years since the coming of the English to Britain, and seven hundred and thirty-one years since our Lord's incarnation. May the world rejoice under his eternal rule, and Britannia glory in his Faith. Let the countless isles be glad, and sing praises to the honour of his holiness!

In the twilight world which arose in the British Isles after the retreat of the Roman legions from their province of Britannia, Celtic languages and literatures continued to flourish. As fate would have it, the only Gaelic author from this period to gain worldwide prominence was the victim of forgery. As is now known, Ossian was the product of one of the great literary scams of history. If he existed at all, he was a Scottish bard from the times before Scotland was born. He certainly was not the author of the melancholy verses which the Reverend James Macpherson (1736–96) claimed to have discovered and translated into English in 1762. Yet the fakery, which was soon exposed, did not prevent him from becoming a cult figure in the budding Romantic movement. He fooled Goethe, who quoted him widely, and he beguiled Napoleon, who carried a copy with him on all his campaigns. (As a Corsican who had lost his native culture Buonaparte was obviously waiting to be seduced by a long-lost bard of the Dark Ages.) Even so, good imitations can create great appeal in any medium, and Macpherson was an imitator of the top class.

My love is a son of the hill. He pursues the flying deer.
His grey dogs are panting around him: his bow-string sounds in the wild.
Whether by the front of the rock or by the stream of the mountain
   tough liest;
Then the rushes are nodding with the wind, and the mist is flying over
   thee,
Let me approach my love unperceived, and see him from the rock . . .[14]

Though my upbringing was Christian, my historico-religious education was limited by the usual English horizons of the day. I was sent every Sunday afternoon to Bible class, where the Old Testament was viewed on a par with the New, and where the history of the Jewish people ended with the arrival of Jesus Christ. No one mentioned a word about the extraordinary diaspora of the Jews which might have explained the presence in my school of Jewish children like David Lentin or Nina Garvin; and nothing was said about Hebrew being a language both of the Bible and of the emerging State of Israel.

So when I wrote *Europe: A History*, I was keen to make amends. In the chapter on ancient Rome I made space for a Hebrew quotation from the Torah. I obtained it from a friend who once invited me to speak at his synagogue in Glencoe, Illinois:

עֵץ־חַיִּים הִיא לַמַּחֲזִיקִים
בָּהּ וְתֹמְכֶיהָ מְאֻשָּׁר:
דְּרָכֶיהָ דַרְכֵי נֹעַם וְכָל־
נְתִיבוֹתֶיהָ שָׁלוֹם:

ETZ CHA-YIM HI
LA-MA-CHA-ZI-KIM BA
V'TOM-CHE-HA M'U-SHAR.
D'RA-CHE-HA DAR-CHEY NO-AM,
V'CHOL N'TI-VO-TE-HA SHA-LOM.

The Torah is a tree of life to those
who hold it fast, and those who
cling to it are blessed. Its ways
are ways of pleasantness, and all
its paths are peace.[15]

Islam, too, was off the map. As a boy, I don't think I met any Muslims at all, although one of my scoutmasters, who had served in the Indian Army, could speak Urdu and he told me a bit about the emerging state of Pakistan. Until I read Gibbon and learned about Charles Martel and the battle of Tours, I had no idea that Islam had an unbroken presence in

Europe for some 1200 years. So I equally made space in the chapter 'The Birth of Europe' to quote the muezzin's traditional call to prayer in Arabic. I obtained it from our neighbourhood grocer, Mr Mahmud Khan, who provided a wonderfully artistic text from his mosque on the Cowley Road:

اذان کا بیان

Allāhu akbar
ašhadu 'an lā ilāha illā llāh
ašhadu anna Muhammadu 'rasūlu 'llāh
'alā 'l-salāh
hayyā 'alā 'l-falāh
Allāhu akbar
ašhadu 'an lā ilāha illā llāh[16]

Despite the childhood enthusiasm, I never got a proper grip on Welsh. Though the borders of the Welsh-speaking part of Britain lay little more than a cycle ride away from my home in Lancashire, there was no trace of Welsh studies in our syllabus, and no respect for Welsh culture. I bought the books and the tapes, and I listened fervently to Welsh choirs singing fervently in Welsh but, to my lasting chagrin, I never reached take-off nor broke the linguistic barrier to join them. I was left with a deep sense that part of me belonged to that brave, defeated country, and a still deeper sense of inferiority when I met colleagues at Oxford, like Robert Evans or Rees Davies, whose Welsh credentials were so much better than mine.

It took me a long time to realise the extent and the perfidy of English propaganda against Britain's non-English peoples. The English boast incessantly about the length of their own history. They wilfully confuse what is English and what is British. At Oxford, they force all students of the English faculty to read *Beowulf*, just as the historians must read Bede, 'in order to know their roots'. They never encourage a glimmer of aware-ness of the fact that Britain has numerous and diverse cultural roots. At some point it struck me that the Welsh word for England, *Lloegr*, meaning 'The Lost Land', had centuries of sorrow behind it. I also learned that the 'Welsh of the Old North', who lived in what was to become southern Scotland, held out in so-called Strathclyde to the end of the first millennium. If modern British students were serious about studying their roots, therefore, they would not read just Bede and *Beowulf* but should equally be encouraged to look into the oldest British literature, including *Y Gododdin*, which tells of a battle at Catraeth (Catterick) in AD 600:

> Gwŷr a aeth Gatraeth, oedd ffraeth eu llu,
> Glasfedd eu hancwyn a gwenwyn fu,
> Trychant trwybeiriant yn catáu,
> A gwedi elwch tawelwch fu.
> Cyd elwynt lannau i benydu,
> Dadl ddiau angau i eu treiddu.

> Warriors went to Catraeth, their host was swift,
> Fresh mead was their feast and it was bitter,
> Three hundred fighting under command,
> And after the cry of jubilation there was silence.
> Though they went to churches to do penance,
> The certain meeting with death came to them.[17]

Old Welsh of course, is not remotely intelligible to modern British students, but neither is *Beowulf*, which refers to events in distant Jutland and Frisia and which was composed in a language that is completely undecipherable. 'Olde English', in fact, is a misnomer. It may be old, but it isn't recognisably English. 'Pre-English' might be closer to reality:

Āð wæs geæfned,   ond incgegold
āhæfen of horde.   Here-Scyldinga
betst beadorinca   wæs on bǣl gearu;
æt þǣm āde wæs   ēþgesȳne
swātfāh syrce,   swȳn ealgylden,
eofer īrenheard,   æþeling manig
wundum āwyrded   – sume on wæle crungon.
Hēt ðā Hildeburh   æt Hnæfes āde
hire selfre sunu   sweoloðe befæstan,
bānfatu bærnan,   ond on bǣl dōn
ēame on eaxle.   Ides gnornode,
geōmrode giddum;   gūðrinc āstāh;
wand tō wolcnum   wælfȳra mǣst,
hlynode for hlāwe.   Hafelan multon,
bengeato burston   ðonne blōd ætspranc,
lāðbite līces.   Līg ealle forswealg,
gǣsta gīfrost,   þāra ðe þǣr gūð fornam
bēga folces;   wæs hira blǣd scacen.

The pyre was erected, the ruddy gold
brought from the board, and the best warrior
of Scylding race was ready for burning.
Displayed on his pyre, plain to see,
were the bloody mail-shirt, the boars on the helmets,
iron-hard, gold-clad; and gallant men about him
all marred by their wounds; mighty men had fallen there.
Hildeburgh then ordered her own son
to be given to the funeral pyre of Hnœf
for the burning of his bones; bade him be laid
at his uncle's side. She sang the dirges,
bewailed her grief. The warrior soared:

the greatest of corpse fires coiled to the sky,
roared before the mounds. There were melting heads
and bursting wounds, as the blood sprang out
from weapon-bitten bodies. Blazing fire,
most insatiable of spirits, swallowed the remains
of both nations. Their valour was no more.[18]

One of several other non-English strands in Britain's make-up was Norse. The Vikings are generally presented by English historians, echoing Bede, as savage sea-raiders. Which they were – just like Francis Drake. But they were also determined colonisers, whose settlements dominated large parts of coastal Ireland, northern Scotland and eastern England. The Danelaw, which stretched from the Thames to the Tyne, filled more time and space in English history than the English perspective would allow. And it was literate, at least if literacy includes the oral traditions. The great Norse sagas, not written down till the High Middle Ages, are an underrated source for events in earlier times.

Rekit telk Rǫgnvalds dauða,
rétt skiptu því nornir,
nú 's folkstuðill fallinn,
at fjórðungi mínum.
Verpið, snarpir sveinar,
þvít sigri vér róðum,
skatt velk hónum harðan,
at Háfœtu grjóti.

The folk-lord is fallen
the fee paid for Rognvald;
sweetly the Norns shaped
for me my quarter-share.
Cast the stone, keen
lads, on Long-leg's cairn
as we celebrate here
the settling of the Scot.[19]

My introduction to Italian at school was to bear further fruit at university. I chose to read the Special Subject, 'The Age of Dante', which carried a huge reading list of works in both Latin and Italian. In preparation, I headed off for a term at the Università per stranieri in Perugia and began the long task of working through the *Divina Commedia* in the original. Nothing has ever given me such breathtaking delight. No other writer has ever succeeded in assembling such a dazzling and comprehensive picture of the intellectual world in which he lived. For some reason, when my *Europe: A History* was being edited, the quotation from the closing canto of *Paradiso* was cut. So I can restore it here:

> Quel è 'l geomètra che tutto s'affige
> per misurar lo cherchio, e non ritrova,
> pensando, quel principio ond'elli indige;
> tale era io a quella vista nova:
> veder volea come si convenne
> l'imago al cerchio e come vi s'indova;
> ma non eran da ciò le proprie penne;
> se non che la mia menta fu percossa
> da un fulgore in che sua voglia venne.
> All'alta fantasia qui mancò possa;
> ma già volgeva il mio disìo e il *velle*,
> sì come rota ch'igualmente è mossa,
> l'Amor che move il sole e l'altre stelle.[20]

Like a geometer wholly dedicated
    to squaring the circle, but who cannot find,
    think as he may, the principle indicated –

so did I study the supernal face.
    I yearned to know just how our image merges
    into that circle, and how it there finds place;

but mine were not the wings for such a flight.
    Yet, as I wished, the truth I wished for came
    cleaving my mind in a great flash of light.

Here my powers rest from their high fantasy,
  but already I could feel my being turned –
  instinct and intellect balanced equally

as in a wheel whose motion nothing jars –
  by the Love that moves the Sun and the other stars.

French was the foreign language in which I received the most thorough grounding and in which I achieved the greatest all-round competence. A signal triumph in my career as a schoolmaster was to land a post at St Paul's teaching French by the direct method to boys at England's most prestigious day school. Thirty years later, one of my former pupils[21] was to reveal that a French boy in the class had assured the rest of them that, in spite of his name, 'Monsieur Daviès' was also French. Yet the point at which French ceased to be 'foreign' but became an internalised feature of my own make-up had occurred a bit earlier. I had obtained a faithful pen pal, Henri Viguié, who lived in a ravishing medieval village called Chanonat in Auvergne, which I visited. And in the year between leaving school and going to university, I travelled on my own initiative to follow a diploma course in French language and literature at the University of Grenoble. Lodging for several months with the family of Madame La Baronne Dela-marche at 5, rue du Lycée, I went native. I learned to drink wine, to dress salad, to relish the '*trois cent fromages*', to wear my coat on the shoulders. And I completely lost myself in the language. Still a teenager who had never left home before, I was lonely. I wallowed in Lamartine, and wandered round the shores of Le Lac de Bourget.

O temps suspends ton vol, et vous, heures propices
  Suspendez votre cours!
Laissez-nous savourer les rapides délices
  Des plus beaux de nos jours.

Eternité, néant, passé, sombres abîmes!
Que faites-vous des jours que vous engloutissez?
Parlez: nous rendres-vous ces extases sublimes
  Que vous nous ravissez?

Que le vent qui gémit, le roseau qui soupire,
  Que les parfums légers de ton air embaumé,
Que tout ce qu'on entend, l'on voit ou l'on respire.
  Toute dise: 'Ils ont aimé.'[22]

Oh Time! suspend your flight, and you, favoured hours,
  Halt your course.
Let us savour these all too rapid delights
  Of our most beautiful days.

Eternity, Nothingness, the Past, Dark abyss.
  What do you make from the days that you engulf?
Speak! Will you ever restore the sublime ecstasies
  Which you have torn from us?

May the wind that groans, and the reeds that sigh
  And the gentle perfume of your scented air
May all that one hears, one sees or one breathes
  Say in unison: 'They were in love.'

Above all, I didn't speak English for months on end. I made close friends
with the two sons of the household, Christian and Bernard; I accompanied
Madame Delamarche on trips in her tiny Renault; and I helped the
daughter, Marie-Josèphe (Choupette) to learn her homework:

Heureux qui, comme Ulysse, qui a fait un beau voyage
Ou comme cestuy là qui conquit la toison,
Et puis est retourné, plein d'usage et raison,
Vivre entre ses parents le reste de son âge!

Quand revoiray-je, hélas, de mon petit village
Fumer la cheminée: et en quelle saison
Revoiray-je le clos de ma pauvre maison,
Qui m'est une province, et beaucoup d'avantage?

Plus me plaist le séjour qu'ont basty mes ayeux,
Que des palais Romains le front audacieux:
Plus que le marbre dur me plaist l'ardoise fine,

Plus mon Loyre Gaulois, que le Tybre Latin,
Plus mon petit Lyré, que le mont Palatin,
Et plus que l'air marin la douceur Angevine.²³

Happy is he, who like Ulysses, has completed a fine journey
Or like the man who conquered the Golden Fleece
Returned home, full of experience and wisdom
To dwell among his kin for the rest of his days.

Alas! When shall I see my little village again,
And the smoke of its chimney? In what season,
Shall I see the enclosure of the poor house
Which, for me, is a province, and much more besides?

I am better pleased by the dwelling which my ancestors built
Than by the imposing facades of Roman palaces.
Fine slate pleases me more than hard marble:

Better my Gaulish Loire than the Latin Tiber,
Better my little Liré than the Palatine Mount,
And better than the sea air, the gentleness of Anjou.

Where is Choupette now?

Polish was actually my second Slavonic language; I started to teach myself
whilst a postgraduate at the University of Sussex in Brighton. Quite by
chance, I found myself lodgings in the house of a retired Polish gentleman
and his wife at 8 Adelaide Crescent, Hove and Mr Horko (aided by his
house-guest, the poet Antoni Słonimski) made strenuous efforts to persuade
me that 'an intelligent lad like you' should not be learning Russian. My
solution was to do both. It was a happy decision. Thanks to my existing
knowledge of Russian grammar – which shares with Polish many of the
same brain-teasers like verbal perfectives and verbs of motion – and my

acquaintance with pure, Italian-style vowels, I was able to make rapid progress, and the slightly awkward slogan written on the cover of my exercise book – *'Ja będę umieć mówić po Polsku'* (I shall be able to speak Polish) – became a reality. Three years spent in Cracow after leaving Sussex permitted me to gain a high level of both oral and written fluency. Thanks to my Polish wife, whom I met in Clermont-Ferrand, Polish, alongside English and French, became a household language.

My adventures with Polish literature are too numerous to be briefly recounted. My apparent prowess in the subject is largely due to my wife, who is a professional literary historian and who has constantly pointed me in the right direction and supplied me with the necessary guidance, quotes and references. I could not have covered a fraction of the ground without her. Even so, I was not badly prepared. Having entered myself for the Polish A-level exam, which I took as the sole candidate in Brighton Town Hall, I was obliged to study a selection of authors between the Renaissance and the twentieth century. Given that Polish literature has a longer run than either German or Russian, this was no mean undertaking. Before I left for my lengthy stay in Cracow, I had already read Kochanowski's *Laments, Pan Tadeusz* by Adam Mickiewicz, and an anthology of modern Polish poets. Thereafter, my familiarity with this vast corpus grew considerably. And, with time, I began to try my hand at translating.

Like all English-speakers who have immersed themselves in the wonderful cosmos of Polish literature, I often wondered why it was not better known. The answer has to lie partly in the unfamiliarity of a difficult language, partly in the hostility of neighbours who would have been happy to see Polish culture suppressed, and partly in the coded allusions and allegories by which the Polish classics convey much of their message. If one doesn't know the history of Poland's politics and society, one can't easily decipher the allusions even in translation. And, of course, the vast majority of educated Westerners are blissfully ignorant of Polish history. So for them the book remains closed.

In one of my early forays into translating Polish I made an attempt to render into English some lines of Słowacki that personalise Europe. And I made a couple of bad mistakes. So I am happy to present the improved version here:

Jeśli Europa jest nimfą – Neapol
Jest nimfy okeim błękitnem – *Warszawa*
Sercem – cierniami w nodze: Sewastopol,
Azow, Odessa, Petersburg, Mitawa –
Paryhż jej głową – London kołnierzem
Nakrochmalonym a zaś Rzym . . . szkaplerzem

If Europe is a nymph, then Naples
is the nymph's bright-blue eye – Warsaw
is her heart, whilst Sevastopol,
Azov, Odessa, Petersburg and Mitau are the sharp points of her feet.
Paris is her head – London her starched collar –
and Rome the holy scapular.[24]

German is a language that I long resisted. To be frank, I didn't like the
sound of it. Forty years on, I can still recall my horror at a newspaper
article which said that the German place names of South Tyrol were 'infinitely more melodious than the Italian ones'. The prejudice can partly be
explained by my love affair with Italian, then at its height, and partly by
negative feelings about everything German. A favourite uncle, who wielded
a strong influence on my upbringing, had been badly maltreated in a
German POW camp, and my boyish revulsion lasted for many years. I did
not know at the time that my uncle had spent his years in the camp
studying the German language, reading up on German literature and
acquiring a taste for Wagnerian mythology. The prejudice also cost me the
first serious girlfriend of my life, who was a student of German and who
rightly resented my grimaces about her singing Mozart's 'Queen of the
Night' in the despised original.

Decades passed before the revulsion subsided, and I came to regret
this major loophole in my linguistic armoury. When I decided to write a
history of Breslau/Wrocław, the capital of Silesia, I played safe by taking
on a former student of mine, Roger Moorhouse, a fluent Germanist, as
co-author. And the partnership worked well.

Yet the bridge of prejudice had been crossed some time earlier when,
in preparing *God's Playground*, I felt it necessary to include a section on
the lost German culture of Silesia. With the help of companions, of ency-

clopaedias and books of German verse, I set out to establish the outlines of a remarkable tradition that stretches from Angelus Silesius in the seventeenth century to moderns like Gustav Freytag and Gerhart Hauptmann. My favourite was, and still is, Joseph Freiherr von Eichendorff:

> In einem kühlen Grunde
> Da geht ein Mühlenrad,
> Mein' Liebste ist verschwunden,
> Die dort gewohnet hat.[25]

> O Täler weit, o Höhen,
> O schöner, grüner Wald,
> Du meiner Lust und Wehen
> Andächt'ger Aufenthalt!

> [...]

> Da steht im Wald geschrieben
> Ein stilles, ernstes Wort
> Von rechtem Tun und Lieben,
> Und was des Menschen Hort.[26]

> Ins Leben schleicht das Leiden
> Sich heimlich wie ein Dieb
> Wir alle müssen scheiden
> Von allem, was uns lieb.[27]

> In a cool and gentle valley
> The mill-wheel still is turning.
> But my sweetheart has departed,
> And will not be returning.

> O valleys broad! O soaring crags,
> And fair green woods below!
> My refuge for reflecting
> On all life's joy and sorrow ...

[. . .]

Deep in the forest stands engraved
The quiet, telling truth
Of how aright to live and love,
Of where lies man's real wealth . . .

Misfortune and pain, like familiar thieves
So stealthily overtake us;
For everything that we hold most dear
Must surely be parted from us.

I never even attempted to learn Finnish. It is not an Indo-European language and is unlike almost anything else that one can meet in Europe. I once spent a day in Helsinki, during a stopover on a Baltic cruise, and I opted to visit the municipal sauna instead of seeking out a copy of *Finnish for Foreigners*. Yet I had colleagues in London University who taught Finnish, and from them I knew that the *Kalevala* was a literary work which no one interested in the growth of European culture could possibly avoid:

> Siitä vanha Väinämöinen,
> Laskea karehtelevi
> Vehehellä vaskisella,
> Kuutilla kuparisella
> Yläisihin maaemihin
> Alaisihin taivosihin.
> Sinne puuttui pursinensa,
> Venehinensä väsähyti.
> Jätti kantelon jälille,
> Soiton Suomelle sorean,
> Kansalle ilon ikuisen
> Laulut suuret lapsillensa.

> Then the aged Vainamoinen
> Went upon his journey singing,
> Sailing in his boat of copper,

In his vessel made of copper,
To the land beneath the heavens
Sailed away to loftier regions.
There he rested with his vessel
Rested weary, with his vessel,
But his kantele he left us,
Left his charming harp in Suomi,
For his people's lasting pleasure,
Mighty songs for Suomi's children.[28]

My inclusion of this particular piece in the typescript of *Europe: A History* provoked a memorable confrontation with one of the editors at OUP in New York. The editor said, 'This Finnish verse is absolutely useless,' or words to that effect. 'Ninety-nine point nine, nine per cent of the readers will be unable to understand a single word.' My reply followed the lines of 'That's the whole point. Readers must sometimes be faced with the unintelligible. They can't be fed everything in cosy English translation. Somehow one has to convince them that there are large expanses of European culture beyond their reach, especially if all they know is English with a smattering of French or German.'

Russian is a magnificent language. It possesses a hugely rich lexicon, wonderful rhythms produced by the 'fleeting stress', and a phonetic harmony that most of its Slavonic relatives do not share. One of my first teachers – who was born in Harbin in Manchuria, and was said to be the daughter of the last tsarist director of the Trans-Siberian Railway – made the class write a quote from Dostoevsky about 'our beautiful, melodious, resonant and могучий русский язык' (могучий is a powerful word in itself). I was drawn to Russian initially for purely practical purposes, so as to be able to read some Soviet textbooks and to write a diploma dissertation, 'The Teaching of History in the USSR'. But fate took me further. At St Paul's I was drafted to take over a class whose teacher was on the sick list; I pedalled across west London on my bicycle two or three days a week in order to attend night school; I completed the Cambridge intensive Russian course under the formidable Professor Elizabeth Hill; and I eventually took an MA in Russian studies at Sussex University. So my grasp of the basics was fairly sound. Unfortunately, there was little chance of regular conversations after graduating, and a growing competence in Polish ruined my spoken Russian, which rapidly declined. Even so, I kept up with reading skills. In 2002, when I travelled to Moscow after a very long break, I was pleased to find that I could still read archival documents without too much difficulty.

My adventures with Russian literature, spread over many years, were also quite extensive. I read something from most of the major poets and novelists – Pushkin, Lermontov, Tolstoy, Dostoevsky, Pasternak – but I jibbed at Sholokhov's *Quiet Flows the Don*, and preferred to tackle Solzhenitsyn in translation.

Of course, the world of Russian letters is a mutual admiration society, and I found myself increasingly out of step with some prevailing attitudes. It was hard to be a member of Slavonic (or Slavic) departments and not be committed to the supremacy of everything Russian. I liked Russian, but not if it meant downgrading a dozen other Slavonic cultures. I admired Dostoevsky, but did not rate him the only Slavonic writer worth consideration. Above all, whilst celebrating Russian literature and especially Russian music, I found that the enthusiasm did not stretch as far as Russian politics or Russian imperialism. In those days, in the middle of the Cold War, one always came across types who were learning Russian in order to feed their communist inclinations. Oddly enough, when pressed to choose a subject for an MA dissertation, I chose Vladimir Mayakovsky, one of the most political of Russian authors:

> – Поэзия° – вся! – °езда в незнаемое.
> Поэзия – °та же добыча радия.
> В грамм добыча, °в год труды.
> Изводишь, °единого слова ради,
> тысячи тонн° словесной руды.

> Poetry – all of it – is a journey into the unknown.
> Poetry is like mining radium.
> For every gram extracted, you toil for a year.
> For the sake of every single word, you sift
> A thousand tons of verbal ore![29]

Spanish is another noble tongue. Unlike English, which is noted for the complexity of its vowels, Spanish has a very subtle variety of consonants together with a characteristic technique of delivery that gives its practitioners a lofty even supercilious air. It is the flamenco of the mouth. (Or is flamenco the Castilliano of the dance floor?) At all events, since its vocabulary, its orthography and its grammar are all neo-Latin, any speaker of French or Italian can readily acquire a working knowledge. I first came across it at the age of twenty-one, when I crossed the Pyrenees from France with a group of student friends and was as surprised by the extraordinary sound of the language as by the sight of the black patent-leather cocked hats of the Guardia Civil. I settled down to study it a bit more seriously when doing some work on the Spanish Civil War, and before long I was reading Lorca with the help of a parallel English crib:

> Los caballos negros son.
> Las herraduras son negras.
> Sobre las capas relucen
> manchas de tinta de cera.
> Tienen, por eso no lloran,
> de plomo las calaveras.

> [...]

> Oh, ciudad de los gitanos
> En las esquinas, banderas.
> La luna y la calabaza
> con las guindas en conserva

> Their horses are black.
> The hooves are black.
> Under their capes they glisten
> with ink and wax.
> They weep not, having
> skulls of lead.

[...]

Oh city of the Gypsies
where flags [fly] on the corners.
The moon is preserved in aspic
with pumpkins and cherries.[30]

Nonetheless, my Slavonic expertise grew faster than my neo-Latin interests, and it opened several further vistas. Most of them I have never had time to follow. I would love to take a closer look at Serbo-Croat, for instance, which the Serbs write in a Cyrillic alphabet and the Croats in a modified Latin alphabet. It was the first Slavonic tongue which ever reached my ears – on the dockside at Rijeka in 1957. Even so, I have had cause to make some interesting forays. On more than one occasion I have tried my hand at Old Church Slavonic, a supposedly dead language which sounds very much alive when you hear it in the liturgy of the Orthodox and Uniate Churches. It is thought to derive from an old form of Macedonian since its instigators SS Cyril and Methodius were Macedonian Slavs in the service of the Byzantine emperor. It is an essential element of the European scene. An extract from the Gospel according to St Matthew relating to the Nativity may not be inappropriate:

Old Church Slavonic

Russian

Глава́ в҃.

І҃и҃с҃8 же ро́ждш8са въ ви_ лееме́мъ і8де́йстѣмъ во дни́ йрwда царл̀, сѐ, волсвѝ ѿ восто́къ прїидо́ша во і҃е҃рли́мъ, глаго́люще:

в҃. гдѣ̀ е́сть рождейса ц҃р҃ь і8де́йскїй; ви́дѣхомъ бо звѣ_ зд8 е́гẁ на восто́цѣ ѝ прї_ идо́хомъ поклони́тиса е́м8.

ГЛАВА 2.

Когда же Іисусъ родился въ Виѳлеемѣ Іудейскомъ во дни паря Ирода, пришли въ Іеруса-лимъ волхвы съ востока и говорятъ:

2. гдѣ родивщійся Царь Іу-дейскій? ибо мы видѣли звѣзду Его на востокѣ и пришли по-клониться Ему.

Now when Jesus was born in Bethlehem of Judaea in the days of
Herod the Tsar, behold there came wise men from the east to Jerusalem, saying: Where is he that is born Tsar of the Jews? for we have
seen his star in the east, and are come to worship him . . .[31]

The Ukrainian lead was followed more assiduously. Since Ukrainian
and its near neighbour Byelorussian were the main languages of Poland's
eastern provinces, I had good reason to gain a knowledge of them as part
of my researches into Polish history. Ukrainian and Byelorussian belong
to the East Slav family, so they have much in common with Russian. But
they have their own special forms, their own pronunciations and a strong
admixture of Polish vocabulary. When writing *Europe: A History*, I
decided to encapsulate the history of Ukraine on a single page: and, as
part of the exercise, to make my own translation of the moving verse by
the national bard, Taras Shevchenko:

TESTAMENT
When I die, make me a grave
High on an ancient mound
In my own beloved Ukraine
In the steppe land without bound,
Whence one sees the endless
Expanse of the wheatfields
And the steep banks of Dnipro's shore:
Whence one hears the stentorian roar
Of the surging river
As it bears away to the far blue sea
Our oppressors' blood.
Then will I leave hills and fields for eternity
To stand before God Almighty
And to make my peace in prayer.
Till that time, it's my destiny
To know nothing of God
First make my grave. Then arise
To sunder your chains

And bless your freedom
In the flux of evil foemen's veins!
At last, in that great family
Young and free,
Do not forget. But with good intent
Speak quietly of me.[32]

And so, full circle, to the native English. Despite its mainly chronological chain, the above selection must seem rather haphazard. I suppose it is. On the other hand when T.S. Eliot set out in 1922 to describe the contemporary state of European culture, he, too, saw a wasteland of scattered fragments:

London Bridge is falling down falling down falling down

Poi s'ascose nel foco che gli affina
Quando fiam ceu chelidon – O swallow swallow
Le Prince d'Aquitaine à la tour abolie.
These fragments I have shored against my ruins
Why then Ile fit you. Hieronymo's mad againe.
Datta. Dayadhvam. Damyata.

Shantih shantih shantih[33]

They say that the first three foreign languages are the hardest. To some extent this is true, since one learns how to learn and the muscles of one's mouth, like the circuits of one's brain, grow more supple. But it's never a simple business, and unfamiliar languages even from familiar linguistic groups can present formidable difficulties.

One year, I decided to go to a summer school of the University of Bucharest and learn Romanian. It's a neo-Latin language with considerable Slavonic accretions, and my hopes were high. (The word for 'yes' is *da*, as in Russian; whilst the word for 'no' is *nu*.) Ventures of this sort were always a leap into the unknown, but they also offered an effective way of getting inside the more secretive communist dictatorships. In Sinaia, where the summer school was held in a former royal palace in the glorious setting of the Transylvanian Alps, the Securitate issued us all with little red cards saying: NO PERMISSION TO SPEAK WITH ROMANIAN CITIZENS. So verbal intercourse with the natives was virtually nil, and my competence in Romanian stayed very rudimentary. Nonetheless, I learned to count from *unu, doi, trei* (one, two, three) to *douăzeci şi unu* (twenty-one) through endless games of table tennis; I scored the winning goal in a football match, held before a huge crowd in the town stadium between 'The Roman World' team and 'The Rest'; and I learned a great deal about the inner fear-ridden mechanisms of Soviet-style societies, by talking at length with the other participants, especially the Russians. They told me, for example, that the KGB agent in their delegation – who, like the rest of us, was pretending to learn Romanian – had immediately put me on his 'watch list' when he heard that I could speak Russian. I also discovered that the ordinary members of the Soviet delegation couldn't work out who their leader really was. By befriending the staff at the local hospital, where I was treated for an eye infection (in the presence of a policeman), I gathered much information about the persecution of Romania's Greek minority. At the end of the month we were taken on a bone-shaking coach tour from one end of the country to the other. The guidebooks at the various sites had not been translated. One morning, I sat by the sea in the ruins of Tomi (Mamaia), Ovid's place of exile, tackled the one Romanian brochure available, and realised that I could just about read it.

Another year, I signed on for a summer school at the Charles University in Prague; the results were similarly mediocre to those in Romania. Since I already knew Polish (another member of the West Slavonic family) I was put into the advanced class. It was a mistake. A little knowledge proved irritatingly dangerous. The accentuation of Czech is consistently different from Russian or Polish; the case endings are baffling. And there are many 'false friends' (*zachód* means 'the West' in Polish, and 'the lavatory' in Czech). So I soon realised my limitations. I cut more and more of the lessons, and spent much of the time with an English colleague from Cheltenham, who introduced himself as an aeroplane buff. He had a strange desire to hang around in districts close to the flight path of Prague's military airport, and an uncanny ability to recognise Soviet military aircraft by the sound of their engines. I presume that he was HMG's answer to the KGB man at Sinaia. Together, we made the most of the opportunity to test conditions in Czechoslovakia after the suppression of the Prague Spring. We met some dissident historians; we observed an illegal demonstration which was stoned by the police; and we were very nearly arrested when hiking on the border in the Krkonoše Mountains. We escaped thanks to the refusal of the Czechoslovak border guards to hand us over to some Polish soldiers who had grown suspicious of our presence. Nonetheless, at the end of it, I tested out my new-found skills by working for a few days in the city archive at Opava. I was interested in the Czech–Polish border war of 1919–20, and as a Britisher I managed to gain access to a document collection from which Polish scholars had been excluded for fifty years.

All of which reminds me of a seminar which was organised in the Vatican in 1990 on the personal initiative of Pope John Paul II. The pope, who was well versed in history, had long prayed for a reconciliation between the Christians of west and east, and in particular between the Roman Catholics, Greek Catholics and Orthodox of 'his part' of Europe. He was also a formidable linguist in his own right, and the seminar observed a rule which allowed any participant to speak in his native tongue, so long as it was a recognised language of the old Polish-Lithuanian Commonwealth. The result was a linguistic riot, a new Tower of Babel. The only language missing was Tatar. The opening speech was presented by a learned monsignor in Latin. A Lithuanian colleague insisted on saying his piece, which no one else understood. And there was a lecture in German – the language of the city-state of Danzig/Gdańsk. The Poles, Ukrainians and Byelorussians talked to each other with varying degrees of intelligibility. (Old Byelorussian, known as *Ruski*, was the official language of the grand duchy of Lithuania.) There was even a contribution in Yiddish. Nothing could have better reconstructed the realities of cultural life in Poland-Lithuania prior to the partitions of the late eighteenth century. What is more, since the USSR was still intact, many of the participants had never been abroad and were having their first taste of the freedoms which everyone now accepts as normal.

To be honest, however, the collector's approach to language learning brings diminishing returns. The more one knows, the better one sees that there is infinitely more to know. And the point comes when there seems to be no further point. To the uninitiated, familiarity with a score of languages may seem impressive. In reality, it represents a mere drop in the linguistic ocean. Europe can boast a hundred languages at least, and hardly anyone comes near to a passing familiarity with half of them.

Two things would seem to be important. The first is a clear awareness of the sheer volume and diversity of Europe's linguistic heritage. The second is a sense of confidence that language learning can be both fruitful and enjoyable. If the need arises, all European scholars need to feel in their bones that a new language can be tackled, and, though not easily mastered, at least readily accessed for the lower levels of utility. In forty years of rambling round Europe, I have encountered dozens of languages from Catalan to Romanche, and from Danish and Dutch to Wendish and Kashub that I can roughly decipher on the basis of existing skills. At the same time, I am always meeting others – like Basque or Hungarian or Turkish – which completely defy understanding.

In the last analysis, literature proves a stronger attraction than language itself. Once one senses that there is something worthwhile to be read on the heights, one gains the energy to gird one's linguistic loins, to plod through the low-lying thickets of syntax and vocabulary, to climb through the foothills, and finally to gaze on the world below from the sunlit uplands.

In this sort of endeavour I have greatly benefited from the company of inspiring colleagues. For many years I was a junior member of an academic department of London University headed by Professor Hugh Seton-Watson. Hugh had unrepeatable advantages: he was brought up in a milieu where multilingual proficiency was taken for granted; he had accompanied his father before the war to almost every east European country; he spoke all the main languages with great ease – French, German, Italian and Russian – and he delighted in his mastery of Romanian, Hungarian and Czech at levels that hardly anyone else could match. When he retired at sixty-five he was learning Farsi. And the last time I saw him, as he boarded a bus in Russell Square, he was carrying a copy of Camoens – in the original Portuguese, of course. I was not short of role models.[34]

After all this, one might be tempted to ask if any language has completely defeated me. I would have to say, 'Japanese.' In 1982–3 I spent a year in Sapporo at the Slavic Research Center of the University of Hokkaido. Before leaving for Japan, I met a young Japanese man in

London, who promised to teach me the language in two weeks flat. His special method was highly interesting but totally ineffective since there was no ready way of remembering the complicated patterns that he expounded. Even so, when I settled in at Sapporo, I did an hour's hard study every day reading grammars, practising the three alphabets and trying to learn vocabulary. A young lady called Mikiko dropped in from time to time for elementary conversation. But the brain did not respond. It may be that I had other things on my mind. It may be that I had passed the age barrier, after which language learning becomes much harder. I simply did not retain what I took in. Japanese, for example, has a very simple phonetic system, with only thirty-five syllables to master. This makes everything sound confusingly similar. I kept calling my friend Yutaka, which means 'Autumn', by the word for a housecoat, *yukata*. And I constantly made other mistakes of the same sort. Eventually, I realised that I was fighting a losing battle. By the end of the year I could easily have presented a fascinating lecture on the problems of mastering Japanese but I could barely string two sentences together. Anything which I undertook in the art of *haiku* (or is it *hukai?*) would have to be done in some other language:

Old Ozzie abo
Calls history man from Oxford
'White fella dreamin'[35]

One niggling question remains: in what circumstances is it appropriate to use literary extracts to enhance historical narratives? Many historians would answer, 'Few.' But my answer would be, 'Many.' It is obviously appropriate if the extract can be used as a contemporary source directly relevant to the events under review. It may also be appropriate, in my view, to deploy a poem or a literary reference which is not immediately illustrative of established fact. For example, when writing about King Macbeth of Scotland, who reigned in the eleventh century, it is perfectly legitimate to quote Shakespeare's play *Macbeth*, which was written in the early seventeenth century. The condition would be that the reader should be left in no doubt about the nature and provenance of the reference made.

I would also maintain that some fictional reconstructions of the past can succeed in conveying historical reality as accurately and as effectively as many an academic analysis. In this regard, *Il Gattopardo* (*The Leopard*) by Giuseppi Tomasi di Lampedusa, first read in student days at the instigation of a girl from St Anne's, evoked lasting enthusiasm. 'When this book opens,' the translator's note explained, 'the Bourbon state of Naples and Sicily, called the Kingdom of the two Sicilies, was about to end. King Ferdinand II ("Bomba") had just died; and the whole Italian peninsula would soon be one state for the first time since the fall of the Roman Empire.' From there one plunges straight into Lampedusa's own 'Introduction to the Prince'.

> May 1860. *Nunc et in hora mortis nostrae, Amen.* The daily recital of the Rosary was over. For half an hour the steady voice of the Prince had recalled the Sorrowful and the Glorious Mysteries; for half an hour other voices had interwoven a lilting hum, from which, now and again, would chime some unlikely word: love, virginity, and death; and during that hum the whole aspect of the rococo drawing-room seemed to change; even the parrots spreading iridescent wings over the silken walls appeared abashed . . .[36]

This is a genre which the author called *Romanzo*, but it is deeply and genuinely historical. Its reconstruction of political attitudes, especially of the conservative prince, is as true and precise as the descriptions of art, manners and landscape. '*Se vogliamo che tutto rimanga come è,*' he declares, '*bisogna che tutto cambi.*'[37] (If we want things to stay as they are, things will have to change.)

The really controversial cases arise when literature is used not as a particular source of reference but as a vehicle for conveying either the *genius loci* or perhaps a touch of period ambiance. Here one must be careful. It is easy to conceive of literary insertions grossly inappropriate to the historical passages they are supposed to adorn. Yet I would plead a measure of tolerance. A pithy quote or a colourful verse can often create resonances that push the reader into enquiring more deeply. And dissonances may well be as effective as harmony. The worst of all solutions is a historical text that contains nothing at all to arouse the reader's imagination. For the past, like nature itself, reverberates to countless, strange evocative echoes:

> La Nature est un temple où de vivants piliers
> Laissent parfois sortir de confuses paroles;
> L'homme y passe à travers des forêts de symboles
> Qui l'observent avec des regards familiers.
>
> Comme de longs échos qui de loin se confondent
> Dans une ténébreuse et profonde unité,
> Vaste comme la nuit et comme la clarté,
> Les Parfums, les couleurs et les sons se répondent.
>
> Il est des parfums frais comme des chairs d'enfants,
> Doux comme les hautbois, verts comme les prairies,
> Et d'autres, corrompus, riches et triomphants,
>
> Ayant l'expansion des choses infinies,
> Comme l'ambre, le musc, le benjoin et l'ancens,
> Qui chantent les transports de l'esprit et des sens.[38]
>
> Nature is a temple, whence living pillars
> Sometimes emit confused words;
> Men travel there through forests of symbols
> Which watch them with familiar looks.
>
> Like long echoes which mingle from afar
> Into a deep and shadowy unity,
> Vast as the night, and, like clarity itself,
> Perfumes, colours and sounds reverberate.
>
> There are smells as fresh as the skin of babies,
> Gentle as oboes, green as the fields:
> And others – corrupted, rich and triumphant,

Endowed with infinite expansive powers,
Like amber, musk, benjamin and incense
That sing of the ecstasy of spirit and senses.

IX

1000 YEARS OF POLISH–GERMAN CAMARADERIE

MANY authors share a foible for which I also confess a weakness. They like to go to public libraries and check that their own books are on the shelves and frequently used. When my own history of Poland, *God's Playground*, was published, therefore, I used to creep into various libraries to see if my book was there. After one or two such visits, I discovered a curious phenomenon. Volume I of *God's Playground* nearly always fell open in my hands at exactly the same, well-thumbed spot – at page 493. I eventually realised that the reason for this lay in the fact that page 493 carries the opening lines of one of the more risqué passages of the book, devoted to the amorous adventures of King Augustus II the Strong (reigned 1697–1733). Augustus II has the distinction of featuring in the *Guinness Book of Records* as the man who fathered the largest number of children in history. It is a nice coincidence that he is known in German as Friedrich-August der Starke.

Ramshackle dynastic states were commonplace in eighteenth-century Europe, and there is no *a priori* factor which explains why some of them, such as 'England-and-Wales/Ireland/Scotland/Hanover' should have thrived, whilst others like 'Poland-Lithuania/Courland/ Saxony' should have floundered.

Apart from that, Augustus the Strong was an interesting prospect in himself. As Duke of Saxony, Meissen, and Lusatia, he possessed the means to live of his own. As an Elector of the Holy Roman

Empire, he wielded influence in the world, but not unlimited power. As commander of imperial armies in the campaigns of the Holy League he had a distinguished military reputation. As the father of some 300 children, including the famous Maurice de Saxe, Marshal de Saxe, Marshal of France (1696–1750), his personal prowess was beyond reproach. He looked a fitting successor to the great Sobieski.

Augustus the Strong's amours formed one of the wonders of the age, attesting no less to his catholic and cosmopolitan taste than to his phenomenal stamina. After a series of youthful adventures in Madrid and Venice, where he had variously disguised himself as a matador and a monk, he returned to Dresden in 1693 to the charms of his bride, Eberdine, Princess of Bayreuth, to the labours of the Electoral Office, and to the cultivation of a bevy of concubines – official, confidential, and top secret. Maurice de Saxe was the Elector's son by his one-time Swedish favourite – Aurora, Countess of Königsmark. He received his name, it was said, in memory of the famous victory that was gained over his mother at the royal hunting-lodge at Mauritzburg. His half-brother, Count Rotowski, was the son of Fatima, a Turkish girl captured at Buda in 1684. His half-sister, Countess Orzelska, Princess of Holstein, was the child of Henriette Duval, daughter of a Warsaw wine-merchant. In Poland, the new King left no stone unturned. When the Countess d'Esterle, who had journeyed with him to Cracow to witness his coronation, was surprised *in flagrante* with Prince Wisniowiecki, she lost her place to Princess Lubomirska, wife of the royal Chamberlain and niece of a cardinal. The latter, having changed her name to Mme Teschen, soon yielded to the businesslike Mme Hoym, who negotiated a legal contract and a salary of 100,000 RM per annum. This professionalism was copied by most of her successors, not least by Mme Cosel, who insisted on the erection of a suitable palace for herself in Dresden, and by Maria, Countess of Denhoff, daughter of the Polish Crown Marshal, whose interests were astutely managed by a mother-in-law intent on recovering her family's insolvent fortunes. The most extraordinary story of all concerned the abandoned mistress of the British ambassador to Saxony, who, having turned for comfort to

the Elector-King, scored the only known non-event in fifty years of
gallantry.

Yet unlike his spermatozoa, most of the political ventures of
Augustus the Strong failed to reach their target . . .[1]

The hilarious world of that licentious monarch, who reigned simultaneously in Dresden and in Warsaw, provides an apt introduction to the
theme which I now intend to develop. It suggests that the history of
Polish–German relations is not quite so uniformly sombre as many modern
historians would have us believe.

God knows, Poland and Germany have lived through a very long period
when mutual hatred and contempt have been all too common. Frederick
the Great of Prussia, who appeared on the European scene shortly after
Augustus the Strong had left it, undoubtedly changed the tone for the
worse. As a comment on the nefarious role which he played in the dismemberment of the old Polish commonwealth, he quoted the Latin tag, *vita
mea, mors tua*. In other words, he cynically calculated that Poland must
die so that Prussia could flourish. From then, growing hostility marked
the attitudes of the nascent German and Polish nations. In the hands of
Prussian leaders, German identity was nurtured with a sense of superiority
over Germany's eastern neighbours. In the Nazi era, it reached the nadir
of all international relationships when occupied Poland was turned into
the *Lebensraum* laboratory and the home of the Holocaust. Over several
generations from the days of Bismarck, Germans were led to believe in
the official stereotype of the Pole as a lazy, incompetent and incorrigibly
rebellious savage. Official Prussian and German historians joined their
Russian colleagues in the thesis that the destruction of Polish statehood
had rendered a great service to humanity, for Poland was the habitat of
anarchy and of *polnische Wirtschaft* – a common German expression
meaning 'a right old shambles'.

For their part, the Poles were increasingly taught both to fear Germany
and to despise it. By their most influential modern nationalist leaders,
such as Roman Dmowski, they were told that Germany was a still more
dangerous enemy for them than Russia. Not least in the People's Republic
after 1945, they read in their history books about an unending national

struggle as their forebears fought for survival against medieval colonists, Teutonic Knights, the armies of Frederick the Great, the school inspectors of Wilhelmian Germany and the Nazi SS.

Such was the dialectic of German and Polish nationalism that each side developed a mirror image of the other's prejudices. Both sides cultivated the myth of the '1000-year war of Teuton and Slav'. Both sides gave central prominence to Germany's centuries-old *Drang nach Osten*, the Germans being taught to think that their 'drive to the east' was one of the great civilising missions of European history. Poles were encouraged to think of it as one of the most sustained campaigns of unrelieved evil and oppression that could be imagined.

The purpose in presenting a less conventional selection of elements within the history of German–Polish relations is to show that the stereotypes do not contain the whole story. To argue my case, I have taken five themes.

Prehistoric Lusatian Culture

In the early nineteenth century, archaeological pioneers digging in the district of Bautzen (Budisyn) west of the River Oder discovered a series of sites belonging to the same unmistakable prehistoric culture. Their finds were soon linked to further sites over a wide area ranging from Pomerania in the north to Upper Silesia in the south and to Masuria and to Mezovia on the Vistula in the east. This 'Lusatian' culture flourished for at least a millennium, *c.*1400–400 BC, spanning the transition from the late Bronze to the early Iron Age.

One thing which archaeology could not definitively prove, however, was the ethnic associations of these prehistoric Lusatian people. In imperial Germany it was taken for granted that the Lusatians had been Germanic, thereby consolidating the assumption that the eastern lands of the modern German empire were founded on native German soil. The assumption automatically turned the Slavs of Prussia into a tribe of alien parvenus.

Such conclusions were quite unacceptable to Polish archaeologists. In the twentieth century a Polish 'Aboriginal' or 'Autochthonous' School took immense pains to show that the Lusatians were proto-Slavs and that the expanse of the European Plain between the Oder and the Vistula formed the prehistoric Polish heartland. Their findings, which automatically demoted the prehistoric Germanic tribes recorded in the region to the status of transients and intruders, were formally upheld after 1945 by the communist censorship of the Polish People's Republic.[2]

Caught between conflicting Prussian and Polish versions, the cultural authorities of the German Democratic Republic encouraged the equally dubious view that Lusatian culture should be attributed to the ancient Illyrians.

Of course, neutral observers might wonder why such a large tract of Europe had to be exclusively awarded to the forebears of only one of the modern claimants. Surely, there had been room enough on the Great European Plain for tribes of all hues to cohabit in harmony. After all, apart from Germanics and proto-Slavs a suitable place has to be found for the ancient Celts. If present-day political backing for the Celtic claim is weak, evidence for a Celtic presence in the prehistoric German–Polish border-lands is extremely strong.

The Hanseatic Tradition

The Hansa was one of the major international institutions of medieval northern Europe. First recorded in 1161 at Visby on the Baltic island of Gotland, it started as an association of individual merchants, but soon grew into a far-flung league of commercial cities spanning many countries. Its most westerly member was Dinant in Brittany, its most easterly Novgorod. Lübeck became the site of its annual assemblies, which, despite a long period of decline, did not come to an end until after the Thirty Years War. The league's objectives were to enforce the freedom of the seas, to suppress piracy, to reduce tolls and tariffs, to oppose the restrictive practices of princes, and generally to promote the liberties and prosperity of its members. Since several major cities within the kingdom of Poland belonged to the league – notably Wrocław, Cracow, Gdańsk (Danzig), Elbąg (Elbing) and Toruń (Thorn) – it exercised an important influence on the development of Polish–German relations over several centuries.

Not surprisingly, German historiography traditionally stressed the German character of the Hansa. For similar reasons, Polish historiography either minimised or totally ignored the Hansa's role in Poland. In my view, it is a serious anachronism to view the league's activities through modern national perspectives of any ilk. What is more, the ethos of the Hansa cities long survived the active period of the league's history. In Royal (West) Prussia, for example, the German burghers of Danzig, Elbing and Thorn stayed intensely loyal to the Polish commonwealth right to its destruction during the partitions at the end of the eighteenth century. They did so for the same reasons which had inspired them to escape from the Teutonic state in 1466 and to seek protection of their municipal liberties from the Polish king. Like their most famous son, Nicholas Copernicus, who was born in Toruń only seven years after the city's incorporation into Poland, they took pride in their Polishness, not from any sense of modern ethnic identity but from their view of Poland as the land of freedom where their Hanseatic virtues were valued. By the same token, they were intensely fearful and contemptuous of the militaristic and coercive spirit of Prussianism, which was fostered by Hohenzollern rule in the neighbouring duchy of Prussia and, from 1657, in the united states of Brandenburg-Prussia. It was entirely predictable, as proved to be the case, that when the Hohenzollerns eventually annexed the great Danzig, the German burghers promptly rebelled in the best Polish (and Hanseatic) fashion.

Two hundred years on, when the German Federal Republic is animated by an ethos much closer to that of the Hansa than of Prussia, it may not be too fanciful to think that the Hanseatic tradition still has a part to play, not least in relations with its most immediate eastern neighbour.

Migration, Assimilation and Cohabitation

Just as medieval Poland saw a great influx of German merchants and colonists, so the nineteenth and twentieth centuries have seen huge tides of Polish migration into Germany. The result in both countries is a complicated ethnic mix, and varying degrees of assimilation which modern nationalists (and racists) have been loath to explore. Indeed, thanks to the pervasive nationalism of imperial Germany, the institutioned racism of the Third Reich and the strongly anti-German and nationalistic bias of the post-war communist regime in the so-called People's Poland, this is a subject which has been suppressed for generations. Yet it is vital to any proper understanding of Polish–German relations.

It is a simple fact that not only is there still a substantial German minority in present-day Poland, but also that large numbers of Polish families can claim German descent. The high incidence of German names in Poland gives a clue but does little to uncover the real rates of intermarriage and assimilation over the centuries when women not only adopted their husbands' family names but also their culture and identity. The same can be said on the other side. Not only is there a substantial Polish minority in Germany, topped up by regular waves of immigration since 1945, but there are a large number of German families who knowingly or unknowingly are descended in whole or part from Polish stock. Friedrich Nietzsche the philosopher, often thought of as the most Germanic of Germans, is a good case in point.

This is a complex and sensitive subject which demands many nuances and refinements. For one thing, it is necessary to stress that ethnic purity is a myth. Both the Germans and Poles have been forged from the most variegated ethnic elements. The impact of the Thirty Years War on Germany's gene pool is well known. The impact of two world wars on occupied Poland can hardly have been less. Secondly, in the Polish case one has to take account of an important Jewish element within the population. For six centuries, from the time of the Black Death, Poland provided the principal refuge for Europe's persecuted Jews – at least 10 per cent of the total population. Since many of those Jewish refugees originated in medieval Germany, the majority of Polish Jews continued to speak Germanic Yiddish right to the end of the community's existence during the Holocaust. When the time came for those Polish Jews to migrate westwards again, particularly to imperial Germany and to Vienna, they assimilated very rapidly into modern German culture and society. At the same time, like many neophytes they rapidly turned their backs on the world which they had left, frequently adopting hostile attitudes both to the traditional religion of the *Ostjuden* and to their memories of Poland.[3]

A very particular history also needs to be told about those border provinces where substantial communities of Poles and Germans lived alongside each other for centuries. Pomerania, Wielkopolska, Kujawy, Silesia and Galicia all have a long pluralistic past which has been almost completely forgotten admist the nationalist whirlwinds of the twentieth century. One of the trick questions which I love to put to Polish audiences is, 'Who is the most famous son of the city of Poznań?' No one ever remembers Field Marshal Paul von Hindenburg in this context. Similarly, it is fascinating to read in the first chapter of General Guderian's war memoirs that he took time off during the opening offensive of the invasion of Poland in September 1939 to visit the ancestral home of his family at Gross-Klonia.[4] In the same way, millions of men conscripted into the armies of imperial Germany continued to think of themselves as Poles despite their German uniforms. The collected war correspondence of Joseph Iwicki, who wrote daily letters in Polish to his mother from his billet on the Western Front in 1914–18, is an eloquent testimony to the lot of such men. Iwicki, who came from a Polish village in Pomerania, had been sent to fight the British in Belgium, whilst hoping nonetheless that the war in which he was involuntarily engaged would somehow result in an independent Poland.[5]

His thoughts closely reflect those of the young poet, Edward Słoński, whose lines record the hopeless predicament of Polish soldiers in the Austrian army on the Eastern Front ordered to fire at Polish soldiers fighting in the Russian army.

> We are kept apart, my brother,
> By a fate that we can't deny.
> From our two opposing dugouts.
> We're staring death in the eye.
>
> So when you catch me in your sights,
> I beg you to play your part,
> And sink your Muscovite bullet
> Deep in my Polish heart.
>
> For I see the vision clearly,
> Caring not that we both will be dead;
> Since that which has not perished
> Shall rise from the blood that we shed.[6]

That was in 1914. And 'that which has not perished', from the words of the national anthem, was Poland.

The ethnic kaleidoscope of the Polish–German borders was considerably more varied than modern descriptions permit. It can be amply illustrated, for example, from the history of Silesia. Since the bloody confrontations of the three Silesian risings in 1919–21 and the forcible mass expulsion of Germans after 1945, Silesian history has often been reduced to a simplified dialectic of German versus Pole. Post-war Poles have been fed tales of endless German oppression in Silesia as if all Germans had been Nazis, and the Silesian *Vertriebenen* (expellees) have lived for fifty years on tales of endless Polish barbarity as if all Poles had belonged to the communist security service. In reality, Silesia's past was not two-sided but many-sided. Neither Poles nor Germans displayed any high degree of uniformity. There was a world of difference between the old-established German Catholic communities of rural Silesia, with its baroque monasteries and peasant villages dating from Austrian and Bohemian times, and the pushy Prussian Protestants and bureaucrats who built and organised Silesia's burgeoning industrial cities. Similarly, the proletarian Polish Catholic parishes of the Upper Silesian mining region who sent Wojciech Korfanty to the Reichstag before the First World War had no more in common with the Polish Protestant towns of neighbouring Austrian Silesia, like Cieszyn, than with the great estates of the German 'smokestack barons', like the Hohenlohes or the von Donnersmarcks, who ruled their lives from on high. There were many Silesian families who were perfectly bilingual, who spoke their own peculiar dialect at home and who had no desire to be forced into one exclusive German or Polish compartment. Many Silesians, like their most eminent poets, Angelus Silesius and Joseph Freiherr von Eichendorff, wanted nothing more than to savour their own inimitable *Heimat:*

> Die Ros' ist ohn' Warum,
> sie blühet weil sie blühet,
> Sie acht't nicht ihrer selbst,
> fragt nicht, ob man sie siehet.[7]

There's no 'why' about the rose;
it blooms because it blooms,
paying no heed to itself,
not caring whether it is seen.

O Täler weit, o Höhen
O schöner, grüner Wald,
Du meiner Lust und Wehen
Andächt'ger Aufenthalt![8]

Oh valleys broad, and heights!
Oh fair green forest.
You are the pensive refuge
Of all my joys and sorrows!

When old Silesia came to an end in 1945, the scourge arrived in the form of the victorious Red Army and the vengeful communist security forces which followed in its wake. Prior to their expulsion, many German Silesians were beaten, raped, pillaged, tortured, imprisoned and killed. At Lamsdorf (Łambinowice) an ex-Nazi camp was reopened for the incarceration of German civilians. Germans tended to blame Poles; they had no reason to know or to care that in reality the Poles were being scourged no less viciously than they were themselves, and by the same communist agencies. Indeed the notorious Security Office of those days, the UB, was run by the Soviet authorities, and was not under Polish control.[9] Strangely enough, though they perceived the tragedy differently and suffered in different ways, both the Poles and the Germans of Silesia were sharing a common fate for the last time. What better epitaph than one pronounced three centuries earlier at the end of the Thirty Years War: *'Wir sind doch nunmehr ganz, ja mehr denn ganz verheeret!'*[10] – We are now wholly, nay more than wholly, devastated!

Polonophilia and Pro-Germanism

Notwithstanding the deepening animosities of the late nineteenth century and the atrocities of the mid twentieth, it is worth recording that none of the adverse events put an end to the strands of sympathy for Poland in Germany and for Germany in Poland.

German Polonophilia is undoubtedly the thinner strand, perhaps because in their era of power and prosperity Germans paid little attention to their eastern neighbours. It is still in a relatively disadvantaged position for the simple reason that, whilst many Poles speak German, very few Germans bother to learn Polish. Even so the record is not entirely blank. Poles would have been heartened to read the *Polenlieder* of the 1830s, when German opinion strongly supported the November Rising against Russia, just as they were in the 1980s, when West Germany organised the largest campaign of food aid to Poland's near-starving citizens.

Polish pro-Germanism has taken many forms. In the political sphere it has traditionally been followed by those Polish leaders who, trapped by Poland's unenviable dilemma between two powerful empires, judged Russia to represent the greater threat. Such was the position of Józef Piłsudski, whose legions fought for the Central Powers in 1914–17 and who took part in the German-sponsored government of the restored kingdom of Poland but only to the point when he was pressed to sign an unconditional oath of loyalty to the kaiser. After his refusal, he found himself a political prisoner in Magdeburg Castle. Generally speaking, Poles from the east were most impressed by the Russian danger and were most prepared to consider cooperation with Germany. Poles from the western provinces, in contrast, who knew the German menace at first hand, were least reluctant to work with the Russians.

In the economic sphere, where Poland traditionally acted as the bridge between the dynamic German economy and the vast Russian market, Poles were simultaneously tempted by admiration for the quality of German achievements and fear of domination by German interests.

In the cultural sphere German influences were steadily growing stronger from the Enlightenment onwards. As Polish universities declined, or in the nineteenth century were suppressed, increasing numbers of Polish students were sent to Germany to be educated. German philosophy, German science, German art and German music were all well known, widely disseminated and carefully imitated in Poland. Numerous Polish intellectuals, from August Cieszkowski, the philosopher, to Aleksander

Brückner, the historian, preferred to write and publish in German. Not until the twentieth century did the cultivation of German culture acquire the negative, unpatriotic overtones of more recent times. One of the curious questions still to be answered is whether Polish nationalism of the *Blut und Boden* variety was not itself the product of Poles who invented an anti-German ideology from too much familiarity with German ways of thinking.

Polish individualism and the instinctive mistrust of authority which crystallised in the long stretch of statelessness were rooted in conditions which few Germans experienced. Even so, they could appeal to German radicals and dissidents, who were themselves uneasy at the ingrained conformism of their compatriots. For a poet like Günter Grass, Poland possessed all the quiet, dotty charm of Don Quixote:

> I have always said that Poles are gifted,
> Perhaps too gifted. But gifted for what?
> They are masterly kissers of hand and cheek,
> And what is more, past masters of melancholy and cavalry.
> Don Quixote himself, you know, was a highly gifted Pole,
> Who took his stand on a hillock near Kutno
> With the rays of the sunset carefully at his back.
> Lowering his lance with its red-and-white pennants,
> He mounted his highly ungifted charger,
> And quite dependent on such beastly horse-power
> Rode straight at the flank of the field grey ranks ...
> Whether it was done in masterly fashion or otherwise,
> And whether they were sheep, or windmills, or panzers
> Which kissed Don Quixote's hands, I cannot tell.
> At all events he was embarrassed, and blushed in masterly fashion,
> So I cannot say exactly – but Poles are gifted.[11]

The story of Polish cavalrymen charging German tanks in 1939 is a myth which many Poles are willing enough to share. But in the eyes of Günter Grass, there is sympathy and affection as well as irony.

The Catholic Connection

Thanks to Poland's proximity to Protestant Prussia and her subjection to German eastern policies strongly inspired by the Prussian legacy, the picture of Polish–German relations has often been dangerously oversimplified. 'Catholic Poland' was seen to have faced 'Protestant Germany' much in the way that it faced 'Orthodox Russia'. In reality, though predominantly Catholic in modern times, Poland sheltered a rich variety of religious communities right up to 1939. And Germany, though predominantly Protestant in the north and east, is predominantly Catholic in the south and west. In the Third Reich, when the German state was in the hands of pagan Nazis, the inclusion of Austria significantly raised the Catholic percentage in the Reich's population. Catholic Poles have never been bereft of Catholic allies in Germany. Their popular identification of Germany with Prussia and Protestantism is a false one. How effective the Catholic connection has been in practical politics is another matter.

Prior to the Reformation, the Polish Church naturally turned to its German bishops to help it with its difficulties with the Teutonic Knights. Pawel Włodkowic (Vladimiri), rector of the Jagiellonian University, formulated an elaborate treatise on the unchristian 'crusading' activities of the knights of Prussia and presented it to the Council of Constance (1414–18). Unfortunately the empire could no more curb the knights than the Church council could. So cutting the Teutonic state down to size was left to the valour of Polish-Lithuanian arms. (Modern Polish audiences are surprised to find that the Virgin Mary was the patroness of the order, as she was of Poland.)

After the Reformation, when the rise of Prussia posed a strategic threat to Poland, the Holy Roman empire was Poland's natural ally. Though the Polish *szlachta* disliked the Habsburgs' absolutist instincts, especially after the suppression of Bohemia, and no Habsburg candidate ever won a Polish royal election, the Polish–imperial frontier was one of the quietest in Europe. In the empire's greatest hour of need, in 1683, when Vienna was besieged by the Ottomans, it was Jan Sobieski and his winged hussars who rode to the rescue. Poland's union with Saxony (1697–1763) was inspired by common fear of Prussia.

Bismarck's *Kulturkampf* gains a prominent place in Polish history books as an instrument of Prussia's policy of Germanisation (which it was). But, as Poles forget, it was primarily used to attack the Catholic states within Germany itself. After all, it led to the imprisonment not just of the Polish archbishop of Breslau, but also that of the archbishop of Cologne.

In the First World War German policies towards Poland were undoubtedly pursued with an eye to the empire's advantage. On the other hand, with the restoration of the kingdom of Poland in 1916 and the creation of an autonomous Polish government and administration, they also revealed a degree of enlightened self-interest. It was German concessions in 1916–18 that paved the way for a viable independent republic in 1918. Archbishop Kakowski, as chairman of the German-sponsored Regency Council in Warsaw, was the very first Pole to hold a position of authority in Warsaw for almost fifty years. Of course, since the German empire soon collapsed, the relative generosity of its dispositions was soon forgotten.

German policies towards Poland in 1939–45 bore little relation to those pursued in 1914–18. Since the Nazis planned to reduce the Poles to a nation of illiterate helots, their plans for the racial reconstruction of the *Lebensraum* involved the genocide not only of the Jews but also of the Polish intelligentsia, including the Catholic clergy. In the territories of the New Reich, for example in Łódź in the Warthegau, and in Silesia, the SS immediately carried out a wholesale purge of Polish priests. Some 3000 were sent to Dachau alone. (According to the US chaplain, who interviewed the handful of survivors on the day of Dachau's liberation in 1945, they begged not for bread but for breviaries.)

All in all, some 2–3 million Polish Catholics were killed within the Greater Reich by the Nazis, to the deafening silence of the Vatican. This tragedy may be seen as just another example of Nazi inhumanity. It may also be seen as one of the worst episodes in the shared humiliation of Catholics in Germany.

It certainly sets the context for the remarkable initiative taken by Poland's Catholic hierarchy in 1966. For twenty years the post-war communist regime had covered up its own crimes by relentlessly harping on the crimes of the fascists, and of the fascists alone. The celebration of Poland's millennium had caused a split between the interpretation of the Church, which stressed Poland's membership of the universal Christian community, and the propaganda of the communist state, which was banging the drum about the 1000-year war of Teuton and Slav. Then, without warning, the Polish bishops issued a public address to their brother bishops in Germany. It extended forgiveness for Germany's sins against Poland, and asked forgiveness for Poland's sin against Germany. Its aim was unerring. No other step did more to dissolve the hatreds of the Cold War. Nothing could have better set the two divided nations on the path of reconciliation. Within four years, Chancellor Willy Brandt was on his knees in Warsaw. Within a dozen years, solidly backed – as it was reported – by the votes of German cardinals, the archbishop of Cracow found himself on St Peter's throne.

Over the centuries, Polish–German relations can be classified as good, bad and indifferent. There are patches of black and white, and every conceivable shade of grey. To talk of a 1000-year reign of bonhomie or camaraderie is certainly eccentric. But it is no more inaccurate than the tale about a 1000-year reign of unmitigated antagonism. Indeed, only one of ten recorded centuries can be said to have been characterised by entrenched mutual conflict. The decades from 1870 to 1970 were dominated by xenophobic nationalism, and encompassed some of the most atrocious acts of inhumanity in European history. But they can hardly be judged typical.

Historians, like politicians, must sometimes resort to affirmative action. After generations of fear and suspicion, it can do no harm to point to the silver lining among the clouds, and to raise one's glass to the old Polish toast, 'Kochajmy sie!' – Let us love one another! It is a toast which Augustus the Strong, king of Poland and elector of Saxony, must have drunk many times with relish.

X

THE ISLAMIC STRAND IN
EUROPEAN HISTORY[1]

IN European History, Islam has traditionally been regarded as the great
'other', *le grand Contraire*, the opposite: the definer of what Europe was
not. Very often you see the contradistinction of Europe and Islam as West
and East: Europe as opposed to Asia, Christendom as opposed to the
parallel great religious sphere of Islam. This dichotomy obviously contains
considerable substance. The first version of Europe in the middle of the
first millennium of the Common Era saw the Christian world concentrated
geographically in the European peninsula; and the cause lay in the rise of
Islam, which had overrun most of the countries of the eastern Mediterranean previously under Christian influence. It is in this regard that the
Belgian historian and medievalist Henri Pirenne wrote, '*Charlemagne sans
Mahomet serait inconcevable*' – Charlemagne without Muhammad would
have been inconceivable. It is Islam which defines the boundaries of the
Christendom of the Middle Ages.

More worryingly, perhaps, the dichotomy has been carried over from
the medieval Age of Faith into contemporary politics. Here again we
frequently meet the historic dichotomy of the West, meaning familiar to
Europeans, and the East, meaning something alien, something almost, if
you like, anti-Western or anti-European. I am sure you are all aware of
what I am writing about, for there is a whole vocabulary of discussion
especially about the Middle East, where the dichotomy is inbuilt. For
example, Westerners talk of Islamic fundamentalism as if there wasn't
a Christian fundamentalism or a Jewish fundamentalism, or of Arab

terrorism as if there wasn't terrorism in Belfast or the Basque country or elsewhere. It is presented as though negative activities were specifically related to others and to parts of the world, but not to us.

This brings us to another basic point, which is the presence within the confrontation of Europe and Islam of the third monotheistic religion – Judaism and the Jews. It is quite an interesting paradox that historically the Muslim lands were often the tolerant host of Jewish communities, whereas in Europe the Jews met with varying degrees of intolerance and, during the Second World War, a programme of extermination. Since the war this historic scenario has changed. The West, now led by the United States of America, has become the chief patron of a separate Jewish state, whilst the Islamic world is seen once again as the other, sometimes even as the enemy.

I should say that having written a monster tome on Europe and having talked to many audiences about it, some of the most frequent questions are about Islam. But it did strike me that very few people talk of these issues in the broad historical context. They talk of present threats and dangers. If, for example, you browse through the computerised library catalogues, and you key in the words 'Islam' and 'Europe' you come up with three or four subjects which are related to history but which do not present an overview. For example, there is a huge literature on the relations between Islam and Christianity. It appears in comparative theology, in the history of the Christian Churches and their relations with the Muslim and Jewish worlds. There is quite a lot on European attitudes to Islam. Edward Said's book *Orientalism* – which is a study of Europe's distorted perceptions of the Arab and Islamic world – is a key item.[2] Or Bassam Tibi's books on the challenge of fundamentalism.[3] There are also quite a lot of local studies which have a historical character very often inspired by current politics. You may have seen Noel Malcolm's recent book on the history of Kosovo,[4] or his previous one on Bosnia.[5] But you don't easily find a guide to the basic historical landscape. Hence, the present subject.

One should add that the underlying intellectual debate which prompts this sort of historical enquiry usually concerns the nature of cultural identity, the extent of Europe's undoubted debt to Christianity, the possibility of contradictory belief systems within one civilisation and the competing virtues of homogeneity and pluralism. The debate is also extremely relevant to questions of contemporary politics and international relations. The most influential text in this particular field is Samuel P. Huntington's *The Clash of Civilizations and the Remaking of the World Order* (1996).[6] Huntington is professor of government at Harvard, and betrays all the earnest, no-nonsense thinking that one would expect from that quarter. His civilisations – Western, Slavic-Orthodox, Islamic, Hindu, Confucian, Japanese – are all clean-cut entities with distinct frontiers. They are not messy. They don't overlap. As one of his critics noted, 'The crooked and meandering alleyways of the world are straightened. With a sharp pencil and a steady hand, Huntington marks out where one civilisation ends and the wilderness of "the other" begins.'[7] The present essay, I would hope, adds one more little nail into the coffin of such oversimplifications.

What I have done is to isolate ten moments or themes in the Islamic strand of European history. They all recall times when the Muslim presence has been prominent.

Moorish Spain

The Islamic strand in European history begins in 711, when the Berber Muslim commander Tariq ibn Zayid crossed the Straits of Hercules, as they were still known, and landed close to the rock which now bears his name (Jebel Tariq). He led an invasion which not only overran almost the whole of the Iberian peninsula but also the larger part of what is now France. The tide of expansion reached the River Loire before it was stopped in 732 by Charles Martel, mayor of the palace to the king of the Franks. Of that event, the great English historian Edward Gibbon wrote, 'But for Charles Martel, the truths of the Koran would be now taught in the schools of Oxford, and a circumcised people would learn the Revelations of the Prophet.'

The emirates of Iberia represented the geographical but not the political periphery of the Muslim world. They were, at one or two periods, the absolute centre. The caliphs, the successors of Muhammad and leaders of the entire Muslim world, resided in Granada on more than one occasion, and the wonders of that civilisation are reflected in the Alhambra and in other monuments.

Muslim Iberia was not a closed world. It was a civilisation where many elements met, where, among other things, Judaism flourished as in few other places. Many of the great Talmudic rabbis like Moses Isserles came from Spain. It was also the civilisation where many works of the classical world were translated from Greek or Arabic into Latin, having come from Alexandria, and then being transmitted to Western Europe via Spain. It was also the place whence the decimal counting system of ancient India, having been adopted by the Arabic world, was brought to Europe.

This was an extremely lively and tolerant place, and it wasn't just a flash in the pan. It lasted for 800 years, twice the duration of the Roman empire in the west. Those 800 years ended in 1493 with the expulsion of the Jews who refused to convert and later of the Moriscos, the Moors who had accepted conversion. The contrast between the extremely intolerant ethos of Catholic Spain with its inquisition and the world of Moorish Spain which preceded it, is fairly obvious.[8] Yet when that judgement is made, many other things have to be questioned. For instance, much of the medieval literature dealing with Europe's relations with Iberia is based on the assumption that Christian champions, like Roland and Oliver, were fighting for unadulterated truth and freedom. In the *Chanson de Roland* the battle at Roncesvalles in the Pyrenees in 778 is presented, yes, as a clash of civilisations, of the good facing the dark forces of evil. Needless to say, a more sophisticated gloss needs to be put on the story nowadays.

The Southern Frontier

The southern frontier covers a huge sweep of time and space, yet from the foundation of the Muslim emirates in North Africa in the seventh century right to the present day, the southern boundary of Europe has been in the middle of the Mediterranean Sea. The European shore in southern Europe faces the Islamic world on the northern coast of Africa, and the Muslim presence in Africa has spilled over into southern Europe on numerous occasions. Provence in the south of France, for example, hosted Muslim settlements for centuries. I remember writing about the first crossing of the Alps by Pope Stephen II in the year 753 and describing how he climbed over the Great St Bernard Pass. I noticed that if he had taken a more westerly route over the Montgenèvre and had descended into what is now Dauphiné, he would have been entering Muslim territory. The Muslim communities in the valleys of the southern Alps in the eighth and ninth centuries are reflected in modern Provençal place names.

Similarly, Sicily, once Greek, had a flourishing Muslim civilisation, which was conquered in the eleventh century by the Normans. Expeditions from Normandy conquered both England from the Anglo-Saxons and Sicily from its Muslim inhabitants at more or less the same time. One remnant is the famous Marsala, the sweet wine of Sicily the name of which comes from Marsa-Allah, the port of God. Yet Muslim culture was not wiped out. It was still evident in the thirteenth century, in the time of the great *stupor mundi*, Frederick Hohenstaufen. The Christian emperor ran a court in Palermo where, as in Moorish Spain, Catholic, Jewish and Muslim cultures intermingled. The splendid results can be seen in the mosaics of the Abbey of Monreale.

One might equally talk of the Balearic Islands. Not everyone has come across the figure of Raimon Llull (1235–1315), who was born in Majorca. Sometimes called the First European and also the first novelist – he is the author of 200 books – he was noted, among other things, for his familiarity with Islam and for conducting religious disputations with Muslims. He spent a lot of his time in North Africa and further east.[9]

The more one thinks of this southern frontier of Europe, the more one becomes aware of a different perspective. Most people tend to think of the great divide in Europe as being between east and west. And yet, if one belongs to southern Europe, the most important divide is between north and south. This is reflected very strongly in discussions in the European Union of the present time. Is priority to be given to the problems of the east, the expansion and enlargement to Central Europe? Or should more importance be attributed to the problems of southern Europe and its relations with North Africa? The French, the Spaniards, the Greeks and the Italians tend to have a very different standpoint from that of the northern Europeans.

The Crusades: Four Centuries of Holy War

The Christians like the Islamicists have their own concept of jihad. It was put into regular practice from 1095 until 1444. The former date saw the preaching of the First Crusade at Clermont-Ferrand by Pope Urban II. The latter saw the last Crusade, in which a Christian army was defeated at Varna in Bulgaria where the king of Poland and Hungary was killed. Throughout those four centuries Europe was in the grip of a militant religious ideology in which a very unchristian road to salvation was preached. Military efforts against the infidel were seen as a good in themselves. If you ask yourself who were the victims of these Crusades against the infidel, the answer can be surprising. Of course the Muslims were victims; there were several notable massacres, especially when brawlers like Richard Lionheart, king of England, put in an appearance. Equally, the Crusaders massacred large numbers of Jews on their way to the Holy Land. But in terms of numbers the most people killed were probably Orthodox Christians. The 'great betrayal' is the label given to the Crusaders' conquest of the famous city of Constantinople in 1204 – at that time the capital of the Byzantine empire – and it was followed by a very nasty massacre. And last but not least the Crusaders themselves are to be counted among the victims. Hundreds of thousands of Christians who set out for the holy war never reached it. In the terrible story of the Children's Crusade, for example, most of the innocents persuaded to join simply died or were eventually sold into slavery. They, like most of the Crusading armies, perished long before they ever reached the Holy Land.[10] And yet there can be no doubt that the Crusades have provided the background to standard Western attitudes until very recently. I myself, as a child in the 1950s, was sent to a Bible class called The Crusaders since the phrase conjured up nothing but positive associations. One may assume that in the Islamic world 'Crusader' is a term of abuse for any Westerner who interferes unnecessarily.

Ottoman Europe

That last Crusade of 1444 consisted of an expedition sent against the Ottoman Turks, and the Ottoman presence has to be one of the major features in any survey of European history. The Ottomans crossed the Dardanelles in the 1320s and their empire was only dissolved in 1920. So here is another 700 years of Islamic presence. The spatial dimension is also impressive. Ottoman expansion in Europe probably covered as much territory as the lands conquered by Napoleon or the lands occupied by Hitler. From our western European perspective, we tend to forget that most of eastern Europe, all the shores of the Black Sea and the Caucasus were overrun at one time or another by the Ottomans. Ottoman expansion into the Balkans, therefore, is only part of a much bigger involvement. On two occasions the Turks reached Vienna. The high point came in 1683 when the capital of the Habsburgs was besieged by the Ottomans for the second time. On that occasion it was saved by the winged hussars of King Jan Sobieski of Poland, who rolled down from the Kahlenberg Mountain, galloped through the sultan's camp and dispersed the Ottoman armies. Sobieski drove them into a retreat which never ceased until the Ottoman empire itself ceased to exist 350 years later.[11]

The Ottoman Line is a name for the mark on the map of Europe which divides those countries which have a history of Ottoman rule and those which don't. It is one of the main dividing lines of European civilisation. The countries which possess an Ottoman legacy are numerous – Ukraine, Russia in part, Georgia, Armenia, Romania, Bulgaria, Hungary, Poland in part, Serbia, Bosnia, Albania, Macedonia, and Greece all have it. All are still concerned, not to say obsessed, with the ongoing consequences. One can see it today in the sorry history of Cyprus, or in the break-up of Yugo-slavia. The parts of the former Yugoslavia which were formerly under Ottoman rule – Serbia and Bosnia, but not Montenegro oddly enough, or Kosovo – have different historical memories from Croatia or Slovenia, which were outside the Ottoman sphere. It is a very complicated, very profound story which is still being worked out.

Islamic Islands in a Christian Sea

Numerous Muslim communities have survived in Europe in isolation from their neighbours. There are the Tartars, for example, who are of Mongol origin, and who settled in what is now southern Russia and Ukraine in the thirteenth century, and adopted Islam a couple of hundred years later.

I can think of three Tartar communities: one is Tatarstan on the Volga, which is one of the autonomous republics of Russia; there are the Crimean Tartars, who were deported en masse by Stalin in 1943 and are still struggling to restore themselves to their ancestral land which is now part of Ukraine; and there are the Polish Tartars, who by now are few and far between.[12] When I went to New York for the first time in the 1970s and visited the Piłsudski Institute, I was amazed to meet the secretary of the institute, Pani Zarema, who was entirely Polish but introduced herself as a Muslim. Her father had been a colonel of the pre-war Polish army and her grandfather had been commander in 1939 of the Tartar cavalry. These Tartars were entirely polonised in secular culture, but were still practising Muslims. A handful of settlements and mosques still survive in the region of Białystok.

Prior to the recent break-up of Yugoslavia, Albania was the only recognised European state to possess a Muslim majority in its population. It broke free from the Ottoman empire in 1913 and enjoyed a brief spell of precarious independence before falling in 1939 into the hands of Mussolini's fascists and in 1945 into the grip of the extreme and extremely eccentric communist regime of Enver Hoxha. For most of the post-war decades, therefore, the religious traditions of the country were largely irrelevant, since religion was abolished. All mosques and churches remained closed until 1991. Having followed Tito out of the Soviet camp and having then rejected Titoism, the regime then developed a tenuous link with distant China and with Maoism. Albania was for years the most mysterious, the most isolated and possibly the most miserable country in Europe.[13]

In the 1990s, as Albania slowly emerged from the shadows, the most important question focused on its relations with the neighbouring Serbian province of Kosovo. At one time it looked a near certainty that Kosovo, which has a 90 per cent ethnically Albanian majority, would opt to secede from Serbia and join Albania. After all, Kosovo had been integrated into Albania during the Second World War, and the Kosovans made no secret of their dislike of Serbian rule. Things have worked out differently. When the Kosovo Liberation Army (KLA) began to operate in the province, demanding separation from Serbia, the Serbian army was sent in to neutralise the KLA and restore Serbian supremacy. This time, however,

A Jewish *shtetl*, German-occupied Poland, *c*. 1915–16.

Arthur Balfour visits a Zionist settlement in the British mandate of Palestine, 1925.

Abu Abdullah, 'The Unfortunate', the last Moorish emir of Granada, 1492.

King Jan Sobieski relieves the Ottoman Siege of Vienna, 12 September 1683.

The Cossacks reject Ottoman rule and turn to Moscow, 1676: *The Zaporozhye Cossacks Writing a Mocking Letter to the Turkish Sultan Mehmet IV* by Ilya Repin.

RAF reconnaissance flight over the mountains of Kurdistan, Iraq, March 1934.

Leopold von Ranke (1795–1886):
the star of German history.

Nikolai Mikhailovich Karamzin (1766–1826):
the founder of Russian history.

Heinrich Himmler (1900–45):
totalitarian of the west.

Lavrenti Pavlovich Beria (1899–1953):
totalitarian of the east.

KL Auschwitz-Birkenau, 1941–5.

Vorkutlag, 1929–*c*. 1980.

Birth of the European Movement: Winston Churchill at The Hague Congress, 29 May 1948.

Death throes of the USSR: Boris Yeltsin addresses the people, 19 August 1991.

Robert Schuman (1886–1963).

Pope John Paul II (1920–2005).

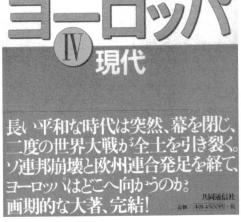

The cover of the Japanese edition of
Europe: A History.

The Italian jacket for *Rising '44*.

Master and pupil:
A.J.P. Taylor and
Norman Davies.

Norman Davies receives the honorary DLitt from the University of Sussex, 2006:
(*left to right*) Chancellor Richard Attenborough, Norman Davies, Professor Rod Kedward
and Vice Chancellor Alasdair Smith.

fearful of the ethnic cleansing that had disfigured preceding Serb campaigns in Croatia and Bosnia, the international community was alerted in time. NATO was not only to bomb the Serbian army and force its withdrawal but also to support a political truce whereby an autonomous Kosovo was to return to its formal link with Serbia.[14]

Bosnia, which is separated from Albania by Montenegro, provides a different variation on the same theme. The majority of Bosnians, like the Albanians, are Muslims, but they speak the same Serbo-Croat language as their Serb Orthodox and Croat Catholic neighbours. They are descended from a medieval Bogomil community, which, having resisted Catholic and Orthodox advances over many centuries, decided to take a third way and to accept Islam from the incoming Ottomans. They formed a civilised, tolerant and by Balkan standards unwarlike enclave, a haven of refuge in the middle of the seething sea of Yugoslav hatred. It did not save them from a terrible ordeal. In 1992 the Yugoslav army laid siege to Bosnia's capital, Sarajevo, in retaliation for the declaration of independence made by Bosnia and its sister province of Herzegovina. The siege was to last for four years, and the cruel, entirely man-made suffering was to cost many thousands of innocent lives. To the north, the Bosnians were engulfed by attacks from militant Croats in a conflict symbolised by the wrecking of the world-famous Ottoman Stari Most or Old Bridge at Mostar. To the south and west, they were attacked by the forces of the Republika Srbska, who at Srebrenica in 1995 were responsible for the worst act of genocide in Europe since the Second World War. Unlike Croatia and Slovenia, which were also attacked by the rump Yugoslav government of Slobodan Milosevic, Bosnia was unable to defend itself and was plunged into the chaos of civil war and inter-communal bloodletting. This appalling fate, which revealed the impotence of the European Union in foreign relations, was eventually terminated by the intervention of the USA and the Dayton Peace Agreement of November 1995. The independence and formal unity of Bosnia–Herzegovina was maintained but only by recognising the continued existence of the autonomous Republika Srbska alongside a Muslim–Croat federation. Only time will tell whether this complicated formula can provide the basis of lasting peace.[15]

The unhappy stories of Bosnia and Kosovo inevitably provide food for thought on the position of Islam in Europe. At the international level, the

USA and NATO would like to take credit for the fact that they came to
the rescue of embattled Muslim minorities. At the regional level, however,
one observes signs of older and less welcome instincts. On the one hand,
Germany's haste to recognise Croatia and Russia's support for Serbia
hinted at the re-emergence of traditional, faith-based alignments. On the
other, it was evident that several generations of communist rule had done
nothing to heal the more extreme forms of sectarian nationalism. Indeed,
the chief offender in this regard, Milosevic, is an old-fashioned communist
boss who did not hesitate to appeal to the medieval heritage of Kosovo
Field and of Christian Crusades against Islam.

The Eastern Question

This is the label usually given to the long diplomatic and military crisis in
the nineteenth century caused by the decline of the Ottoman empire or
Turkey, 'the Sick Man of Europe', as it was called. I have no idea how to
summarise such a subject in a few sentences, but I wish to underline the
very peculiar combination of the imperial designs of the powers and, at
the same time, the appalling campaigns of propaganda. Among the imperial designs, the most blatant was tsarist Russia's ideology centred on
the claim that Russia was the third Rome – that Russia was the natural
successor to Byzantium, the second Roman empire, which was the
successor in turn to the first Roman empire – and on these grounds that
the tsar had a long-standing aim to conquer the straits of the Bosporus
and to restore the city of Constantinople, a great Orthodox symbol.
Hence, for Russia, the wars against the declining Ottoman empire were
of prime ideological importance. Furthermore, since Russia was a great
Christian empire, much of the Eastern Question involved rather crude
Christian propaganda denouncing the misdeeds of the Muslim Turks.[16]

The Russians, however, were not alone. Perhaps the most obvious case
is the famous outburst of William Gladstone, the British premier, about
the 'Bulgarian horrors' of 1876, which were used as a prop to justify
intervention to prevent Constantinople falling into Russian hands. Why
this particular atrocity was singled out from all the others is the essence
of politics. One should also mention a baleful legacy of that time, the
Balkanisation of the peoples of the declining Ottoman empire. The

machinations of the powers encouraged an infusion of ultranationalist ideology, then very current in Europe. The resultant conflicts were thereupon blamed on the victims. We could still hear a British foreign minister not very long ago talking about the hopelessness of trying to stop people 'who want to kill each other'. This sort of comment has a long history going back to the nineteenth century. The association of the 'Sick Man' with the leading Islamic state in the world did irreparable damage to Islam's image.

The Cyprus problem, which is still with us, is a direct result of unscrupulous imperial diplomacy. The island had been in Ottoman hands since 1571, and its mixed population of Greeks and Turks had shown few signs of discontent, but the British were keen to obtain a base which would cover the approaches to the Suez Canal. In 1878, therefore, after secret negotiations they published the details of a convention whereby the sultan had handed over the administration of Cyprus in return for protection against Russian aggression. They also announced that the Porte was to receive an annual tribute calculated at £92,799 11s. 3d. Needless to say, the locals were not consulted. In effect, Cyprus had become a British colony, although it did not receive that status officially until 1925. The tribute was never sent to Constantinople, being used instead to offset unpaid Ottoman debts to the Bank of England dating from the Crimean War. The whole episode was a disreputable scam. But it had consequences. From the very outset, the Greek party looked for enosis or union with Greece, whilst the Turks looked to the British to stop it. Agitation grew inexorably. Independence, granted in 1960, led to inter-communal violence and to a state of emergency. A Greek coup in 1974 led to a Turkish invasion and to an impasse that lasts to the present day. Perhaps 200,000 Greeks lost their homes in the north, and the Turkish Republic of Northern Cyprus is recognised by no one except Turkey.[17]

Islam and European Imperialism

I remember asking my twelve-year-old son how many European empires had Muslim subjects. I started off with the British empire, which ruled over Muslims from northern Nigeria to Brunei, and the French empire. Then we thought of the Russian empire. Then he came up with the Dutch empire, which I'd forgotten, in the East Indies. And we ended with the Spanish empire in North Africa and the Italians in Libya. We forgot the Portuguese in Timor, but six out of seven is not bad. And the number of Muslim peoples round the world affected by European imperialism must run into hundreds of millions. The withdrawal of European imperial control from many parts only happened in our lifetime.

But it's not only direct imperialism. The various League of Nations mandates in Syria, Lebanon and elsewhere blessed colonialism under a new name. These too came to an end and the legacy is enormous. It means that for most of the Muslim nations in the world today their independence, their present identity, was achieved in contestation with the former European imperial powers, who in some cases have been substituted by the new informal American version of imperialism. It does mean that, for many millions, Europe has gained the significance of alien oppression. 'Europeanisation' is connected with socio-economic modernisation and the destruction of traditional cultures and societies. As far as Europeans go, the imperial encounter with Islam has the very obvious connotation that Muslims are not seen as bearers of a great civilisations but rather as former colonials. The Muslims that most Europeans see are people who have been connected with their late empires. Russia has had probably one of the largest Muslim contingents of any of these empires, although in 1991 the whole of Soviet Asia – Kazakhstan, Kirghizstan, Turkmenistan and Uzbekistan – broke away to form independent nations.

France has had a more intense relationship with parts of the Islamic world than any other European country. Three factors can be noted. The North African countries of Tunisia, Algeria and Morocco were geographically close to France. French policy chose to treat the *Departements d'Outremer* not as colonies but as integral elements of the metropolitan republic. And French republican principles insisted that the state be strictly separated from the religious authorities. As a result, France became intimately involved in transforming traditional Muslims into standardised secular French citizens. In some respects the experiment was admirable. It was surprisingly free of racial prejudice. Yet not being pushed to a conclusion, it provoked a fearsome reaction. Protests were treated as mutiny and met with vicious repression. After 8 May 1945, when the rest of the world was celebrating VE Day, Algeria was left mourning the death of 8000–9000 townsfolk of Sétif, who were killed by French forces in retaliation for an uprising by separatists. Violence bred violence. Tunisia and Morocco were released in 1956, but Algeria's agony was prolonged through round after round of civil war. In the end, with hundreds of thousands dead and a million *pieds noirs* driven out to France, there was little to rejoice over. The nationalists were victorious, but it is sad to see that independent Algeria has seen no let-up in violence. In French eyes, Algeria stands for a clash of incompatible civilisations.[18]

One doesn't think of Britain being on the front line facing the Muslim world, but in the early twentieth century its involvement became very extensive. Egypt and Sudan, northern India (Pakistan and Bangladesh) and Malaya were prominent Muslim areas. And then, in the course of the First World War, the British played a key role in the break-up of the Ottoman empire in the Middle East. Through Lawrence of Arabia, they spurred on the Arab revolt that led to the formation of the Saudi and Jordanian kingdoms. Through General Allenby, they captured the Holy Land and were rewarded with the mandate for Palestine which included present-day Jordan. Through forces that moved up from India into Mesopotamia, they planted a stake that gave them the post-war mandate in Iraq and a dominant voice in Persian affairs. Through the persuasive power of the Royal Navy, they established a string of forts, coaling stations and outposts from Aden to Bahrain that gave them decisive influence in the Red Sea, the Indian Ocean and the Persian Gulf. Through the takeover of former German colonies in east Africa, they completed a great strategic arc stretching from Zanzibar to Singapore.

Britain's interest in the Middle East began with sea-borne commerce, but in the century between the Indian Mutiny of 1857–8 and the Suez crisis of 1956, the main concern was to safeguard communications to India and the approaches to the Suez Canal. In the 1920s an additional factor arose from the need to protect oil supplies, initially from Persia. Yet the loss of India broke Britain's will to bear the burden of controlling the Middle East, and it was happily offloaded to the Americans.

Britain's involvement in the Middle East may have been short but it wasn't sweet. Repeated revolts broke out in each of the mandated territories. In Palestine both Arabs and Jews took to arms. In Iraq the most dire means were used to crush the insurgents. And in Egypt the rise of

Arab nationalism under Colonel Nasser proved unstoppable. The British simply did not possess the military muscle to attempt the scale of rearguard actions that the French were to mount in Indo-China and Algeria. So the edifice crumbled quickly. Yet it's interesting that the British did not often fall foul of the religious authorities. They had a long tradition of respecting local institutions and beliefs, and they did not arouse the ire of Islam. Unlike the Americans who followed they did not earn the label of 'The Great Satan'.

The Islamo–European Borderlands in the East

Whereas Europe had become the main base of Christianity and the Middle East of Islam, there existed between them a broad borderland where influences from both sides could be felt. In the Caucasus, for example, which lay for centuries between the Christian empire of tsarist Russia and the Muslim empires of Persia and the Ottomans, Christian peoples like the Georgians and Armenians lived alongside Muslim groups like the Azeris, Chechens and Ingush. Further west, the main body of Turkish settlements straddled the European mainland and Asia Minor. When the Ottoman empire came to a close in 1920, Turkey's largest city, Istanbul, the former Constantinople, was left as a living link between Turkey-in-Europe and the larger part of the Republic of Turkey on the eastern side of the Bosporus.

Turkey, which experienced an intense period of Europeanisation under its first president, Kemal Atatürk, was to become one of the most problematic candidates for entry into the post-war European Community. Most of the trappings of traditional Islamic life, from Arabic script to the veiling of women and the merger of religious with political authority, had been abandoned in the 1930s, and Turkey's first application to join the EC was made as early as 1959. In other words, Turkey applied before Britain did – before Spain and Portugal, before Greece, before Scandinavia. Yet the application did not thrive for a number of reasons. Turkey may have been a loyal member of NATO and a secular democracy with marked economic potential, but its credentials continued to be met with scepticism. Turkey's military was said to interfere too often and too arbitrarily in political life. Turkey's human rights record was excoriated. Turkey's treatment of its ethnic minorities, especially the Kurds, was judged to fall below European standards. Turkey's espousal of other Turkic groups, especially in central Asia, was thought to conflict with its pro-European tendencies. And all the while the suspicion lurked that the criticisms, however justified in themselves, were put forward as a screen for underlying prejudices. When pressed, many Europeans, including their political leaders, continued to express fundamental opposition to the accession of a predominantly Muslim country. Their assumption was that Europe was not compatible with Islam, even with regard to applicants where state and religion were strictly separated. As a result, for decade after decade Turkey's associate membership failed to lead further. Turkey was not included in any of the four waves of enlargement that took place between 1973 and 1995. As the end of the twentieth century approached, no progress was noted.[19]

Chechnya, situated on the northern slopes of the Caucasus range, suffered from far more acute problems. It has been fighting for its very existence for longer than anyone can remember. Attacked and invaded by the forces of imperial Russia in the early nineteenth century, this nation of mountain clans saw its outlying lowlands appropriated by Russian settlers and a Russian administration imposed in the new capital of Grozny. Even so, Chechen fighters held out in the hills for over fifty years, and their fearless leader, Shamil, passed into legend. In their own eyes they were defending a way of life in which Islam played an essential role. In Russian eyes they were ingrates, primitives, bandits and outlaws who had forfeited all rights to decent treatment. One attempt to regain independence was crushed after the Russian Civil War, and in the Second World War Stalin, taking no chances, ordered the entire nation – men, women and children – to be deported to the depths of central Asia. After the war the depleted survivors returned to a land where all the most productive districts had been given to Soviet intruders and where the oil-based economy was totally integrated into the USSR. Resistance was impossible as long as the Soviet Union lasted, but in 1991 the Chechens rose again. Isolated from all outside support, branded as terrorists and subjected to an all-out Russian onslaught which killed 70,000 people in Grozny alone, they forced President Yeltsin to regret his war policy and to negotiate. This brief interval in the mid-1990s did not last, and Yeltsin's successor, President Putin, has resorted to measures that look like a war of extermination. As the continuing tragedy unfolds, the Russo–Chechen conflict has demonstrated two things. One is that state terrorism can be every bit as inhuman as anti-state terrorism. The other is that the comfortable powers of this world cannot be counted on to speak out in defence of the oppressed, especially if the oppressor has a place at the top table.[20]

Israel and Palestine

Strictly speaking, Israel lies in Asia not Europe, but from the historical point of view one can easily see the Israeli–Palestinian conflict as Europe solving its problems at the expense of the Arab/Muslim world. A hundred years ago there were hardly any Jews in Ottoman-ruled Palestine, and most of those who lived there had arrived during the preceding decades. In 1898 the Zionist movement was holding its founding conference, and the idea of transferring the Jewish masses from Eastern Europe to the Levant seemed a totally impractical proposition. Similarly, for much of the time during the British mandate, which came into being in 1920, the authorities were committed to an even-handed policy to all communities – Muslim, Christian and Jewish – and it looked highly unlikely that the Zionists could somehow gain a dominant position. It was only during and after the Second World War that the prospects began to change. Trying to force the issue, the extreme Zionists turned to terrorism. The tide of Jewish refugees fleeing the Holocaust grew into an unstoppable flood, and in 1948 the State of Israel came into being unilaterally, through force of arms.

To the Zionist way of thinking, the creation of Israel cannot be seen as a hostile act towards Islam. Jews believed that the land had been theirs since biblical times and that by recovering it they were righting a wrong that had been caused long before Islam existed. Yet Palestine was not an empty country; millions of its native inhabitants were driven out of their homes and Muslims the world over felt both injured and insulted. Jerusalem, whence the Prophet ascended into heaven, is one of Islam's holiest sites, and its loss to the Israelis in 1967 was another intolerable blow. What is more, the Jewish advance was being achieved with the collusion of the Christian world, especially of the USA. It was also greatly assisted by the political divisions of Islam, exacerbated by the rise of

Arab nationalism and the intervention of the USSR. Yet these divisions have been part of the continuing barrier to resolution.

In the 1990s, following the extended Palestinian intifada and the assassination of the Israeli premier by a Jewish extremist, long-promised peace talks seemed to make progress. They were sponsored by the US, whose president presided over a symbolic handshake on the White House lawn, and were rewarded with the Nobel Peace Prize, jointly awarded in 1994 to Yasser Arafat, Shimon Peres and Yitzhak Rabin. Both sides were in agreement on the basic formula of land for peace – Israeli concessions of occupied land in return for guarantees of a Palestinian state and permanent Israeli–Palestinian peace. Yet the millennium came and went with no peace.[21]

Contemporary Migration

The colonials' revenge, if that's not the wrong way of putting it, has taken the form of the mass migration of millions of people from their distant homelands to the countries of Europe which once ruled them. Some of the biggest groups are the Pakistanis and Bangladeshis in Great Britain, the North Africans in France and Spain and the Turkish *Gastarbeiter* in Germany, but there are many others and, recently, there has been the migration of Albanians, Kosovans and Bosnians from within Europe, escaping the danger spots of the 1990s. This is one of the great phenomena of our time and numbers can be extremely large. I was talking the other day, for example, to a Welsh television producer. The culture and language of Wales was preserved by the Methodist religion. It was in Methodist chapels that people read the Bible in Welsh, sang their hymns in Welsh and held their communities together. Today there are more Muslims in Wales than there are Methodists.

Yet one should draw attention to the exceedingly inaccurate, not to say strange, language in which these issues are often discussed. The Muslims in the United Kingdom, who are overwhelmingly either Pakistani or Bangladeshi in origin, are often described as part of the 'black community', or, if one wants to be very subtle, one talks about the 'black and Asian community'. In other words, racial terminology is applied where it has no place. In reality, the Pakistanis have nothing in common with the Jamaicans, who are also called black. They have also nothing in common with the Chinese, who are Asian but not 'coloured'. Putting Pakistani Muslims and Indian Hindus into the same bracket and saying this is one community reveals gross ignorance of culture and history, and to many of us history and culture are the most important things there are.

What is more, the culture of Islam is far more diverse than many Westerners are willing to notice. Nor are the divisions limited to that between the Sunnis and the Shias, who have been feuding within Islam for longer than the Catholics and Orthodox within Christianity. None of the secular states in the Islamic world – Egypt, Syria and Iraq – has attempted to suppress religion, and each has established its own mix of secular and religious cohabitation. Similarly, each of the monarchies supports a different brand of Islam. The Saudis, for example, sponsor the extreme, conservative Wahhabi sect, which is not well viewed in Jordan or in the Gulf sheikhdoms. There is little sense of common purpose even among the Islamic radicals who seek to overturn the existing order and to introduce theocratic systems based on sharia law. The Islamic revolutionaries of Ayatollah Khomeini who overthrew the shah of Iran in 1979 are Shias; they do not belong to the same strand as the Muslim Brotherhood in Egypt or the Front Islamique du Salut in Algeria. The al Qaeda organisation, which grew out of the war of the Afghan mujahideen against Soviet occupation, is rare in that it tries to coordinate the scattered Islamicist movements that exist in various parts of the world.

In any major European city – in London, Paris or Rome – all these branches of Islam will have their advocates and their faithful followers. The great variety of mosques does not fall far short of the variety of Christian churches. In many city centres and in many provincial towns, especially where industrial decline has been accompanied by a relative decline in housing prices, one can find compact ethnic communities of immigrants from the principal groups – Pakistani, Arab or Turkish. They can be as separated and isolated from fellow immigrant communities – of Chinese, Indian or Afro-Caribbean origin – as they are from the general public. They wish to work, to prosper, to practise their religion, to live in peace and, within prescribed limits, to assimilate. The only thing likely to unite them is the hostility of their hosts.

Indeed, the danger of intra-communal violence is very real; for the intolerance of a majority will inexorably fuel reaction among a minority that perceives itself badly treated. One or two outbreaks have already occurred. There are small white supremacist and anti-immigrant groups, like the BNP, which are raring to inflame existing tensions. And, sad to say, there is a small trickle of radical Muslim youngsters who have travelled to Afghanistan or Pakistan for training and who may be dreaming of revenge. One can only hope and pray that the trickle does not swell into a flood.

The conclusions will be brief. The first is a very obvious one, and it is that Islam is, and always has been, for the last 1300 years, an integral part of the European experience. Muslims are not just the aliens outside; they are part of the social and cultural fabric inside Europe. They are part of the diversity which many historians of Europe have chosen to praise. They are one of several permanent minorities, including the Jews, whose toleration and integration, though not necessarily assimilation, has always been a test of the kind of liberal, pluralistic society on which democratic culture rests.

Secondly, even this briefest of surveys of the Islamic strand in Europe should make people realise that the world of Islam is every bit as diverse today as it has been in the past. I have talked about the caliphs of Granada, Sicily, the Chechens, the Tartars of Poland, the Muslims of Bosnia, the Albanians of Kosovo, the Turkish *Gastarbeiter* in Germany, the Pakistanis and the Bangladeshis in Britain, the Algerians in France and the central Asian Muslims in Russia. And I have only just scratched the surface. Islam is no more of a monolith than Christendom, and it is only monoliths that can be presented as frightening monsters. By the same token, it is knowledge of this rich variety within each others' worlds that defends us best from the injustices of stereotyping.

Thirdly, it is possible to look at the Islamic strand both as a threat and as a great opportunity. In the United Kingdom, for instance, Muslims are making a contribution out of all proportion to their numbers. One has only to pick out three current political issues. One is the appearance of an underclass and of welfare dependency – of people who have lost the enterprise to look after themselves. Then there's the question of family breakdown, which is a major social plague. The UK has the highest percentage of unmarried mothers and lone-parent families in Europe. And lastly education: the state education system is in deep trouble. Yet in all these spheres the Muslims have a relatively good record. In education it's quite stunning to see that Muslim girls in particular are performing exceptionally highly because they are well motivated – because of their family background, their desire to succeed and perhaps also a desire to liberate themselves from family controls. A whole generation of Muslims has moved from immigration to the professional middle classes in a remarkable space of time.

Finally, one would hope that Europeans' familiarity with the Muslims in their midst would help them to play a moderating role in the general counsels of the West. Nowadays, the leadership of the West has passed to the United States of America, which has had a much shorter and more superficial contact with Islam. Both the Arab and Muslim presence in America is weaker than it is in Europe. In several European countries, notably in France and the United Kingdom, one would like to think that familiarity with the Islamic world encourages a more balanced approach.

Naturally, no one can put an exact measure on these things. All one can say for certain is that the European heritage does have a greater Islamic component than is often imagined. The clear-cut dichotomy between Europe and Islam is a false one – the boundaries of the two civilisations are considerably blurred; the overlap is extensive. There are many Muslim Europeans of very ancient vintage, just as there are many new Muslim communities. Their existence in Europe's past and in Europe's present can only serve as a healthy counterpoint to unjust stereotypes, to partisan judgement and to myths of our own exclusivity.

XI

THE JEWISH STRAND IN
EUROPEAN HISTORY[1]

PERHAPS I should start with a statement of affirmation. I felt moved to make such a statement in Chapter 3 of *Europe: A History*. I had reached the period after the collapse of the western Roman empire when something recognisable as Europe first came into being. It so happened at the time I was writing this chapter that I had been invited by a friend in America to give a talk in his local synagogue, in a suburb of Chicago called Glencoe. Of course, it was very moving to be asked to talk about the Second World War in such a setting and at the same time to attend a service. I came away with the service sheet from this Reform synagogue and I incorporated a small quotation from it into my chapter to under-line the continuous presence of Jewry in the whole European story from beginning to end. I had just been talking about the great length of time which it took for Judaism and Christianity to diverge; for several centu-ries the two religions stayed entangled with each other. But what I stressed was this:

> Whatever the date of the final split, the Jewish presence in Europe, alongside Christianity, was never extinguished. Every week, for two millennia, the celebration of the Jewish Sabbath on Friday evenings has always preceded the Christian Sabbath on Sundays. After the lighting of the candles and the prayers for peace, the service culmi-nates in the opening of the Ark of the Covenant and the reading from the book of the law, the Torah: 'The Torah is a tree of life to

those who hold it fast and those who cling to it are blessed. Its ways are ways of pleasantness and all of its paths are peace.'[2]

However, neither 'Europe' nor 'Jewry' are fixed entities. Each of them has been changing over time and the relationship is not a simple one. The complex Jewish strand weaves to and fro throughout Europe's past.

So I will start with the birth of Europe. The first version of Europe was to be found in the theocratic community and the geographical concentration which at the time was called Christendom. It arose in the middle centuries of the first millennium of the Common Era, partly from the Christianisation of Europe's pagan peoples and partly from the physical isolation of the European peninsula by the advance of Islam. It was the rise of Islam which set the defining limits on Christendom and which presented it with its main ideological 'other'. For many centuries Jewry too was defined exclusively as a religious community. Unlike today, when definitions of Jewishness range from the legal and the national to the cultural and, in Britain's current Crime and Disorder Bill, the ethnic, the position of Jewry as a religious community was very largely governed for many centuries by its relations with the dominant Christian Church.

Very particular complications arose from the fact that Christianity sprang from the same religious root as Judaism. It is because of this that the Jewish presence within Christendom has always been of special and fundamental importance, creating rivalries which sometimes are harder to manage than other sorts of antagonisms. Judaism has been the numerically smaller but chronologically senior partner within the Judaeo-Christian tradition throughout the whole of European history. Pope John Paul II was well aware of this seniority when he addressed the Jewish community as 'Our Elder Brethren'. Jews and Christians are divided members of the same spiritual family.

Within this framework the geographical distribution of the Jewish diaspora was for long an important consideration. Just as the rise of Islam cut off many Christians from the main body of Christendom, so too the main Jewish concentrations were long situated in Asia, not in Europe. Europeanists often forget that in the long formative period of Jewish–Christian relations, the Jewish presence was strongest outside Europe.

Throughout those first dozen centuries when the apostles, doctors and fathers of the Christian Church, from St Paul to St Thomas Aquinas, were formulating and refining the Christian faith, the immense labours of the *tannaim, amoraim* and *geonim* were proceeding in parallel in Palestine and even more prominently in the academies of Babylon. First the Mishnah and then the two versions of the Talmud and the subsequent generations of Talmudic scholarship, right up to the closure of the last Babylonian academy in 1058, were undertaken by Jews in the Orient. I am no expert at all in this field but I think that the first European Talmudist of distinction was the French scholar Rashi Salomon Ben Isaac, who died in 1105. Certainly the great Rabbi Moses ben Maimon (the Rambam), otherwise known as Maimonides, who in some ways is the Talmudic counterpart to St Thomas Aquinas, lived the whole of his life in the Muslim world, first in Cordoba, then in Morocco and Egypt. It was not until the expulsion of the Sephardim from Spain in the fifteenth century that the northern Ashkenazi Jews came to the fore.

Geographical distance indeed may be one reason why Christian–Jewish relations were relatively harmonious throughout those early Middle Ages. And it is very important that all aspects of the Christian–Jewish relationship – good, bad and indifferent – be always kept in mind. It is very easy, as was the complacent Christian custom for too long, to pretend that everything in the garden was rosy. There is a very ancient story of hatred and false accusations and spasmodic persecution. But it is equally misleading to ignore the shared traditions, to pretend that common ground and goodwill never existed, and to harp exclusively on the ugly, accusatory angles. Among other things, a vital distinction needs to be made between attitudes and actions. Hatred, like compassion, can be harboured by all sides in a dispute. But policies can only be put into practice by the powerful. It is the greatest of ironies that the Gospel of Love, the religion of the weak, the slaves and the oppressed, became the official ideology of the Roman empire and thereafter the official religion of almost every European state until recent times. Power politics had little time for Christ's commandment about 'loving thy neighbour as thyself'. And it is small comfort that Christian rulers often treated other Christians, heretics and nonconformists even worse than they treated non-Christians.

*

In this regard, I would like to place a gentle question mark under the tone and vocabulary in which these ancient issues are nowadays discussed. In particular, I have come to wonder whether the concept of anti-Semitism, which tends to dominate modern discussions, is entirely adequate to its task. It is not that I doubt in any way the reality of the appalling prejudices and events, from the opinions of Tacitus to the ultimate tragedy of the Holocaust, to which the label 'anti-Semitism' has been applied; Jew-hatred is an old and well-evidenced emotion. Nor do I rest my query merely on the suspicion that the label has been so overworked that it has been rendered increasingly meaningless. When anti-Semitism is used to characterise everything from the unique instance of genocide that is the Shoah to petty or personal disagreements with Jewish individuals or to well-meaning criticism of the State of Israel, we may well be in need of more precise terminology. The main defect of anti-Semitism as a conceptual tool undoubtedly lies in its dialectical nature. Like all other products of dialectical thought, from the 'anti-Americanism' of McCarthyism to the ubiquitous 'anti-Sovietism' and 'class warfare' of communist debate, it demands a bipolar, conflictual vision of the world, where all contending elements are reduced to friend or foe, to us and them, to right and wrong. Intelligent gradations are discounted; honest differences are not respected; one-sided prejudices are encouraged. In my view the science of dialectics, the fascinating but false philosophy of opposites, does not provide a very fruitful means for exploring the complexities of Christian–Jewish history.

Many of us will have forgotten, or perhaps will never have known, where the concept of anti-Semitism came from. According to the very best authorities it was invented in 1879 by a notorious German racist and Jew-hater, Wilhelm Marr, founder of the Anti-Semiten Liga. An anarchist and an atheist, Marr had earlier authored a particularly sarcastic work called *The Victory of Jewry over Germanity Seen from the Nonreligious Perspective (Der Sieg des Judentums)*, in which he replaced the traditional terms 'Jew' and 'Judaism' by 'Semite' and 'Semitism'. 'There must be no question of parading religious prejudices,' he wrote, 'when the real difference lies in the blood.' He then launched the League of Anti-Semites in order to foster his sick and dialectical scenario of 'the Jews versus the Rest'. Is that really a battlefield that we wish to prolong? To my mind it is very odd that the brainchild of a racist bigot should have found its way into the mainstream of supposedly liberal discourse. It strikes me as particularly incongruent that Marr's deliberately unreligious construct should now be applied to the Age of Faith, serving theories which try to retrace a continuous pedigree running from the genocidal practices of godless fascists to the ancient disputes of two kindred religions.

If, after all that, I am allowed to use a dialectical term myself, a suitable antidote may possibly be found in the story of the Maccabees, who resisted Seleucid rule in Palestine and restored Jewish political and religious life in the second century BC. One of the largest tracts of common ground in the Judaeo-Christian tradition is found in the Old Testament, sacred both to Jews and to Christians. Yet, having been raised as a Bible-reading Protestant, I can still remember my surprise when I first saw a Roman Catholic Bible and noticed that, unlike its Protestant equivalent, the Catholic Bible includes the first two books of the Maccabees. On further enquiry I found that the Catholic Church recognises two of the four Maccabean books as part of the canonical Apocrypha. Even more interesting – since Judah Maccabee and his family performed their valiant deeds almost two centuries before the life of Christ – the Catholic Church decided to honour the Jewish heroes as official martyrs. The Festival of the Maccabees was fixed in the Catholic calendar on 1 August.

When one reaches the High Middle Ages one is dealing with a period that I would extend into the sixteenth, if not into the middle of the seventeenth century. Nothing is more medieval and theocratic to my mind than the age of Luther and the Counter-Reformation. The Reformation had a very immediate impact. The Renaissance and the scientific revolution, which were going on concurrently, did not really have a widespread effect until much later. The leading question here would be: what made late medieval and early modern Europe less tolerant and more militant than the preceding period? Historians come up with various explanations: they talk about the Crusades; they talk about the rise of cities, the rise of urban classes and the rivalry between Christian and Jewish commercial elements; they talk about the fading of Christendom's wars against the external pagans and hence its turning in on itself. Certainly the active persecution of Jews started surprisingly late. The first wave of 'pogroms', if one may use an anachronistic term from imperial Russia – the massacres of Jews – occurred at the time of the First Crusade in 1096. The first case of the Blood Libel occurred in 1144 here in England in the case of the so-called St William of Norwich, who was much more likely to have been a victim of the same sort of crime as James Bulger. The first instance of public burning of the Talmud occurred in Paris as late as 1242. That date is interesting. The Emperor Justinian had already formally condemned the Talmud and its supposedly subversive influence on Christians in the sixth century, but one has to wait for the thirteenth century before any Christian ruler did anything about it. And even in the instance of 1242 the king of France was the only Christian monarch to pay any attention to the pope's instructions to have the books burned.

I have to race through the centuries and can only draw your attention to a couple of significant features. One, I think, is the strong contrast between Western and Eastern Europe. Almost all the great persecutions, the burnings of Jews and the expulsions occurred in the west. If you look through the list of expulsions starting with the decrees of the Visigoths in Spain in the seventh century right up to the long series of expulsions in the fifteenth century, almost every one of them was started in the countries and cities of Western Europe. The Jews, true enough, were expelled from Muscovite Russia because of the so-called Judaising heresy, but there were very, very few of them in Russia to be expelled. England expelled its Jews in 1290. In contrast to that, the great refuge for Jews in Europe was to be found in the east, in the former Poland-Lithuania, at the time the largest state in Europe. Especially after 1349, as a result of the Black Death, Jews were widely accused in Germany of spreading the plague. So Poland became the great place of exile for Yiddish-speaking Jews right until the Second World War. The name for Poland in Hebrew, *Polin*, means 'Here I rest'. Some of the topics on which I could enlarge include the mutually agreed separation of the two religious communities, the important political and social alliance between the ruling Polish nobility and the Jews, and the long story of Jewish autonomy in Poland. Not all historians seem to know not only that the Jews of Poland formed their own local *kahals*, or communes, but also that a central Jewish parliament, the Council of the Four Lands, continued right until 1764 when the Russians took direct control over Poland's affairs.[3]

The other prominent feature to be mentioned in this period of the late Middle Ages and the early modern age is the wider context of superstition within which the persecution of Jews took place. I think it was no accident that the peak of persecution of Jews in Europe, in the fifteenth and sixteenth centuries, coincides exactly with the rise of the 'witch craze'. In my book *Europe: A History* I recount, for example, the story of Dr Benedikt Carpzov, a seventeenth-century Lutheran pastor who has the distinction of being the all-time star witch-hunter, who boasted of having personally procured the deaths of 20,000 persons. One can always wrangle over the numbers, but I suspect that it is not very surprising that Jews should have been maltreated in a continent which was systematically burning and killing its women and its freethinkers on an altogether grander scale.

With the Enlightenment we reach a period which undoubtedly saw a sea change in European attitudes. This, incidentally, is the period, starting in the late seventeenth century and going on into the late eighteenth, in which the name 'Europe' itself emerges, largely from a sense of shame among Christians about the community of Christendom, which had been so rent asunder by their fratricidal wars. In one of its emanations the Enlightenment was distinctly hostile to Judaism, as it was to all forms of traditional religion. The philosophers of the Enlightenment put forward reason as the great guide. They were turning a cold shoulder, not to religious belief as such, but to all forms of bigotry, superstition and, if you like, unconsidered belief. Again, in *Europe* I quoted a few lines from the English poet John Dryden, a soundbite of the Enlightenment's attitude to traditional Jewry. 'The Jews,' he wrote, 'a headstrong, moody, murmuring race, God's pampered people, whom, debauched with ease no king could govern nor no God could please.'[4]

The traditionalist Orthodox Jewish communities of the age were treated with the same disdain as the traditionalist Christian Churches. And yet the general Enlightenment of those *philosophes* was matched by a related movement, the Haskalah, within Jewry itself. The Haskalah is usually referred to as the Jewish Enlightenment, and its philosophers, the *maskilim*, sought to bring Jewry out of its isolation and into mainstream European society. In particular they wanted to educate Jews in a way that would make them, as somebody said, 'Europeans in the street and Jews at home'. The early focus of this movement was Prussia. The name most frequently mentioned is that of Moses Mendelssohn (1729–86), who was the model for Lessing's Nathan der Weise. And of course the Haskalah saw great success. But in the eyes of some Jews it was seen as the start of a slippery slope. It took the first step away from the traditional Jewish community towards assimilation. And after assimilation there waited conversion and, at the end of the line, atheism; in other words, the complete disappearance of Jewishness.

Once more, just a couple of passing comments about this whole period. It was the Enlightenment, with its stress on reason, tolerance and moderation, which prepared Europe for the key steps of the next century in the life of Europe's Jewry, especially Jewish emancipation and the winning of full civil rights. To this day, many secular and educated Jews revere the Enlightenment as the key moment in the history of European civilisation. The widespread adoption of enlightened rationalism by educated and emancipated Jews is one of several causes of the phenomenal prowess of Jewish scholars, scientists and thinkers in the subsequent era. One only has to mention names like Marx or Freud or Einstein to see how strong these connections were.

But the anti-Enlightenment also existed, and it was not necessarily backward or retrograde. In describing the anti-Enlightenment in *Europe: A History*, I wrote one paragraph about the rise of Methodism in England and Wales, and the next paragraph about the emergence of the Hasidim in Poland. I was describing the reaction of a fervent form of religion against what was seen as an ossified, traditional, religious structure, both in traditional Jewry and in the Church of England.[5]

In *Europe* I gave labels to each of the chapters, and when I reached the nineteenth century I attached the label 'Dynamo'. I was referring to Europe as the home of the Industrial Revolution, the powerhouse of the world in its day, both technologically and ideologically. There are very definite Jewish links to each of the main themes of that century. There is the important and interesting story of the rise of Jewish industrialists and Jewish bankers. The best-known story is that of the Rothschilds, who came originally from Frankfurt, but there are still more from Eastern and Central

Europe.[6] Personally, I am perhaps more concerned with the realm of ideas. Here I will just mention three great currents of the nineteenth century: liberalism, socialism and nationalism.

Liberalism has several variants. There is political liberalism – rule by consent. There is economic liberalism – laissez-faire, free trade. There is cultural pluralism – a liberal cultural policy which protects the identities and interests of the minorities against those of the majority. Jewish emancipation naturally became one of the main goals of the great liberal movement of the nineteenth century. During the French Revolution in 1791 there was a decree giving full citizenship to Jews, and this was gradually extended across Europe in the nineteenth century. This was a two-way operation. It meant that many Jews, as the beneficiaries of liberalism, themselves became the active promoters of liberal causes. And you see how many Jews were active in liberal politics and in wider liberal issues, including the promotion of cultural pluralism. I mentioned the Rothschilds. There was an interesting footnote here in England, in that one of the Rothschilds was elected Member of Parliament for the City of London in 1847, 1849 and 1852 but could not take his seat because of the then-binding rules of Parliament concerning the oath. It was only in 1858, after a long delay, that Lionel Rothschild was able to benefit from the full emancipation which in theory had been granted twenty years before. His son, Baron Nathan Rothschild, was created a peer.

Socialism, one of the great streams of nineteenth-century thought, had many currents within it, all of them in one way or another with Jewish links. Marxism itself was founded by a person certainly of Jewish pedigree. Social democracy was still more important. Not long ago I saw the still-existing tomb of Ferdinand Lassalle in Wrocław, the former Breslau, where both of the old Jewish cemeteries have survived, and, believe it or not, there still stands the tomb of the founder of the most important of the social democracies of the nineteenth century, the German Social Democratic Party. And, at the end of the century came communism. Marxism-Leninism, as it was officially defined in the Soviet Bloc, seems to have had a particular attraction for what Isaac Deutscher called the 'non-Jewish Jew': one could only become a true communist by rejecting one's Jewish heritage.[7]

An absolute majority of the top Bolsheviks in Lenin's circle were ex-Jews of that sort, as were many of the leading cadres in some of the later east European communist regimes. Even Lenin himself, whose mother was Jewish, would have been counted a Jew according to Talmudic rules.[8] It was not until very late in his rule that Stalin turned against the Jewish comrades. He appears to have been preparing an anti-Semitic purge at the time of his death. The Nazis were quick to exploit the presence of an ex-Jewish element within the communist movement. They pushed it to absurd extremes, trying to maintain that communism was nothing more than a Jewish conspiracy, which is nonsense. Even so, it is impossible to deny that the group of ex-Jews played a significant role within communism, and that their activities have had some baleful consequences. (Names such as Henryk Yagoda or Jakub Berman belong in the roll of infamy.) The important thing to stress is that, as atheists and so-called internationalists, they had completely rejected the values and loyalties of the Jewish community. They showed no more scruples in persecuting Jews than in persecuting anyone else.

Nationalism, probably the most potent of all nineteenth-century movements, is still with us, whilst many of the others have fallen by the wayside. Nationalism, like socialism, came in many variants. In its most extreme form, it took on the attributes of what is usually called integral nationalism or exclusive nationalism – a form of ideology which aims to create a national community purged of all 'alien elements'. It is the sort of movement which coins slogans like 'France for the French', 'Italy for the Italians', 'Lancashire for the Lancastrians' or whatever; and anybody who does not match the identikit image of the dominant group is liable to be regarded as alien and undesirable. Within the many streams of nationalism, Zionism fits perfectly normally and logically. Zionism also possessed many variegated streams, as national movements always do. It was in many ways a typical nineteenth-century nationalist movement, demanding a national home for the Jewish people. At the time it was founded there was no certainty as to how, when or where its goals could be achieved. As we all now know, they *have* been achieved after a terrible struggle, and the State of Israel has been the result. It is absolutely fair to say, however, that the fundamentalist element within Zionism, which preaches an extreme and exclusive brand of nationalism, and which sees little place for non-Jews within the Jewish state, is as negative and disruptive as any of the older integral nationalisms that it resembles. The tolerant and visionary founders of Israel, like David Ben-Gurion, whose strong national sentiment was coupled with socialist principles and a broad humanity, would wince at some of the antics of his recent successors. In my view there can be no peace in Israel, perhaps no future for Israel, until the Jewish state can modify its policies to take account of the interests and sensitivities of all the inhabitants of the Holy Land.

When we come to the twentieth century, few people would contest the assertion that our own times have witnessed the nadir, the pit, of European civilisation. Within that pit, the fate of Europe's Jews at the hands of Nazi Germany must surely be located on the very lowest rung. Nothing learned in the last fifty years has been able to dent the findings of the Nuremberg tribunal regarding the Nazis' war crimes and their still more heinous crimes against humanity. However, political circumstances at the end of the Second World War determined that the only crimes that could be investigated were those perpetrated by the defeated enemy. The fact that the largest of the combatant powers, the Soviet Union, had emerged victorious and was thereby able to conceal its own mass crimes caused enormous imbalances in our knowledge and our consciousness. For fifty years the world has been only half-informed. The Nuremberg tribunal had nothing to say about Stalin's crimes. In Eastern Europe all crimes were automatically attributed to fascism. Even during the Cold War, many people in the Western democracies were reluctant to shed their illusions about 'good old Uncle Joe', whose troops had played the decisive role in the defeat of Hitler. Fascist apologists were run out of town and sometimes prosecuted. Communists and communist apologists, protected by democracy, operated in the highest circles of government and academe. Nazi-hunting flourished and still does. The hunting of communist criminals has never even started. In the United Kingdom, the British War Crimes Act of 1991 was carefully drafted so as to eliminate the legal possibility of Soviet crimes being judged criminal. If ever there were a move to hold surviving communist mass murderers to account, the United Kingdom would be the obvious place for them to take refuge.

In the 1990s the collapse of the Soviet Bloc, the loosening of tongues and the opening of archives in the former communist capitals have all confirmed many of the worst accusations. Most recently, a weighty chronicle of communist crimes, published in Paris as *Le Livre Noir du Communisme*, has been accompanied by far-reaching moral declarations by some of the most senior French intellectuals and academicians. It is no longer possible to ridicule or to minimise the scale of Stalin's mass crimes and those of his disciple Mao, and Mao's disciple Pol Pot. The ratchet of the debate has now moved up several notches. The totalitarian debate of the 1960s turned on the claim that communism and fascism were not opposites but generically similar. The present-day debate turns on the claim that they are morally equivalent. One French academician has called them *frères siamois*. Another, Alain Besançon, has uttered the fateful words, 'equivalence of evil, *oui*'. But Western opinion is still unprepared for such conclusions. Myths can sometimes prove more resilient than the truth.

Here I don't intend to plunge into quite such deep waters, but I shall try to say something about the implications for the historical debate. Most importantly, no amount of revelations about the scale and nature of Stalin's crimes can change the well-established facts about the Holocaust. I am quite certain that the evidence for the Holocaust and for its five to six million Jewish victims lies beyond the realm of serious dispute. What the growing consciousness about communist crimes will gradually do, I think, is to change the context and the climate within which the Holocaust is discussed. The Holocaust will be seen to have been perpetrated not by the one single, supreme evil force of European history, but by one of the two great evils whose titanic contest generated a much richer range of criminals and victims of all degrees. This is where I would like to outline three 'unacceptables' – three forms of discourse which, in my estimation, will become increasingly untenable.

Firstly, it will become impossible to defend the uniqueness of the Holocaust without making comparisons. As the late Sir Isaiah Berlin once remarked, logic demands that the uniqueness of any phenomenon can only be established after it has been compared with other similar phenomena. I believe that the standing of the Holocaust will emerge unscathed from any such comparisons or scrutiny. For instance, in any overall survey of the history of concentration camps it can easily be shown that the Soviet Gulag system operated a far more extensive network and for a much longer time than did the Nazi SS. But equally the Soviet Gulag knew no equivalent to the Nazi death factories such as Treblinka, Bełżec or Sobibór, or to the notorious crematoria at Birkenau.

Secondly, I suspect it will become impossible to present the Jewish element as the sole point of reference in any number of general issues relating to the Second World War. For instance, in analysing the strange and shameful silence of the Vatican during the war, the question has usually been posed in a form that asks why Pope Pius XII apparently did nothing to assist the suffering Jews. But at some stage it will also have to be asked why he did nothing to assist the millions of Catholics who were being killed. After all, already in 1940, in the years before the Holocaust had even been launched, there were 3000 Catholic priests in Dachau alone. And most of them perished. Similarly, at any one time the largest single group of inmates in Auschwitz-Birkenau (as opposed to the transportees who were immediately gassed and cremated on arrival) were always Polish Catholics. As far as I know, no one in the Catholic hierarchy in Rome ever lifted a finger on their behalf. They were abandoned to their fate. One can hardly argue that the Church's inaction on that front was inspired by anti-Semitism.

Thirdly, I suspect it will become impossible to use ethnic criteria to decide who in the maelstrom of war were the murderers, who were the bystanders and collaborators, and who were the victims and survivors. Judging by press reports, this issue lay behind Harvard University's recent rejection of a proposal to create a chair of Holocaust and Cognate Studies, 'cognate' being the category to which all non-Jewish tragedies were presumably to have been consigned. If one takes the mass crimes of mid-century Europe as a whole, then the company of mass murderers will not be confined to the Nazi SS and their henchmen, or as Daniel Goldhagen would have it, to the German nation as a whole – Hitler's supposedly 'willing executioners'. It will be expanded to include all the planners and operatives of the various communist killing machines. The roll-call of victimhood will have to be extended far beyond the conventional list of Jews, Gypsies, homosexuals, the genetically disabled and communists. It will have to encompass all sorts of groups slated for extinction, from Ukrainian peasants and educated Poles to bourgeois officials and the so-called kulaks. The word 'genocide' was coined in 1944. The term '*classocide*' is now gaining momentum as a result of the French debate. It is very hard to make moral distinctions between the two. Both refer to the killing of categories of human beings simply for who they are.

Similarly, if one looks at the total experience of each ethnic group, one finds that they all provide candidates for inclusion in both the rogues and heroes galleries. In the case of the Jews, one would have to examine the credentials of individuals like Henryk Yagoda, who was the organiser of Stalin's purges before he was himself purged, or Jakub Berman, who ran Poland's post-war security police, and his many subordinates. Both played prominent roles in murderous episodes of mass repression. One would also have to ponder the extraordinarily high incidence of Jews who served in Hitler's *Wehrmacht*, and even in the SS.[9] In the category of bystanding, one will want to learn more of the attitude of Jewish communities in the Baltic States, Romania and eastern Poland, who watched millions of their fellow citizens being deported to the camps in 1939 to 1941 before their own turn came with the arrival of the Germans. In the category of collaboration, one has to count not just the Jewish ghetto police recruited by the Nazis, but also the Jewish groups and individuals who worked as informers and agents for the various Soviet organs of repression. In the category of victim, one needs to explore the fate of innocent Jews killed by the Soviets as well as those killed in the Holocaust. I've always wondered why so few studies have been undertaken about the huge numbers of Jews in the Gulag. One can find a fascinating introduction to that subject in the memoirs of Menahem Begin, the future prime minister of Israel, who as a Polish citizen had the good fortune to benefit from Stalin's extraordinary 'amnesty' of 1941. Begin was then able to escape from the USSR and to reach Palestine as an NCO of the Polish 'Anders Army'.[10]

In the case of other groups, the Ukrainians for instance, one would uncover a similar range of wartime destinies. For some reason, Ukrainians are usually stereotyped as Nazi collaborators, as concentration camp guards or as volunteers in the Galizien Division of the Waffen SS. These stereotypes are extremely unjust. Given the appalling repressions inflicted on the Soviet Ukraine before the war, the surprising thing is how very few Ukrainians signed up for Nazi service. There were far more Ukrainians in concentration camps as prisoners than there were as guards, and there were far more Dutchmen, Scandinavians and Hungarians in the Waffen

SS than there were Ukrainians. And there were many times more Ukrainians fighting against the *Wehrmacht* than for it. Unfortunately one rarely hears anything of the countless Ukrainian soldiers of the Red Army or of the many millions of Ukrainian civilian casualties. It's a well-known dodge. Whenever Ukrainians did bad things during the war they were called Ukrainians. Whenever they did good things they were called Russians.

At all events, ethnicity offers no suitable guide to wartime conduct or misconduct. Nowhere is this truer than in the vexed question of wartime Polish–Jewish relations. Poland lost at least six million of its citizens, more if one includes the eastern provinces annexed in 1939 by the Soviet Union. Half of them in rough terms were Catholics and half were Jews. The losses on both sides were immense. One might expect that mutual sympathy would prevail, but it rarely does, as the continuing and embarrassing wrangles over the museum at Auschwitz testify. I myself can do no better than what I have done before: quote the lines of a Polish-Jewish poet lamenting the passing of the pre-war Polish-Jewish world in which he was raised.

Gone now are those little towns, though the poetic mists, the moons,
    the winds, the ponds and stars above them
Have recorded in the blood of centuries the tragic tales, the histories of
    the two saddest nations on earth.[11]

(As a purely personal afterthought, I might add that the very first time I heard the Polish language spoken in this country – on a dark night on a windswept promenade at Hove – it was being spoken by the poet who wrote those lines, Antoni Słonimski.)

So where have we reached today? Almost sixty years after the Second World War Europe is a very different place and world Jewry is a very different community. In my view, Europe only finally shook itself free from the war in 1989–91. Throughout the Cold War, the conquests of Stalin's armies, which began after Stalingrad in 1943, were held firmly in place until the collapse of the Soviet Union at the start of the present decade. For all that time Europe was kept artificially divided, so much so that west Europeans were ceasing to think of the eastern half as Europe at all. Now, in theory at least, the two halves are reuniting. In practice, while a select part of the former east moves slowly and painfully towards integration, select parts of the former west are pressing rashly and rapidly ahead with monetary union. To my mind the cart is pulling the horse.

The Jewish community has been transformed still more radically. The decimation of Europe's Jews during the Shoah created serious imbalances in world Jewry. Whilst European Jewry held a very prominent position before the war, the centres of gravity have now shifted to North America and to the re-founded State of Israel. The focus of power and influence has moved to the close alliance between the US Jewish organisations and Israel. European Jewry has slipped back into a supporting role. One might almost say that the pattern has slipped back to where it was 1000 years before. The Shoah destroyed the greatest human reservoir of traditional Orthodox Judaism, thereby handing the dominant voice to secular, reformed and assimilated Jews. The traditional communities of pre-war Eastern Europe had preserved their numbers and their distinct identity, among other things, by strict observance of the 613 Talmudic mandates and prohibitions, including the ban on intermarriage. In post-war times many Jewish families have relaxed these prohibitions and are encountering the inevitable consequences. The present-day danger to the survival of the Jewish community comes far less from persecution than from marrying out. As someone put it, 'The main trouble for the Jews today is that everyone wants to love them.'

Post-war Jewish consciousness has been indelibly scarred by the Holocaust. Indeed the initial trauma was so great that the subject was mourned in virtual silence for many years, even in Israel. The great surge in Holocaust studies and Holocaust commemoration did not really begin until the late 1960s and is thus barely thirty years old. Yet its intensity has been so great, and its effects so impressive, that some people might wonder whether the time is not at hand for a change of emphasis. It would be a very great pity if the Jewish presence in Europe were to be remembered primarily for the attempt to extinguish it rather than for its magnificent achievements. Victimisation has not endowed the victims with virtue; it merely makes them the object of pity. This can hardly be a healthy environment in which to raise new generations of secure and well-adjusted Jewish children. The Holocaust must never be forgotten, but there are so many uplifting aspects of Jewish history in Europe to be remembered alongside it.

Present-day European culture can be nothing if not pluralistic, and it is essential that within that richly woven tapestry the colourful Jewish threads be clearly visible. To this end, it is desirable that every European child and university student should know something about Jewish culture, Jewish history and Jewish religion. By the same token, Jewish people need to be assured that the Holocaust is not the whole story, that the Jewish scenes in Europe's past have their clear blue skies, their silver linings, their short sharp showers as well as the terrible storms. In this way, Jewishness and Europeanness can coexist in harmony. Jewishness and Europeanness are not the same thing, although they do overlap. One must hope that all Europeans will cherish the strong Judaic and Jewish strands in their heritage, and that the Jewish world can appreciate, though not uncritically, the European elements in their own heritage. If everyone remembers the story of Judah Maccabee and Hannah and her seven sons, as both the Jewish and the Catholic traditions choose to do, that goal of harmony will be one step nearer.

XII

MISUNDERSTOOD VICTORY[1]

THE sixtieth-anniversary celebrations of the end of the Second World War are likely to be the most verbose, the least reflective and the last. The dubious platitudes which will be uttered in Moscow stand to cement popular belief into the indefinite future. For, in the nuclear age, there is not going to be another protracted world war, and the politicians will be lining up to extract their pound of kudos from the only major victory celebrations on offer. President Putin, the host, will say that Soviet forces played the prime role in defeating Nazi Germany. This will be one of the few tenable claims to be made. The British and the Americans will talk as usual about 'the common campaign against evil' and 'the triumph of freedom, justice and democracy'. No one is going to present a reasonably accurate account of what actually happened.

People don't always realise how much has changed in sixty years. When the British talk complacently of 'how we won the war', they forget that the 'we' of then is no longer the 'we' of now. In 1939–45 Britain was still the centre of a worldwide empire whose members made huge sacrifices for the war effort. Canadians, Australians, New Zealanders, South Africans, Indians and many others were all 'British' in ways that do not pertain today. What is more, we in the United Kingdom had allies – France in 1939–40, Poland throughout the war, the USSR and the USA from 1941, and dozens of others. The war was not a forerunner of the football match in 1966 between England and West Germany; indeed, we were fortunate to survive the early setbacks and to end up on the winning side. We could

not possibly have survived alone. This country, the UK, performed magnif-
icently, but our performance was dependent on many faithful allies. To
make sure of the point, readers could start by asking themselves if they
know the nationality of the pilot who scored the highest number of 'kills'
during the Battle of Britain.[2]

Similar care has to be taken defining the other sides of the conflict. For
Britain, the enemy of 1939–45 was above all 'the Germans', yet the shorthand subsumes a bevy of other states and nations. By 1939, the Third
Reich had expanded into Austria and Bohemia, and one third of the panzers
that launched the blitzkrieg against France had been built at the Škoda
works in Plzno. The Axis powers included fascist Italy, imperial Japan,
Romania, Hungary and various others, as well as the Reich, and in the years
when Britain was under the most severe threat, they were supported by the
Soviet Union. Luftwaffe warplanes attacking London or Coventry were
fuelled by Soviet oil. At the height of its power in 1942–3 the Reich
controlled the human and economic resources of the greater part of
Europe. Two million French prisoners and more than ten million forced
labourers from the east toiled on German farms or in German factories,
releasing manpower for military service. The Waffen SS raised volunteer
divisions from almost every occupied country: from Scandinavia, from
Belgium and Holland, from France and Italy, from Russia, the Baltic states,
Ukraine and Yugoslavia. They even raised a skeleton Legion of St George
from British prisoners. But they got no Poles, no Greeks and no Jews.

The Soviet Union was the largest combatant state of all. It was widely
called Russia by those who didn't understand it. For Russia during the war
was only one of fifteen Soviet republics, and the Russians formed only
55–60 per cent of the population. It was ruled by a Georgian tyrant who
ceded nothing to Hitler in murderous designs, and who only entered the
war against the Reich after being attacked himself. What is more, just as
Germany in its years of success had boosted its military resources by co-
opting men and material from conquered countries, so in 1944–5, the
Soviet Union followed exactly the same policy. Every country 'liberated'
by the Red Army was obliged to supply conscript forces to fight against
Germany under Soviet command.

Above all, an elementary knowledge of geography is essential. In
September 1939, when Hitler and Stalin joined forces to destroy Poland,

the eastern half of Poland was annexed by the USSR and renamed Western Byelorussia and Western Ukraine. All the inhabitants of this large area became involuntary Soviet citizens, and in due course supplied an enormous cohort of Soviet casualties. In June 1941, at the start of Operation Barbarossa, it was not Russia that the *Wehrmacht* was invading but Soviet-occupied Poland. As the German armies spread out, they overran the whole of the Baltic states, the whole of Byelorussia and the whole of Ukraine, but only the peripheral fringes of Russia. At various times they approached the outskirts of Moscow, Leningrad and Stalingrad, but they never captured a major Russian city. As a result, by far the heaviest civilian casualties of the war were incurred in the western, non-Russian borders of the USSR: among Balts, Byelorussians, Jews, Poles and Ukrainians. These are not territories or populations over which President Putin presides today. But Westerners have rarely noticed such niceties.

Western attitudes to the Second World War crystallised in the immediate post-war years, and they have never budged. They were moulded by information from Western sources, by the accounts of Western commentators like Winston Churchill or Chester Wilmot, and concentrated on those aspects of the war in which the Western powers were most active. The political framework was provided by the ideology of anti-fascism, which had held the Grand Coalition together between 1941 and 1945. And their moral foundations were supplied by the Nuremberg tribunals, whose shortcomings, though observed, were not widely discussed amidst the near-universal revulsion against Nazi crimes.

One needs to ask, however, why more comprehensive and realistic overviews of the war failed to gain acceptance. In particular, it is something of a puzzle to see that, even during the onset of the Cold War, when Western opinion lost most of its earlier illusions about Stalin and the Soviet Union it still failed to apply its new-found knowledge to assessments of the Second World War. One reason is undoubtedly connected to the shame felt at the discovery of traitors and Soviet agents, like Burgess and Maclean, who had penetrated Western governments. A second reason must be linked to US domestic politics, where the primitive methods of Senator Joseph McCarthy succeeded in turning a valid line of enquiry into a distasteful witch-hunt. A third reason lies with the very slow tempo of revelations about wartime Soviet realities.

For many years the horrific realities of the war in Eastern Europe remained largely concealed. The world only began to get a hint about Stalin's maltreatment of his own people after Khrushchev's 'Secret Speech' of 1956. The extraordinary scale of wartime mortality in the USSR – now estimated at twenty-seven million – did not begin to emerge until the first post-war Soviet census in 1959. It was the 1960s before Solzhenitsyn revealed the true nature and chronology of the Gulag, before Hannah Arendt provoked the debate on totalitarianism, before Robert Conquest published his pioneering studies of the Great Terror, of the Ukrainian famine and of the 'Nation Killers', and before awareness of the Jewish Holocaust began to be energetically promoted. We had to await the collapse of communism before President Gorbachev admitted to the Katyn Massacres or *Le Livre Noir du Communisme* was compiled, or news filtered out about the Trophy Archive or about ethnic cleansing in Volhynia and Galicia. Antony Beevor's superb studies of the battles for Stalingrad[3] and Berlin,[4] which described such things as the Red Army's contempt for its own men and the systematic mass rapes of German women, were treated as revelatory. Many reviews of my own book on the Warsaw Rising[5] reacted as if the complete destruction of an Allied capital in 1944 was breaking news. The mass mortality caused by inter-Allied forced population transfers of Poles, Germans and Hungarians has only become an issue in the most recent years.

The subject deserves a study in depth, but what seems to have happened is that Western opinion was only informed about the war in Eastern Europe in dribs and drabs over forty to fifty years, and that this drip-feeding was insufficient to inspire much radical rethinking of the overall framework. It was also significant that we learned about Stalin's world in the context of the Cold War when we no longer identified with the Soviet Union as a common partner. Western intellectuals were ready enough to accept the incoming information and in some cases to use it for anti-Soviet political purposes, yet the Western public at large was too emotionally involved in the existing scenario of the Second World War to consider any major adjustments. The Western democracies had never actually fought the USSR, and for all his 'peccadilloes' Stalin could never compete with Hitler in the popular mind as the evil enemy. In other words, the playing surface was tipped against objective assessments from the start. And all developments in historiography were subject to the same inbuilt bias.

The Jewish Holocaust, for example, which was barely discussed for twenty years after the war, made enormous inroads into Western consciousness from the 1960s onwards exactly because it fitted so snugly into the existing scheme. Indeed, it has rightly become an emblematic episode in the history of human inhumanity. In some countries Holocaust denial has been made a criminal offence, yet Gulag denial is not even an issue. Academics who obstinately and ludicrously maintain that Stalin killed handfuls rather than millions are not fired. The British War Crimes Act applies exclusively to crimes committed 'by Germans or on German-occupied territory', thereby institutionally denying all non-German crimes. And the European Parliament, when recently asked to observe a minute's silence in honour of around 22,000 Allied officers murdered by the NKVD, refused. For the Western mindset has not been conditioned to apply equal standards to all sides in the conflict. Anyone wishing to tell the tale more objectively would need to re-examine the proportions, the ideologies and the morality.

All historians would agree that the Third Reich was defeated by the effective cooperation of East and West. No serious commentators suggest that the Western powers triumphed in Europe single-handedly, or that the military performance of the Red Army was anything but awesome. Yet no one shows much enthusiasm about quantifying relative contributions. I myself have never met anything more precise than statements to the effect that Soviet forces inflicted more German losses than the Western armies combined. German sources, however, are more forthcoming. They state unequivocally that 75–80 per cent of Germany's losses in men and materiel were incurred on the Eastern Front. The unavoidable implication is that all other contributions added up to a maximum of 20–25 per cent. Of this, the Americans might claim the laurels for 15 per cent, and the British for perhaps 10 per cent.

Of course, Western apologists will argue that the Soviet Union received enormous logistical supplies from both Britain and the USA, that the Red Army's campaigns on land were complemented by the Western bombing offensive and the war at sea, and that other aspects of the Western war effort from industrial production to intelligence should not be overlooked. Yet the fact remains: fighting is the essential activity in war. And as an adversary for the Nazi war machine the Red Army greatly excelled its Western counterparts both in quantity and in effectiveness. This is not the perspective to which Western audiences are accustomed.

The scale of Soviet predominance can be illustrated in several ways. Suffice to say that in one single operation in the spring of 1944, when demolishing Army Group Mitte in Byelorussia, Marshal Rokossovsky destroyed *Wehrmacht* divisions equivalent to the entire German deployment on the Western Front. The D-Day landings are the only operation fought by Western armies that might scrape into the top ten battles of the war.

Not surprisingly, both military and civilian casualties incurred in Eastern Europe reached a similar titanic scale. Here one must beware of the notoriously false 'twenty million Russian war dead', which has passed unchallenged all too often. The accepted figure is twenty-seven not twenty million, but it refers to 'Soviet citizens' not to Russians. And the so-called war dead include millions of wartime victims killed by the Stalinist regime itself. Even so, the levels of wartime mortality were staggering. The Soviet command assumed that it would lose two to three men for every German soldier killed. Manpower was a near-inexhaustible resource used with total abandon. The Red Army lost up to thirteen million, and still managed to prevail. Perhaps seven of the thirteen million would have been Russians. British military losses totalled 300,000.

On the civilian side, one only needs to look at the map of the German occupation to see in outline where the remaining fourteen million came from. Around two million were Jews – a recognised Soviet nationality – caught in the Nazi trap during the advance of Operation Barbarossa in 1941. Byelorussia (now Belarus) is the country which, with 25 per cent, lost the highest proportion of its inhabitants, though Poland and the Baltic states were not far behind. Ukraine, which unlike Russia was completely occupied by the Germans, probably suffered the largest total demographic loss, possibly eight to nine million. The Russian city of Leningrad (now again St Petersburg) lost up to one million citizens during the horrendous siege of 1941–4.

Needless to say, all these figures are tentative. The USSR never published any authoritative breakdown of wartime losses, and was averse to ethnic or regional sub-totals. Soviet historians and demographers had no reliable statistics to work with. The catastrophes of the 1930s and the 1940s were so colossal that no accurate records could be kept. All figures derive from deductions, projections and informed guesswork undertaken many years later.

In the case of Ukraine, for example, the post-war census could identify a vast demographic black hole but it said nothing about the hole's many different causes. It could not differentiate between the unborn progeny of millions of victims of the pre-war terror, famine and collectivisation, the millions of military deaths, the millions of civilians killed either by Hitler or by Stalin, and the millions of deportees who may or may not have perished in the Reich or in camps and relocated factories within the USSR. Historians can be fairly sure of the general categories but not of the precise figures for those categories. The most important thing to remember, however, is that all the major groups of wartime losses in the east overlap; they are not discrete entities. The massive total of twenty-seven million Soviet citizens who perished contains groups and individuals who also feature in parallel calculations of Ukrainian losses, Polish losses and Holocaust losses.

On the ideological front, Westerners are accustomed to thinking of the Second World War as a two-sided conflict, of good fighting evil. The Soviets had a similar dialectical view. They were the authors of the concept of anti-fascism, which caught on in the West, encouraging the illusion that all opponents of fascism were inspired by similar values. In reality, Soviet communism was every bit as hostile to Western democracy as it was to fascism, and principled democrats were bound to recoil from its spurious embrace. The conceptual foundations of Stalin's murderous dictatorship cannot be likened to Western ideals. Hence, despite the rhetoric, the Grand Coalition of 1941–5 can only be seen as a temporary marriage of convenience. Europe's ideological arena saw not two but three rival contenders circling for supremacy. It should have been no surprise, once fascism was eliminated, that the Western world moved into a subsequent phase of conflict with Soviet communism.

Stalinist practices, however, present a much deeper problem than does Marxist-Leninist theory: they undermine the entire moral framework within which the Allied cause is perceived. It is extremely hard to maintain that the Allied powers were fighting for untrammelled good if the largest of their members was perpetrating mass murder on the grand scale. Prior to 1941 enough was known about Stalin's concentration camps, purges, show trials, state terror, deportations, aggressions and campaigns for the elimination of whole social classes that Western leaders had no excuse for ignorance. Yet such was the desperate need for Soviet military assistance, such the overwhelming demand for the defeat of Nazi Germany, that all Western suspicions were suspended. Indeed, thanks to the persistent work of fellow travellers, of well-placed Soviet agents and of sheer naivety, a fairy-tale vision was created of 'Dear Old Uncle Joe' and his 'alternative forms of democracy'. Since the Red Army's colossal victories had saved the Allied cause from oblivion, the Western public convinced itself against all the evidence that Stalin was fighting for the same generous aims as they were. During the war there were thousands of people in London and Washington who had been eyewitnesses to Stalin's camps and murders, but they were effectively silenced by war censorship and in some cases by military discipline. Officers caught discussing what they had heard about Stalin's crimes were threatened with courts martial. Even Churchill, who had once been a strident anti-Bolshevik and who openly admitted 'supping with the Devil', warmed to the blandishments of success.

When victory finally came, on a vast wave of relief, very few were willing to count the enormous political and moral cost. At the Nuremberg trials, three categories of criminal conduct were established: crimes against peace (wars of aggression), war crimes and crimes against humanity. Nowadays, these are universally accepted as the standard for judgements on international legality and morality, and by any reckoning Stalin's regime deserved to stand trial on all counts. It had already been expelled from the League of Nations for crimes against peace; whilst defeating the *Wehrmacht*, its forces had perpetrated innumerable crimes against prisoners, civilians, refugees and women; and in pursuing systematic policies of mass murder, mass deportation, wholesale repression and widespread ethnic cleansing, it had manifestly entered the realm of crimes against humanity. Yet in the euphoria of victory it need not have feared a reprimand, let alone a formal accusation. When German defence lawyers at Nuremberg protested on this score, they were cut short by the chairman,

Sir Geoffrey Lawrence QC. 'We are here to judge major war criminals,' he reminded the court, 'not to try the prosecuting powers.'

Above all, one must forget the notion of a universal 'liberation' of Europe. The liberation was genuine enough when the Allies entered Rome, Paris or Brussels, and it was dramatically self-evident when Allied soldiers released the survivors of Belsen, Buchenwald or Auschwitz. But the story doesn't end there. In Eastern Europe Soviet forces imposed a new tyranny as soon as the Nazi tyranny had been crushed. One form of totalitarianism seamlessly replaced another. Buchenwald in eastern Germany was emptied of the Nazis' prisoners, then used for the communists' prisoners. As Auschwitz was liberated in January 1945, other camps like Majdanek were filling up with members of the resistance movement (our allies) whom the NKVD were treating as enemies. Wartime heroes flown into continental Europe by SOE and the RAF were now cast into Soviet dungeons. Democrats were arrested, shot or put on trial. Vast tides of innocents, including all Soviet POWs who had survived German imprisonment, all so-called repatriants handed over by Western forces, and most of the slave workers returning home from Germany, were shipped off to the Gulag. Puppet dictatorships with no popular support were introduced by force into country after country. For all of this, the label 'liberation' is not appropriate.

So historians have a problem. Somehow they must find a way of describing a complicated war in which, after several twists and turns, the combined forces of Western democracy and Stalinist tyranny triumphed over Nazi Germany. They must give pride of place to the role which the Soviet Union played in the military defeat of Germany, just as the USA shouldered the main burden of the war against Japan. At the same time, without minimising the Western contribution, they must emphasise that Stalin's triumph had nothing to do with freedom or justice, and that by Western standards the overall outcome was only partly satisfactory. It is a tall order. To date, no one has succeeded.

XIII

THE POLITICS OF HISTORY[1]

HISTORY and politics have been firmly bound together since the year dot, or at least since dot plus one – I suppose that some short period had to pass before the first historian had something to report. For a very, very long time history as a subject of academic study was essentially political history, and it preceded the rise of political science by centuries. All the other branches of history – economic, social, cultural, scientific, psycho- and so forth – are relatively recent creations. By the same token, the habit of treating history instrumentally for political purposes is as old as the hills. The office of court chronicler must go back to Nebuchadnezzar and beyond, and the job description was to concoct a selective record of events that would please the king. Just as the language of history is full of political statements about who came out on top and who went under, so the language of politics is full of historical references.

Nonetheless, for much of the twentieth century it was often thought that the politicisation of history was far more blatant in Eastern Europe than in the West. After all, Marx's historical materialism formed the basis of Soviet ideology; the Soviet Union professed a very clear, if simplistic view of its pioneering role in modern history; and the official view was enforced by an iron-hard censorship throughout the countries of the Soviet Bloc. We in the West were given to thinking that the Free World possessed both an open-minded approach to history and a superior, democratic system.

Since the demise of the USSR, however, Western countries need to examine their own attitudes more critically. And it turns out that the manipulation of history by Western politicians, though less systematic, can be every bit as shameless as that practised by some of the great tyrants of the past. Not long ago, for example, Donald Rumsfeld, lord of the Pentagon, likened President George W. Bush to Winston Churchill, making a beautifully inept comparison between America's pre-emptive attack on Iraq in 2003 and Churchill's non-pre-emptive stance towards Nazi Germany in the late 1930s; Churchill called for rearmament not for a pre-emptive attack. It would seem, therefore, that American-style democracy provides no sure defence against the mutual subversion of history and politics.

After all, there are few historians who are not themselves political animals. Despite their frequent protestations about objectivity, they can only form a view about the past by drawing on the values and convictions which they have obtained from living in the present. And those convictions can often be decidedly partisan. Eric Hobsbawm, one of Britain's most senior historians, managed for decades to combine membership of the Communist Party with membership of the British Academy. The late E.P. Thompson, author of the influential *The Making of the English Working Class* (1963) also combined left-wing activism with distinguished history writing. On the right wing, my friend and sometime neighbour, Norman Stone, now professor of international relations at Bilkent (Ankara), mixed Thatcherite activism with the chair of modern history at Oxford. The self-promoting Andrew Roberts links unabashed Toryism with writing about *Eminent Churchillians* (1994) or *Napoleon and Wellington* (2001). One can almost guess the political orientation of such people by looking at the titles of their publications.

The same phenomenon can be observed in the past, even among the greatest of historical names. Edward Gibbon, author of the unsurpassed *Decline and Fall of the Roman Empire* (1788) was such an advocate of the Enlightenment that his judgements on religious matters sometimes descended into satire or even ridicule. (His famous description of St Simon Stylites never fails to convert students to history for life.) Jules Michelet (1798–1874), author of the classic *Histoire de France* (1867), was a firebrand republican. Heinrich Treitschke and Nikolai Karamzin, who held similar positions in the pantheons of German and Russian historiography, were unrestrained apologists for the Hohenzollerns and Romanovs respectively. Michał Bobrzyński, author of the most balanced nineteenth-century history of Poland, served both history and, as governor of Galicia, the Habsburg empire. Benedetto Croce, historian of Italy, contrived to combine politics, philosophy *and* history.

Some thinkers have argued cogently that history and politics are so close that complete impartiality is a pipe dream. This is the view of Howard Zinn, a peace campaigner of the 1960s, whose *People's History of America* was part and parcel of his political campaigning.[2] Zinn worked with Noam Chomsky on *The Pentagon Papers*[3] and he is probably best known for the saying, 'One can't stand still on a moving train.' He consistently propounds the idea that historians are involved in a contest whether they like it or not. In his *Politics and History* (1970) he lays into naive academic colleagues who believe in 'objective study', 'disinterested scholarship' and 'dispassionate learning'. He suggests that such phrases are bogus 'bamboozlements' which deceive both the producers and the consumers of history. He writes, provocatively, that traditional historians have worn balanced judgement 'for appearance's sake' and that 'they can no more discard [it] than their pants'. In other words, academic principles concerning impartiality, objectivity and the search for truth are a pretence.[4]

Howard Zinn is a warrior for a cause. The world needs more people with that sort of commitment to principle. But he is not alone. All modern political movements have spawned historians who write accounts of the past to match their views on the present. The feminist movement for instance has had a huge impact, not only fostering gender studies and histories of women, but also adding a fresh dimension to many an established narrative.[5] The gay rights movement has likewise inspired new visions of past realities.[6] The Greens, too, have injected environmental issues into history, from Roman deforestation to the blights of communist planning.[7]

For what it is worth, my own views on this matter are probably closer to those of Howard Zinn than to those of some of the 'scientific' academics. I do think it possible for apolitical historians to write apolitical studies, especially on backwater subjects. At the same time, I agree that complete objectivity is unattainable, and that the search for absolute truth about the past can never end. These postulates present the historian with two duties. The first is to be humble and to recognise one's limitations. The second is to distinguish clearly between uncontested facts and contestable opinions. Under its famous editor C.P. Scott (1846–1932) the old *Manchester Guardian*, which formed part of the diet of my early years, carried a slogan on the title page: FACTS ARE SACRED, OPINION IS FREE. I still think that the slogan is valid.

Nonetheless, when one looks closely at the political uses and abuses of history, one finds that many different factors are in play. As a working list, one can start with seven headings: ideology, propaganda, censorship, nomenclature, mythology, education and international relations. There are undoubtedly more.

Ideology

Almost all political ideologies possess a strong historical dimension. Ideologists construct their schemes with reference to conditions which have been unsatisfactory in the past and which they aim to change in the future. Hence, in addition to looking forward, they also look back. Marxism, for example, arguably the most influential ideology of the twentieth century, is often thought of as an economic theory. In reality, as historical materialism, it is essentially a philosophy of history which uses a dialectical method of socio-economic analysis to explain the development of civilisation over the ages. The struggle between capitalism and socialism, which Marx identified in his own day and which he expected to mature into a proletarian revolution, was but the most recent stage in a series of such class conflicts which had proceeded since earliest times. In each stage of history Marx found an oppressed class – slaves in the ancient world, serfs in feudal times and the working class in his own day – which was programmed to rebel against its lords and masters and, in accordance with 'the spiral of history', to usher in a new stage. The period of socialism due to emerge after the triumph of the proletarian revolution was to be marked by the first classless society since the prehistoric tribal period. Marxism in its original form exercised its greatest influence on the democratic socialist movements of Western Europe, particularly on the German Social Democratic Party (SPD). It had strong advocates among socialists in France, Italy, Poland and elsewhere, but less so in Britain where the labour movement, as was once rightly remarked, 'owed more to Methodism than to Marxism'.

Communism is usually thought of as a refinement or variant of Marxism. It certainly holds Karl Marx and Friedrich Engels to be its founding fathers; and it counts itself the only true form of socialism. (Communist purists do not normally accept the label given to them by outsiders, believing 'communism' to be the name not of their ideology but of the harmonious social system to appear in a paradise of well-being and contentment in the final phase of history.) In the days of the USSR, Soviet leaders always claimed that they had built 'the world's first socialist state' which in turn was 'building communism'. As one wag put it, 'Communism was like the horizon: a distant prospect which invariably recedes as fast as you approach it.'

Be that as it may, Lenin and his disciples introduced so many fundamental changes and add-ons to Marxism that they lost track of its original character. Indeed, it was very fortunate for both Marx and Lenin that Marx was dead long before the Bolsheviks started purloining his legacy. Lenin's relationship to Marx may best be likened to that of a sectarian leader who insists on being the sole true Christian among the worldwide followers of Christ. Marxism-Leninism is essentially a plan for political action. It outlines how power can be seized by a small avant-garde of militants who do not need the full support of the masses and who need not wait, as Marx would certainly have insisted, until the socio-economic conditions are ripe for revolution. The Bolsheviks, therefore, did many things which would have sent Marx to an early grave. They seized control of a largely peasant society in which the industrial proletariat was particularly weak. They overturned the revolutionary government that had removed the tsar. They launched the unrestrained Red Terror, using force and fraud at every turn and provoking the Russian Civil War. In short, they created a bloodbath, and called it socialism. Yet, like all who emerged from the Marxist tradition, they had a strong sense of history. They cultivated violent heroes such as Spartacus, the rebellious Roman slave. They loved extremists, like the Levellers of the 'English Revolution'. And they adored the Jacobins, to whom they likened themselves. Lenin viewed himself as the new Robespierre.

Nationalist ideologies come in many forms, but a long historical perspective is one of the things that they usually have in common. Zionism, for instance, is a typical late-nineteenth-century concoction of the German type. It is fired by a fierce belief in *Blut und Boden* – the unbreakable bond between blood and soil. In the Zionist case, the blood is Jewish and the soil is the ancient land of Israel as defined in the Old Testament. By use of the favourite nationalist device of 'historical right', the Zionists claim that by resettling Palestine in modern times, the Jews are only repossessing what was unjustly taken from them by the Romans after the Judaean Revolt of AD 70. As corollaries, they hold that other Semitic peoples who have inhabited the territory since time immemorial remain there on sufferance, that non-Jews who left or were driven out do not have a right of return similar to their own, and that Israelis must control all the land's resources. According to the Balfour Declaration of 1917, which gave political Zionism its earliest hopes, a 'Jewish National Home' was foreseen on condition that the rights of the indigenous population in Palestine were not abrogated. Yet, more than eighty years later, there is no sign of a shared Palestine containing a 'Jewish National Home' alongside protected Arab communities of equivalent standing. Instead, there is a nuclear-armed Jewish State of Israel, supported by the USA and strong enough to defy all relevant rulings of the United Nations. There is a kingdom of Jordan: but no Palestinian state, and no prospect in the present two-state plan that the Palestinians will gain anything resembling equal status. Incessant hatred, conflict and terrorism emanate from both sides, though the fair-minded might judge that the stronger of the sides bears the larger responsibility. (To date, the largest single act of terrorism was the bomb planted in the King David Hotel by a group including the future Zionist premier, Menahem Begin, on 22 July 1946.)[8]

Israel, of course, prides itself on being a democracy, and it is constantly lauded as such by its American protectors. It certainly possesses an admirable internal framework of political and constitutional structures which guarantee the rule of law, respect civil rights and encourage a vigorous parliamentary system. In this particular respect it may have much to teach many of its Arab neighbours, where a variety of unsavoury monarchies, dictatorships and oppressive religious regimes prevail. Yet, at a deeper level, queries are inevitably raised about the Zionist concept of an ethnically exclusive Jewish state and its compatibility with fundamental principles of human dignity and equality. Thirty years of establishing illegal, affluent and exclusively Jewish settlements inside the Palestinian territories have repeatedly blocked progress on the so-called peace process and obstructed all chances of Israeli–Palestinian reconciliation. The US government would not tolerate such ethnically exclusive programmes inside the USA, and it is relevant to ask why it does so when conducted by its Israeli clients.

Zionism is unusual in that its drive to create a secular state is justified by religious, scriptural affirmations.[9] As it happens, the affirmations of the Old Testament are also accepted as the literal word of God by 40–50 million fundamentalist Protestants in the USA, so the Old Testament Alliance between the Bible Belt and the Zionist lobby thrives. And it goes as far as anything to explain why the American superpower should give the tiny State of Israel such unbending, uncritical support.[10]

When it comes to contemporary affairs, therefore, the foreign policy of the Bush II administration cannot be understood without reference to ideology. It can't be dissociated from economic factors, especially from US oil interests, but it is the ideological factor which differentiates it from the policy of preceding administrations. Two strands of thought complement each other. One is the Christian Zionism long associated with America's Republican right, and the other is the amalgamation of trends best known as neoconservatism. The neoconservative group, which contains names such as Richard Perle, Paul Wolfowitz, Douglas Feith, Elliot Abrams and John Bolton, is drawn almost exclusively from American Jews, and stands behind the Project for the New American Century think tank established in 1997. But it is not by any means typical of the Jewish lobby, and it arrived at its present position by a variety of routes. Some of its members, like Wolfowitz, emerged from ex-Trotskyite circles, whose critique of mainline policies was fired from the extreme left; others were followers of the Neoplatonist philosopher Leo Strauss (1899–1973). What they have in common is a belief that the USA should be an ideological state, admiration for the stance of the government of Ariel Sharon in Israel, and the conviction that the USA should not hesitate to pursue its political goals by the use of military might. These ideas were not very prominent in the Bush II entourage prior to 2000, but they filled an earlier vacuum in strategic thinking and they have capitalised to the maximum on the opportunities provided by the attacks of 9/11.[11]

Propaganda

Propaganda is closely associated with ideology. It is concerned with the means whereby one set of ideas can be promoted to the exclusion of others. In order to operate it needs both a coherent set of ideas and the power to distribute them. The name derives from the Vatican office De Propaganda Fidei, which is dedicated to the propagation of the Catholic faith.

Roman Catholics, however, are instructed to believe not only in the articles of their Christian faith but also in a particular version of Church history. They are told that the apostolic succession was divinely ordained, that the patriarch of Rome succeeded directly to the authority of St Peter, who was martyred in Rome, and hence that the Roman pope has always held precedence over all the other patriarchs. These contentions are a prime example of historical propaganda in the field of ecclesiastical politics. They use a view of the past in order to bolster present claims. They are a permanent barrier to reconciliation with Orthodox Christians and hence to ending the scandalous schism of the Church.

Of course, the art of propaganda long preceded the adoption of its modern name, and secular states were not slow to follow where the Church had led. In England the government of Henry VIII took care to bolster the break with Rome by inventing a new version of English history which maintained that the English crown had never been a dependency of the pope, and that the English Church was directly founded by the disciples of Christ, not by the Roman mission of St Augustine. These contentions, which appear between the lines of John Foxe's *Book of Martyrs*, were written into the preambles of the Reformation Statutes by Thomas Cromwell. Enforced by the state as elements of law, they linked an anti-Catholic version of national history to the articles of Anglican Protestantism, thereby establishing anti-Catholicism as a major ingredient of English, and later British, identity.[12]

In that same period a much grander scheme of politico-ecclesiastical propaganda was being introduced in Russia by Ivan the Terrible. First devised by a Muscovite monk in the late fifteenth century, following the fall of Constantinople to the Ottoman Turks, the scheme declared Muscovy the third Rome. The first Rome had been the empire of Augustus; the second the empire created by Constantine in Byzantium; and Moscow was the third. By extension, the theory claimed that the patriarch of Moscow had assumed the supreme authority of the patriarch of Constantinople, who was now controlled by the Ottomans, and that all Orthodox Slavs should automatically submit to the Muscovite allegiance. Since the greater part of historic Kievan Ruś formed part of Poland-Lithuania, and since the greater part of its Ruthenian inhabitants – Ukrainians and Byelorussians – continued to recognise the traditional patriarchate, the stage was set for the long-running conflict during which Moscow gradually assembled the newfangled dominion of 'Russia'.[13]

If in those early modern times political propaganda drew much of its voltage from the admixture of religion, in the twentieth century it gained much potency through the arrival of new communication media – film, radio and TV – and through techniques borrowed from commercial advertising. For obvious reasons, totalitarian regimes took the greatest advantage. In the 1920s Sergei Eisenstein was commissioned to make a series of historical films of such brilliance that he convinced the world of events, like the storming of the Winter Palace, which never actually happened. In 1938 he made *Alexander Nevsky*, a film about the thirteenth-century war between Moscow and the Teutonic Knights whose unforgettable scenes of the battle on the ice roused the Soviet public to resist the German onslaught when the film was released in 1941. Nazi propaganda followed similar paths. It was not especially memorable in the written form but was unsurpassed in the art of the visual image. The Nazi Party rallies at Nuremberg, using searchlights, martial music, massed marches and high-decibel speeches, all filmed by Leni Riefenstahl, reached new heights of impressiveness. Totalitarian art, whether communist or Nazi, was remarkably similar. In architecture it indulged in grandiose neoclassicism; in painting and sculpture, in gargantuan heroics; and in the much-favoured political cartoons, in grotesque ridicule of its perceived enemies. Its message was one of unrestrained power.

All of which underlines the fact that the Nazis and Soviets were not so much opposites as rivals. In 1939 Stalin ordered the remodelling of Glinka's opera *A Life for the Tsar*. It was given a new peasant hero, a new title, *Ivan Susanin*, and a new magnificent scenario for the seventeenth-century story of invasion and resistance. After a successful première in Moscow, the opera was taken for its first foreign airing in Berlin. The point was: the enemy in *Ivan Susanin* was Poland. And in the era of the Nazi–Soviet Pact, the cry of 'Death to the Poles' delighted Nazi and Soviet audiences alike.[14]

All types of regime indulge in propaganda of one sort or another; it is not a totalitarian monopoly. All governments need to explain their policies, to put on the best face possible, and to present their facts and statistics in a favourable light. There is often a very fine line to be drawn between what may be described as 'honest propaganda' and distorted information. In the early twenty-first century the British government of Tony Blair has been widely denounced for political 'spin', whilst both Prime Minister Blair and President George W. Bush were manifestly guilty of misleading their publics in order to justify the invasion of Iraq. The key issue is accountability. It is a good rule of thumb: the less a regime feels restrained by some independent authority, the more it will be inclined to promote information based on dubious arguments, blatant selectivity or downright lies.

Censorship

Censorship is a natural adjunct to propaganda. The propagandist cannot rest easy until all contradictory information is excised. Not surprisingly, therefore, the Vatican's Office for the Propagation of the Faith was quickly joined by a parallel institution: the Index of Prohibited Books. The first name on the list was Martin Luther's, but in time practically all of Europe's most revered writers and thinkers were given the black spot: from Dante and Erasmus to Copernicus, Descartes and Voltaire. Among the historians, one finds all the greatest luminaries of the profession: Gibbon most certainly, Michelet unavoidably and, as the historian of the popes, Ranke inevitably. Nowadays, aspiring historians can only regret that the index no longer pays them any attention at all.

Censorship comes in two forms: defensive (or excisory) and offensive (or prescriptive). The former aims simply to remove all material judged undesirable from the censor's point of view. It conjures up the traditional image of a merry little man with pince-nez wielding a blue pencil and a pair of scissors. The latter is more ambitious. It aims not merely to prune, but to prescribe: to lay down the detailed guidelines of what is permissible. In effect, it is preparing the raw material for the propagandist. Both forms have existed in all ages, but the prescriptive form became something of a speciality of the totalitarian regimes of the twentieth century.

A good example of the genre surfaced in 1977 when a senior officer of Poland's GUKPPiW (Main Office for the Control of Press, Publishing and Spectacles) defected to the West and published a complete set of directives from the previous year. The resultant tome offers wonderful insights into the communist mind. On the defensive side, it is remarkable for the extraordinarily pedantic calibration of prohibited persons and materials: writers who could be quoted subject to normal censorship; writers who could only be mentioned to be condemned; and writers in the category of what Russians used to call не-лицо or 'non-persons', who could not even be mentioned to be reviled. On the prescriptive side, the *Black Book* provided page after page of instructions on how to treat the American bicentenary. The general message was that the 'American Revolution' should not be condemned out of hand, as long as it wasn't called the American Revolution and as long as the progressive events of 1776 were not used to justify the reactionary regime of the contemporary USA. On no account was any hint to be dropped of the fact that American workers enjoyed much higher standards of living than workers in the Soviet Bloc.[15]

To Western susceptibilities, this all looks comprehensively, monolithically oppressive. But at least in the Polish People's Republic little attempt was made to conceal the work of the censorship. Ordinary citizens were required to apply to the requisite office to get their visiting cards, wedding invitations or funeral notices approved. In the Soviet Union the very existence of the censorship was censored.

Given the demise of totalitarianism, however, it may possibly be more interesting to ponder the ways that information is manipulated in democratic societies. For it is simply not true that democracies do not indulge in censorship. In wartime Britain, for instance, a far-reaching war censorship operated. The Royal Mail was complicit in the opening of letters; the press was subject to strict controls; and the so-called Ministry of

Information was involved in activities which, if undertaken by the enemy, would have been called propaganda. Even in peacetime every country operates restrictions. There are controls on military intelligence, on pornography, on criminal activity, on paedophiles, and increasingly on the Internet. Until very recently, Britain, unlike the USA, had no Freedom of Information Act, which made it much easier for government officials to cover their backs, to weed out records and generally to uphold a semi-secret system. It also makes it relatively hard for historians, who have greater difficulty accessing records than in other comparable countries. One should not equate democracy with equal freedom for all. Democratic states still have their self-preserving establishments, their ruling classes, their rich and powerful elites, their tyrannical majorities and their prevailing myths and ideologies. For all these reasons, though unwelcome or unconventional information cannot be easily banned or suppressed, it can be effectively marginalised.

In this regard, one might be well advised to consider the curious case of John Lingard (1771–1851) who by any objective standards was one of Britain's leading historians but whose work is virtually unknown. Lingard's *The History of England* was first published in 1819–30 in ten volumes, and appeared in several later editions. Unusually for its time, it was largely based on international archival research, it contested received interpretations in a solid, sober fashion and, if it lacked the élan of a Gibbon or a Macaulay, its style and its suitability for educational purposes were indisputable. Lingard's narrative on the Reformation, on the Elizabethan Age and the Civil War is worthy of a modern deconstructionist, yet it was effectively excluded from British debates on national history. The point is: John Lingard was a Roman Catholic. Indeed, he was a Catholic priest at a time when the British establishment was overwhelmingly and imperially Protestant. As a result, he and his works were kept out of the mainstream. They became the staple fare of Roman Catholic schools and seminaries but not of other British schools and universities. They were not read much by the historical profession, not widely reviewed and not recommended. They do not feature in the standard historiographies and were only rescued from near oblivion by a retired schoolmaster almost 200 years after Lingard's birth.[16]

Nomenclature

Nomenclature and personal names are highly political devices. They tell us as much about the people who do the naming as about the places and persons that are named. They show that almost everyone tries to mould the world in their own image.

Elsewhere I have used the example of Stonehenge – which could not possibly have been called Stonehenge when it was built. No one knows the identity let alone the native language of those prehistoric megalithic builders who lived on our shores many millennia before the English arrived. Yet it is especially curious to see how modern commentators are blind to the problem. Some years ago, when a theory emerged about the stones being erected by continental engineers, the press was full of reports that missed the point. 'Stonehenge not built by Britons,' I remember, 'but by burly Bretons from France.' *The Times* did not apparently know that 'Briton' and 'Breton' are both Celtic names and are both inappropriate for the pre-Celtic period. And as for 'France', it is almost as recent as 'England'.[17]

The same considerations apply to the king whom the English now call William the Conqueror (reigned 1066–88) but who could not possibly have used the name himself. He was Guillaume le Bâtard or Guillaume de Normandie. Like all the Norman and Plantagenet kings of England but one, he spoke no English and would have thought of himself among other things as *roi d'Angleterre*. But this historical fact is virtually unthinkable to the modern English mind.

Conquerors rename their conquests as a mark of their dominance. When the English first conquered Nieuw Amsterdam in 1664 they renamed it New York in honour of the duke of York. Many modern New Yorkers are sublimely unaware that the names of their suburbs, like Brooklyn, the Bronx or Harlem, are Dutch. Political conflicts see different parties to the conflict using different names for the same places. Irish nationalists and republicans (and their sympathisers) say 'Derry', which derives from the original Gaelic *Doire,* meaning 'the Oaks'. Irish loyalists and unionists (and their sympathisers) say 'Londonderry', which is the name adopted in 1613 during the Protestant plantation of Ulster. Unfortunately there is no third form, and to use one or the other can easily be taken as a political stance. The same is true of the Israel–Palestine conflict.

Israelis talk of Judaea and Samaria as if to use the contemporary Arab names is to admit the rights of expelled Arab refugees to return to their homes.

Russia has been particularly astute at playing the name-changing game. Every land annexed was given a name that implied not recent annexation but the recovery of territory somehow torn from the motherland. When Ukraine was taken from the kingdom of Poland in the 1660s, for example, the province was renamed Little Russia, and the fiction was launched that Ukrainians and Russians are one and the same people with one and the same language and history. It has taken nearly 500 years for this lie to be nailed. Yet when the editor of *The Times* was recently asked when he intended to give the capital of Ukraine its Ukrainian name – Ki'iv instead of the Russian Kiev – the answer was 'Never'. Once *The Times* adopts what it wrongly believes to be standard form, it holds on to it.

At this point I may be forgiven if I briefly tell the life story of my parents-in-law. They were born subjects of the Habsburgs in Austria, then lived in the Republic of Western Ukraine before spending twenty years in Poland. After that they lived both in the USSR, and in the German Third Reich. And they never moved once. Their home city was called Lemberg by the Austrians and the Nazis, Lv'iv by the Ukrainians, Lvov by the Russians. They, being Poles, called it Lwów (pronounced 'Lvoof'). When in doubt one can always fall back on the Latin form Leopolis.

People change their names for any number of reasons. (Indeed, *The History of Name-Changing* is the prospective title of a book which I would love to write but probably never will.) After my own mother died, for example, I found from her papers that she had changed her first name by deed poll. Women's names in general are a subject of great interest. Until recently the laws of most Western countries insisted that a married woman adopt the surname of her husband. For the husband to adopt the wife's surname would have been regarded not just as eccentric but as an affront to his manliness. It was all a sign of the reigning norms of gender politics, where women legally, as well as customarily, were subordinated to men. Spain was one the few countries to develop a more enlightened system in which double surnames nicely indicate both the dual parentage of children and the full equality of spouses. In the Slavonic countries many women traditionally bear the feminine form of their father's or husband's surname.

If Miss Krakowska, daughter of Mr Krakowski, marries Mr Poznański she becomes Mrs Poznańska, which at least gives recognition to her gender. Yet for officialdom in English- or German-speaking countries these nuances are rarely permissible. Wives' names have to be exactly the same as husbands' names. Many Slavonic women, on entering the USA or Germany, have been obliged to adopt a painfully inappropriate masculine name.

The communists played name games with special fervour. Not even the Nazis could bring themselves to rename Berlin 'Adolf Hitler Stadt', but within a few years of the Bolshevik Revolution, the first capital of Soviet Russia, Petrograd, had become Leningrad. Lenin's birthplace of Samara became Ulyanovsk, and soon there would be scores of Stalingrads, Stalinabads or Stalinos. All the Bolshevik leaders sported revolutionary pseudonyms, partly from their need before the revolution to hide from tsarist police and partly from the heroic bravado which they cultivated. Lenin's real name was Vladimir Ulyanov; Stalin, 'Man of Steel', was Joseph Dzugashvili; Trotsky was originally Bronstein; Kamenev was Rosenfeld; and Zinoviev, Radomyslsky. They called the states which they founded people's republics or socialist republics, which was a neat fiction since power always lay not with the people, the soviets or the state, and always with the party dictatorship that operated behind the scenes. Most of the main squares and boulevards of the cities were given ideological names, often recalling the date of the city's capture by the Red Army in the Civil War or Second World War. Little girls were given names like Ninel – Lenin spelled backwards – and even Father Christmas was turned into Father Frost. This was a vast, vain experiment in the political equivalent of wishful thinking; when the Soviet regime collapsed, most of the changes were reversed. St Petersburg was returned at popular request. So, too, was Samara. Stalingrad became Volgograd. And the world breathed a sigh of relief.

Mythology

Some historians seem to think that one of their missions in life is to fight mythology. They set out to sift fact from fiction and to establish the true course of events. That position is all very well, but it fails to recognise that mythology forms part of the mental framework of any age, and that no 'true course of events' can be reconstructed without it. Historians need to know how myths operate, and to identify the historical and the non-historical elements within them. But to banish them altogether would be to mutilate the past in a totally unacceptable way.

Myths come in many forms, but they often conform to archetypes that recur in many different societies and in many different periods. There are patriotic myths, for example, which serve to boost a nation's sense of self-esteem. There are origin myths which use metaphors and fables to explain things that might otherwise be inexplicable. And everywhere there are myths of a golden age that can never be recovered. All these archetypes are highly political.[18]

English history is full of patriotic myths. Most of them are rarely questioned. A particularly persistent one, beautifully encapsulated by Shakespeare, holds that England is an island:

> This royall Throne of Kings, this sceptred Isle,
> This earth of Maiesty, this seate of Mars,
> This other Eden, demy paradise,
> This Fortresse built by Nature for her selfe,
> Against infection, and the hand of warre:
> This happy breed of men, this little world,
> This precious stone, set in the silver sea,
> Which serves it in the office of a wall,
> Or as a Moate defensive to a house,
> Against the envy of lesse happier Lands,
> This blessed plot, this earth, this Realme, this England,
> This Nurse, this teeming wombe of Royall Kings,
> Fear'd by their breed, and famous for their birth,
> Renowned for their deeds, as farre from home,
> For Christian service, and true Chivalrie,
> As is the sepulcher in stubborne Jewry
> Of the Worlds ransome, blessed Maries Sonne.[19]

There are no more stirring lines in English literature, and none that are less true. For England has never been a 'sceptred Isle ... set in the silver sea'. When Shakespeare wrote those lines, in 1595, the Tudor kingdom encompassed Wales as well as England. But it did not extend to Scotland. And even when Scottish King James VI acceded to the English throne as James I, the projected union of the two kingdoms was explicitly rejected by the Westminster Parliament. In the following century, when the United Kingdom was finally formed, England and Scotland were kept as separate entities within the union, and they have remained so ever since. Unfortunately, it suits the English to forget the other nations that share the island with them and to assume, with an insufferable sense of their own superiority, that England and Great Britain are one and the same thing.

Origin myths are often connected in some way with the names of legendary pioneers or founders. Three Slavic nations, for instance, share the legend of the three brothers – Lech, Czech and Rus – who were born of the same parents and who later went their separate ways to father respectively the Poles, the Czechs, and the Rus (forebears of both the Ukrainians and the Russians). The legend is wheeled out whenever politicians call for solidarity among the Slavs. Lech, the first Pole, walked through the forest until he pitched camp under a spreading pine tree beneath the nest of a white eagle. Poland's first capital city and the seat of the country's primate is called Gniezno, meaning 'the nest'. And Poland's national emblem remains to this day the white eagle.

Just as the Garden of Eden forms a necessary prelude to the doctrine of the fall of man, so myths of a golden age generally arise thanks to a subsequent age of decline and disaster. In England the Tudor century came to be seen as a lost golden age thanks to the decades of conflict and civil war that followed. And such it has remained in all popular and officially favoured interpretations. For it emphasised the vigour of the state and monarchy, the triumph of the Anglican Church and the birth of naval power and of overseas empire. Whether or not the Tudors really headed an era of such pure gold is another matter. It can certainly be argued that the age of the price revolution, of enclosures and of 'beggars coming to town' was as bad for the common people as it was good for the court circles and for the Tudor loyalists who cashed in on the Reformation. And one can draw no simple contrast between Tudor success and Stuart failure. England at the end of the seventeenth century under James II, as portrayed by Lord Macaulay, was undoubtedly a more prosperous, powerful and promising place than it had been 100 years before under Elizabeth I.

The problem of rearranging the past according to the needs of the present becomes particularly acute in countries, unlike England, which have never enjoyed a settled existence. Slovakia, for instance, which is now a full member of the European Union, reached its moment of national independence for the very first time on 1 January 1993. Before that, it had always been a junior partner, not to say an oppressed region, within states dominated by others – for 1000 years by the Hungarians, and 1918–39, 1944–92 by the Czechs. So for the Slovaks the search for a historical golden age could be a long one. Between the great Moravian empire of the ninth century and the ill-fated, semi-fascist and pseudo-independent Slovak Republic of Father Jozef Tiso in 1939–44, there is nothing from which to choose.

Yet one should never underestimate human ingenuity. After the sudden demise of the USSR in 1991, all the ex-Soviet republics had unexpected independence thrust upon them, and all are seeking suitable histories to match their new condition. In Turkmenistan, for example, one of five former Soviet republics in central Asia, the new leader or *Turkmenbashi*, Sapamyrat Nyazov, has made an effortless transition from his former post of communist party secretary and has introduced an official personality cult with a strong historical slant. (He is said to base his approach on a mixture of Kemal Atatürk and Kim II Sung.) His aim is to link the dictatorship with a revival of ethnic Turkmen nationalism. In the capital city of Ashgabat, formerly Ashkabad, a gargantuan, gold-plated, revolving statue of the *Turkmenbashi* presides over daily life; the leader's little book *Rahnama*, or *Book of the Spirit*, is compulsory reading, even to obtain a driving licence; and a lavish new cultural centre is rising to extol the virtues of the new alphabet or the president's poetry or his revisionist history. Though the present phase is presented as a great leap forward from the preceding period of Russian-dominated colonialism, the USSR is not condemned out of hand. Rather, in the best Marxist fashion, it is presented as a regrettable but necessary phase in the spiral of progress. The most marked innovation can be found in the glorification of a medieval golden age prior to the arrival of Genghis Khan, when the Turkmen supposedly enjoyed a pristine era of freedom and prosperity. An obscure Turkmen dynasty, which broke away from the Seljuk empire, has been rescued from oblivion and raised to the status of the nation's first liberator. It has still to be seen, however, how this view of the past and present will play out alongside Turkmenistan's new alliance with the USA and membership of NATO's 'Partnership for Peace'.

Historical Education

Historical education is a subject of great political import. It plays an important role in shaping public attitudes and hence in preparing the ground on which politics, politicians and political systems have to operate. It is directly relevant to issues of civics, social development, culture, national identity, international relations and much more besides.

In the 1960s, when I was a postgraduate student at the Department of Education in Oxford, historical education was in turmoil. A strong reaction was in progress against both the content and the methods of history teaching. With the British empire in terminal decline, the old school syllabi, which had given pride of place to British politics and to the unbroken military and diplomatic successes of the imperial nation, were increasingly judged inadequate. In their place, great strides were being made by social, economic and gender history and by the fashion for left-wing ideology. Out went the duke of Wellington and the house of Windsor (aka Schleswig-Holstein-Sonderburg-Glücksburg-Saxe-Coburg-Gotha) and in came women, the Wall Street Crash and the working class. At the same time educators rejected 'the mere learning of dates and facts', appealing instead to the encouragement of empathy and the analysis of sources. Children were urged to relive the emotions of historical situations – 'What did it feel like to be a young soldier in the trenches of the Western Front?' or, 'What was in the mind of a suffragette chained to the railings of Buckingham Palace?' Pre-prepared textbooks and 'talk and chalk' round the blackboard were scorned. (Hence, no doubt, the damning comment of the inspector on my own teaching assessment: 'Mr Davies makes insufficient use of the board rubber.')

The net result of this classroom revolution was twofold. On the one hand, demands arose for much less central control and for much greater choice by individual schools and teachers. On the other, the breadth of general historical knowledge to which students and schoolchildren were exposed was drastically reduced. It stood to reason that if many class hours were to be spent examining narrow topics in great detail, the overall number of topics to be studied would decrease.

Whilst historical educators wrestled with these issues, sometimes acrimoniously, further problems were creeping up. The world was changing. New needs were emerging. Britain joined the European Community in 1973, and numerous observers deplored the absence of a substantial European dimension in historical studies. Britain was engaged in the Cold War, yet very few schools or universities gave priority to the study of communism, of the Soviet Union or of the countries of the Soviet Bloc. Worst of all, history itself was under threat. The school curriculum was coming under pressure to accommodate a whole range of new subjects: social studies, economics, computer studies, general studies and media studies among them. All too often, history and/or modern languages were forced to give way. The point finally came in 1990 when, in the so-called National Curriculum (which applies to England but not to Scotland or Wales) history ceased to be a compulsory school subject. This, by any standard, was a major political disaster.

One phenomenon that appeared not just in Britain and the USA but in most other Western countries too, was the rise of Holocaust studies. Prior to the late 1960s no one even in Israel had paid special attention to the Holocaust. Indeed, the term itself, widely attributed to Elie Wiesel, was not invented until the 1950s. Yet from 1967 onwards, and the Israeli victory in the Six-Day War, it made rapid advances. The explanation is partly the rise of right-wing governments in Israel and of an ever more strident Zionist lobby in the USA with a passion for educational action, but it was also moral, in that people could see a universal message in Europe's largest genocide, and could welcome a refreshing change from the selfish national histories of the past. In short, the Holocaust story became an emblematic episode in the unending war of good against evil. It was accompanied by a series of heart-rending Hollywood films, by a tidal wave of books and teaching materials, and by a widespread demand for all historians to categorise it as 'unique'.

Of course, nobody in their right mind could wish to deny the Holocaust a prominent place in modern historical consciousness; it is absolutely indispensable to a full understanding of the world in which we live. Yet serious questions must be posed both about the way in which it is often presented and about the frequent lack of political and historical context. To study any historical subject in isolation is dangerous at the best of times, and to study a subject with such obvious contemporary implications is especially risky. For the Holocaust is but one of many monstrous atrocities perpetrated against civilians during the Second World War. And it is often used as a justification for current political programmes.[20]

International Relations

International relations is a subject with profound historical dimensions. All current international conflicts have their roots in the developments of the past, sometimes over centuries; and all perceptions of international issues are the product of our previous corporate experiences. It was Lord Palmerston who said that Britain, then the leading world power, 'has no permanent friends, only interests'. This may be true in the long term. In an absolute sense, no alliances and no enmities can be rated eternal. Yet history is full of persistent friendships and persistent hostilities which have provided fixed points on the shifting international landscape for long periods. England (though not Scotland) sustained a deep-rooted animosity to France that played a key role in the growth of English national consciousness and lasted from the Middle Ages to the Entente Cordiale of 1904. France's traditional animosity towards, and rivalry with, Germany lasted even longer, only coming to an end after 1945. Its cessation provided the starting-point of the contemporary European Movement. In the east, Poland's long-standing fear and suspicions of Russia, which wrested regional supremacy from her at the end of the seventeenth century, can be contrasted with Poland's long-standing solidarity with Hungary, which shared many of Poland's experiences. In this same way, it is beyond dispute that the 500–600-year sojourn in the Ottoman empire of European peoples such as the Serbs, Bulgars and Greeks has left them with an unresolved complex about Turkey and the Turks.

Palmerston had been referring to Britain's deteriorating relationship with Russia, which in his time in the mid nineteenth century seemed to be encroaching on British interests in India. Britain and Russia had been partners in the wars against Napoleon and at the Congress of Vienna, but there was a definite downturn in relations during the era of the Crimean

War and the 'Great Game' in central Asia. But the interesting thing is that
the international 'interests' which Palmerston took to be immutable did
not last any longer than the Anglo–Russian friendship which he took to
be dispensable. Britain fought alongside tsarist Russia in the First World
War and alongside the Soviet Union in the Second, thereby reviving the
configuration of Napoleonic times. And the resultant impact on British
perceptions of the world was considerable.

For the British love affair with Russia – if that's not too strong a term
– has operated in many spheres far removed from the military and
diplomatic. Not only did it create fertile ground for the reception of
Russian culture – to which no one could object – but it also led many
people who should have known better to swallow Russian political myths,
to regurgitate undigested Russian historical narratives and in certain situations to close their eyes to the evident manifestations of Russian tyranny.
It is very curious, for example, to reflect that the biggest and most
damaging ring of British traitors in modern times, in the shape of Philby,
Burgess, Maclean, etc. – the 'Cambridge Five' – betrayed their country for
the benefit of a multiple mass murderer. One explanation for this strange
phenomenon obviously lies in the seductiveness of communist ideology.
Another can be sought in the absence of feelings in British intellectual
circles of that vintage which might have curbed their behaviour. When
John Cairncross, the British official who worked on the super-secret Ultra
project at Bletchley Park, was found handing over vital secrets to the
Soviets, he showed no sense of shame. In his view he was simply sharing
information with Britain's natural ally.[21]

Similar prejudices surrounded the sorry obfuscation of the so-called
Katyn Massacres. As is now known without a shadow of doubt, in March
1940 Stalin ordered the 'liquidation' of around 22,000 Allied POWs, who
were shot in cold blood by the Soviet security police. When the German
army uncovered one of the mass graves in the Katyn Forest in 1943 and
declared it the scene of a Soviet crime, the Soviet Union (by then an Allied
power) led a chorus of protests against this 'crude piece of Nazi propaganda'. It broke off diplomatic relations with the exiled Polish government
in London, which had been searching in vain for its missing officers and
which had dared to appeal to the International Red Cross. At the time,
His Majesty's Government did precisely nothing to comfort its Polish ally

in distress, and in all its official bulletins followed the Soviet line about Katyn being a German atrocity. So much is understandable, if not completely defensible, in the heat of wartime. What defies belief is that for nearly fifty years after the war the British government consistently refused to reveal what it had known about Katyn, repeatedly failed to correct its wartime disinformation on the subject, and obstinately denied all suggestions of a cover-up. In other words, throughout the Cold War when the Western world had belatedly come to recognise the true nature of the Soviet Union, the British establishment proved incapable of conceding the truth or of admitting its faults. Even when President Gorbachev finally produced documentary proof of Stalin's crime, the British response was less than wholehearted. Katyn does not mark the greatest atrocity of the Second World War, but it does provide the clearest illustration of the deplorable tendency, even in democratic countries, for historical events to be manipulated and distorted for political reasons.[22]

Knowing this background, one might have hoped that present-day politicians would have learned their lessons. Unfortunately, the Anglo–American war in Iraq shows exactly the opposite. For the authors of the war, President Bush II and Prime Minister Blair, have given ample proof of wilfully ignoring the guidance which a peremptory glimpse at Iraq's history might have offered. It takes no specialist in Mesopotamian affairs to identify a number of historical certainties which, if respected, could have persuaded the Coalition to act with greater circumspection.

1. Iraq is not a 'nation', as the Americans call it, but an artificial and relatively recent construct assembled after the sudden collapse of the Ottoman empire in 1918 and the subsequent establishment of a British mandate in Mesopotamia by the League of Nations. It consists of three disparate parts each deriving from one of the three former Ottoman provinces of Mosul, Baghdad and Basra. The Mosul region in the north is dominated by ethnic Kurds whose natural affection is for their Kurdish kin outside Iraq, especially in Turkey. The Baghdad region is dominated by Arabs of the Sunni Muslim faith, who, through Ottoman preferment of Sunnis, have traditionally supplied the educated and ruling class. The Basra region in the south is dominated by Arabs of the Shia variant of Islam who naturally resent the political power of the Sunni minority and

who often turn for support to their fellow Shias in Iran.

Conclusion. Nation-building from such disparate elements must be slow and problematic at the best of times. Prior to the growth of a democratic culture, any quick-fix election would be bound to bring victory to the Shias, which would be welcome neither to the Sunnis nor to the USA nor to the Arab world at large.

2. As the British found to their cost during their occupation of Iraq 1917–32, Iraqis do not take easily to Western invaders, and resistance can be fierce. Having been subjugated by the Ottomans for several centuries, they had no wish to be run by yet another wave of foreign power-brokers. Their sense of independence was inspired as much by a deep desire to see the outsiders go as by any hope of finding unity amongst themselves. The British experiment of creating unity by imposing a member of the Hashemite monarchy (which also ruled in Jordan) cannot be rated a success. King Faisal I and King Ghazi attracted no general support; electoral victories by the Shias had to be annulled; and numerous insurrections could only be crushed by the reintroduction of British forces and the application of great brutality. The memory of those pacifications, which were at their height in the 1930s and which involved the strafing of rebel villages by none other than 'Bomber' Harris, was very much alive among the new generation of politicians, like Saddam Hussein, who came to the fore in Iraq in the post-war era. The sovereignty of pre-war Iraq, which was nominally introduced in 1932, remained a sham.

Conclusion. It was never likely that an Anglo–American intervention force, however well-intentioned, would be welcomed as liberators. The Iraqis have often heard Western rhetoric before, and have seen how careless Westerners can be about the loss of non-Western lives.

3. In April 1941, when British interests in the Middle East came under severe pressure from pro-German elements, the royal government in Baghdad was temporarily overthrown by a group of military officers called the Golden Square. Led by Rashid Ali al-Gaylani, a former prime minister and ardent Arab nationalist, the conspirators removed the regent and, with the help of German planes based in Vichy-controlled Syria, attempted to seize the RAF airbase at Habbaniyah. For a few weeks the coup appeared to be creating an important staging post for expanding German influence and for supplying the Reich with oil. Energetic military action by the

British, however, stemmed the tide. Habbaniyah held out, as the Arab Legion under Glubb advanced from Transjordan and the 10th Indian Infantry Division landed at Basra. By the end of May the Golden Square had been defeated, and Rashid Ali was forced to flee, first to Iran and then to Germany. He spent the rest of the war in Berlin, broadcasting virulent anti-British and Arab nationalist propaganda from Berlin.

The episode of the Golden Square was closely entangled with Jewish affairs. The large Jewish community in Iraq, which numbered perhaps 100,000, sided unequivocally with the regent and with the British, whilst the mufti of Jerusalem, a virulent pan-Arabist, arrived in Baghdad to support the anti-British coup. At one point British intelligence released a group of Zionist terrorists from jail in Tel Aviv with a view to using them to sabotage oil installations in the event of the pro-German party consolidating control. As it happened, the British did not lose possession of the oilfields, and their Zionist recruits were used for other purposes. David Raziel, the commander of the Irgun, who had played a prominent part in the inter-communal violence during the Arab Revolt in Palestine, was killed on 17 May 1941 near Fallujah, when a plane said to be German bombed the car in which he was travelling. Two weeks later, on 1 June, when the Jews of Baghdad streamed out of the city to greet the returning regent, they were attacked by a mob which then perpetrated a widespread pogrom. The bloodletting initiated a decade of harassment which ended in 1951 with the expulsion of Iraqi Jews to Israel.

Conclusion. Iraq is not an island, and its complicated politics have been closely entangled with the affairs of several neighbouring countries for most of the twentieth century. The Golden Square, though defeated, may be seen as the predecessor of the Free Officers Movement which eventually toppled the monarchy in 1958. Anglo–American oil interests, which in 1951 blocked the advent of democracy in Iran, have been seen with some reason as agents of reaction and enemies of popular change. The long-standing antipathy towards Zionism and the State of Israel is not a recent development.

4. The regime of the Ba'athist Party, which assumed power in Iraq in 1968, was driven by principles of secularism, of Arab nationalism and of pseudo-democratic socialism. If it followed a model, it was that of Soviet communism, which supported several other similar regimes in the Arab

world. Its sworn enemies were on the one hand the Arab monarchies – in Jordan, in Saudi Arabia and in the Gulf – and on the other the Islamist movement, whose religious radicalism offered an alternative to secular Ba'athism. Its fellow spirits were to be found in Syria, in Egypt and in Libya. Like all branches of Arab nationalism, it was fundamentally opposed to the Jewish State of Israel.

Conclusion. Any occupation of Iraq by a US-led force would seem to most Iraqis as in the interests of the Arab monarchies, of Israel and of US oil companies.

5. Saddam Hussein, who subsequently took control of the Ba'athist Party, continued the general direction of its policies, whilst introducing a cult of his own personality and a much higher degree of coercion. By common consent, he was a bloodthirsty tyrant who did not hesitate to apply the most revolting methods. Yet one should not imagine that he lacked support. He cultivated the clans of the Sunni Triangle from which his leading henchmen were recruited, and among the Sunnis he could be viewed as a strong leader able to control the Kurds and Shias. He could also be seen as the protector of those, including many women, who feared the rise of the mullahs and the imams. And as commander-in-chief he greatly increased the influence and prestige of the armed forces. Whatever his vices – which were many – he held Iraq together.

Conclusion. The removal of the Iraqi dictator was bound to initiate a period of instability, if not anarchy, and would do nothing to further the cause of peace in the Middle East as a whole. Saddam's hostility to the Islamicist movement had meant that Iraq, unlike Afghanistan, did not provide a haven for terrorist organisations like al Qaeda. Indeed, Osama bin Laden could only have shown his face in Baghdad at his peril.

If the so-called War on Terror were the prime consideration, therefore, Saddam's regime should have been left in place. In the early years of his rule, Saddam's regime had undoubtedly been developing nuclear weapons, as had Israel. His progress led Israel to launch a pre-emptive attack and to bomb the Osirak nuclear plant near Baghdad in 1981. It was obvious that Saddam would dream of revenge, but in the late 1990s UN inspectors were unable to determine whether Iraq possessed weapons of mass destruction. Uncertainty on this point was certain to be a major consideration in the formulation of US policy. Indeed, any unilateral attempt at 'regime change' in Iraq could only raise suspicions that the US was acting to protect its Israeli client.

6. Saddam Hussein's wars were an essential element in his overall strategy. They diverted attention from internal problems, opened up prospects of achieving the international goals of Arab nationalism and created the appropriate climate of fear and xenophobia on which all dictatorships thrive. In 1980 Saddam attacked the revolutionary republic of Iran, thereby gaining US approval and military supplies. The war lasted eight years and cost the lives of a million men. There was no clear victory but deep animosity against revolutionary Iran lingered.

In 1990 Saddam attacked neighbouring Kuwait, whose territory (with some reason) he claimed to be a slice of the former Ottoman province of Basra, which had been separated by dictate of the British Colonial Office in 1921. This time he earned active American disapproval. In the First Gulf War, Iraqi forces suffered a crushing defeat. Tens of thousands of Iraqi conscripts were slaughtered by the unassailable supremacy of US firepower. Attempts to fire antiquated Soviet rockets at Israel were a dismal failure. But again there was no clear outcome. Saddam snatched survival from defeat, as President Bush I refused to march on Baghdad. Instead, a harsh UN sanctions regime was imposed, enforced by British and American air power. The extreme deprivations of the Iraqi people persisted, this time with a Western enemy to blame.

Conclusion. In the international arena the vacuum created by the fall of Saddam's regime could only be effectively filled by the US military. If the Americans were to pull out as promised at an early date, their withdrawal could easily suck in Iraq's neighbours – Turkey, Syria or Iran – each of them intent on stopping developments which they might regard as threatening. More likely, since the Americans would fear the prospect both of international and of civil war, US troops would have to stay; and Iraq would have to be ruled as an American client state for the indefinite future.[23]

At the time of writing (December 2004), no sensible solution in Iraq is in sight. The anti-American insurgency continues. The US Marines are turning Fallujah into a wilderness and calling it pacified. There is no certainty that elections will take place, or if they do that they will produce a decisive result. Meanwhile, as Saddam waits comfortably in detention for a trial that may or may not occur, the Iraqi people continue to suffer. Casualties mount. In the course of the last year the number of civilian victims was counted in the tens of thousands. It is a rate of killing that cannot be far short of the annual death toll inflicted by Saddam's butchers and torturers. (Americans only count American casualties.)

At the start of the twenty-first century, the invasion of Iraq, first mooted by American neoconservatives in 1996, was becoming a distinct possibility. Anyone weighing the pros and cons could easily have drawn some elementary conclusions. Yet the warmongers in Washington pressed on regardless. When the history of the Iraq War comes to be written, and historians can pore over the documents, it will be interesting to see if anyone in the US governmental machine prepared a historical summary along the lines of that sketched above. For a couple of pages of historical notes would have sufficed to avoid some of the grosser miscalculations.

For decades during the Cold War the world was split between two rival long-term visions. And when the USSR collapsed, some people imagined that the 'end of history' had been reached. Nowadays, one is tempted to consider exactly the opposite hypothesis. For not only have international rivalries continued, so too has the relevance of historical insights. In a strange way the late Soviet Union is sadly missed. For, despite its monstrous faults, the USSR did propagate a coherent historical vision, and by so doing encouraged its adversaries to challenge its contentions and to maintain a minimal level of sensitivity to historical issues. It was strong, for example, on the history of imperialism and on the consequences of imperialism in the modern world. If the Soviet factor had not been eliminated, it is hard to imagine an issue such as the Middle East being discussed, as it is, in so manifestly ahistorical terms. What seems to have happened is that the emergence of a single global superpower has created the illusion that a coherent historical perspective has become redundant. For the time being at least politics reign supreme, and leading politicians show little sense of embarrassment at their historical illiteracy.

And lastly another shift has taken place. For fifty years the West thought of the East as a region starting in the middle of Europe. Since the fall of the USSR, the border of the East has taken a distinct step eastwards. It has moved from Europe to the confines of Asia, and is back where it was before, in the region that was once called the Levant. It will remain there until the problems which centre on Israel and Iraq find some measure of resolution.

XIV

THE RISE OF
NEW GLOBAL POWERS[1]

HISTORIANS, who are supposed to be specialists in the affairs of the Past, are always being asked to speculate about the Future. Almost invariably, at the end of a lecture, question time begins with a hand being raised and the words being put: 'What is going to happen now?' My usual reaction is to say, 'I'm not an astrologer' or, 'Sources on the next stage of events are rather thin', and then to opine that historians are no more skilled in the art of prediction than anyone else.

Yet the phenomenon is unavoidable. People who have listened to the first part of a story, or who have read the account of an uncompleted theme, are always going to be curious about further developments. And historians who have whetted their appetite should not be surprised if they want to hear more.

What is more, one is inevitably led into the curious field of 'the future in the Past': that is, into the ever-changing panorama of predictions and analyses which were made in a Present that no longer exists. To review these predictions and analyses can be a humbling experience. One is forcefully reminded of long-forgotten circumstances that clouded, or at least influenced, one's judgement. And one can occasionally be surprised by the pleasant realisation that on one point or two the prediction was accurate.

Speculation about the 'super-blocs' of the twenty-first century is in fashion. Globalisation is already here, and it is clearly reducing the competence of

THE RISE OF NEW GLOBAL POWERS

individual, sovereign states. The proposition that the growth of supra-national and multinational organisations and of transcontinental lines of communication will force 'a remaking of the world order' is eminently reasonable. The difficulty, as always, lies with the human interpreters. People tend to rely on their previous experiences. Constitutionalists and political scientists draw up schemes based on existing models. Everyone finds it difficult to imagine a new world where many of the prevailing assumptions about political structures, authority and legitimacy may well be changed.

Much of the current debate was fired by the ideas of the American academic Samuel Huntington.[2] Huntington's approach is refreshing in that it proposes cultural identity, rather than political ideology or economic interest, as the guiding principle of the new groupings. Its weaker aspects include a tendency to rely on loaded stereotypes such as the American version of 'Western civilisation', and by implication on the dangerous notion of 'the West versus the rest'. In relation to Europe, for example, it tries to uphold the rigid opposition between Western Europe and Eastern Europe, as if they were distinct and permanent entities. It implies, among other things, that the Soviet Bloc was a natural creation whose members were somehow predisposed to it by economic backwardness and uniform cultural legacy. Huntington would be lynched if he dared to say such things in Warsaw, Prague or Budapest.

Some thought must be given to the vocabulary, therefore, and to the concepts which lie behind it. Huntington talks of civilisations; but it is more common to talk of blocs or power blocs. Yet the latter terms also call for caution. As memories of the Soviet Bloc should indicate, 'bloc' suggests something cast in concrete and possessing monolithic ambitions, highly centralised control and minimal internal elasticity. Yet these are the very qualities which the new groupings are least likely to display. One might think instead of clubs, circles, confederations, conglomerations or concatenations of countries, which are strongly connected to each other but which maintain a fair measure of autonomous manoeuvre. For the sake of argument, let's settle on concatenations.

There are many reasons why such concatenated groupings are likely to develop; indeed, they are already developing.

- Many features of contemporary life and its associated problems – crime, environment, IT, banking, transport, etc. – know no frontiers. They cannot possibly be tackled by individual countries acting on their own.
- Thanks to globalisation, individual countries feel extremely vulnerable not only to hostile forces but also to the everyday operations of multi-national corporations and foreign networks.
- The world is still too large and diverse for anyone to think in terms of world government.
- Many deep-seated conflicts and rivalries remain unsolved, and in a dangerous but interconnected world, isolationism is neither realistic nor attractive.
- As the concatenations grow, thereby gaining power and influence, the harder it becomes for reluctant countries to stay aloof. The processes of closer coordination possess what physicists would call both dynamic and momentum.

Too little thought has been given to the likely characteristics of future formations, and this is where the guessing begins. Nonetheless, one can at least start an argument from the certain knowledge that global technology in general and computerisation in particular played an important part in destroying the totalitarian structures of communism. Gorbachev's policy of Glasnost, for instance, which he launched initially as a move to encourage internal party discussion, spiralled out of control when he realised that the old restraints were no longer viable. Another lovely example occurred in 1980–1 when the Soviet authorities introduced cheap efficient TV aerials so that everyone could watch the expected Soviet triumphs in the Olympic Games in Moscow. Instead, everyone in the western parts of the USSR found that by turning their aerials round 180 degrees they could pick up the uniquely uncensored programmes from Poland which Solidarity had briefly succeeded in wresting from the state-run TV. No doubt the Chinese authorities are learning similar lessons today through the spread of PCs, though state ability to limit the freedoms of the Internet has confounded many critics. Faced with the vast opportunities of the Chinese market, Western firms will be tempted to collaborate with the state by agreeing to inbuilt filters.

So, totalitarianism is not going to return. Nor are old-fashioned colonial empires. Nor are huge, centralised, *étatiste* and bureaucratic monsters of the sort dreamt up by nincompoops who waste their energies fighting a non-existent European superstate. Rather, one must attempt to imagine types of political organism which have no ready precedent in past experience. Three characteristics are worth considering:

1. *Overlapping jurisdictions.* The old idea that a sovereign state enjoys God-given monopoly of access to its citizens and hence sole authority over them is already going out of the window. Instead, it may be perfectly possible for people to recognise the authority of one government for one purpose and of other governments or agencies for other purposes. In some circumstances people could acquire the right to choose between competing jurisdictions in any given province or region. Of course, the executive council of each concatenation would have to appoint a regulatory body for all such arrangements. (Is this not a solution for Northern Ireland?)

2. *Multilayered, multinational authorities.* The old canon law principle of subsidiarity is much smarter and more flexible than most people realise. It is not merely concerned with bringing order to the relations between a supreme supranational authority and national governments – for example, in the EU, between the central organs in Brussels or Strasbourg and the governments of member states. Its principal concern lies with delegating decision-making to the lowest and/or the most appropriate level on each particular issue. In many if not most cases the best level may turn out to be far below or far removed from national governments. The advantages of subsidiarity, therefore, are worth taking seriously. They are instinctively pooh-poohed by the caste of civil service mandarins, which naturally prefers to keep everything within its own remit, but they stand to empower everything from regional bodies (such as the Council of the Isles) to parish councils and the International Federation of Pigeon-Fanciers. This might be no bad thing.

3. *Multiple concatenacity.* (Sorry, that's gratuitous!) All this means is that the global nature of technology and communications will enable members of one concatenation to belong to other concatenations at

one and the same time. In other words, the world is being overtaken by a highly complex network of networks, each consisting of interconnected and partially interlocking organisations. This sort of set-up is very different from the old system of rival blocs and alliances where a country had to belong either to one grouping or to the other. It is already in evidence in Europe, where one chain of countries in the EU coincides to a considerable degree with the separate chain in NATO and another chain belongs to the euro zone. International politics will become increasingly absorbed in the points of interface between various concatenations, and with the friction of competing interests that will emerge with every new organisation that is created. The European Rapid Reaction Force is a prime example.

One thing will not change – power politics. Francis Fukuyama's notion of 'the end of history' is a nonsense.[3] Whatever form the global groupings of the future take, they will continue to compete, to collide and occasionally to come to blows. The strongest argument for engaging actively in the concatenation of one's choice is that true isolation is no longer possible.

Similarly, too little thought is given to the nature of existing formations and how they might merge into the formations of the future. Everyone likes to think nowadays that they have a nation state in which the overwhelming majority of state citizens identify with the same national community. The United States is undoubtedly a leading role model. It was forged from millions of immigrants with the most diverse origins, and in American usage the concept of 'nation' has been completely fused into the constitutional concept for which others would use the word 'state'. In Europe, France, Germany and Poland, among others, are undoubtedly nation states. (It would be difficult to stop a French citizen in the street in Paris and be told that he or she was something other than French.)

Britain, on the other hand, is not a nation state. Both England and Scotland were nation states at one time, and Ireland made herself into one in the course of the last century. But Britain is a composite dynastic state, which went a long way along the road towards creating a new 'British nation' but which didn't quite reach the final destination. A good chance to forge a new modern form of national identity was missed when the empire collapsed, and as a result we are now facing a dramatic identity crisis. It is probably true that 'Britishness' commanded an absolute majority among UK citizens once the disaffected Irish had departed and the rest had passed through the bonding experience of two world wars. New successful immigrants are enthusiastically British. But since 1945 British-ness has been steadily receding in many spheres, whilst the older English, Scots and Welsh identities have been staging a strong recovery. British society never coalesced to the same degree as French or German society, and it is now in danger of disintegrating into its constituent parts. According to that rare thing, an opinion poll which asked the right ques-tion, we reached the critical point in 1999, when an absolute majority of British citizens no longer thought of themselves as 'primarily British'.[4] Devolution, therefore, was long overdue. If it is well managed, it will stave off further involuntary shifts for a few decades. If it is botched, it will precipitate the very thing that it was designed to prevent.

Furthermore, since the decomposition of Britain is proceeding in the hidden foundations of a building whose visible spaces may well be filled with thriving political, economic and cultural activities, it is masked by our inability to look in the right places. And the decomposition of Britain is extremely relevant to the looming choices which Britishers, or ex-Britishers, will have to make in the relatively near future. To which concatenation do we wish to give priority? Do we intend to engage fully with Europe or not? Do we hope to stay tied to the apron strings of the United States? Which concatenation would be best suited to a Britain that is struggling to stay united? On this last point it may be worth emphasising that the European Union caters for both large and small and that its subsidiarity policies, if implemented, could dovetail neatly with the aims of devolution. In the longer term the EU could easily accommodate either a reconsolidated Britain or a string of ex-British republics. The European Union is the most obvious example of a concatenation in the making. The executive arrangements of its Council of Ministers and the dithering over foreign and security policies leave much to be desired, yet it is rapidly becoming a force to be reckoned with – to coin a phrase, a future superpower but not a superstate. One may regret all sorts of failings – from the lemming-like pursuit of 1985-style integration to the delays of enlargement and the 'democratic deficit'

– and one may fear an imminent crisis if priorities are not changed, but one has only to look back twenty years to realise that the momentum is startling.

One aspect is often overlooked. At a certain stage in its crystallisation any organisation needs a lingua franca, and in the last decade, irrespective of the francophone elite in Brussels, the unstoppable advance of English is self-evident. Within the next generation bilingual and trilingual education will probably be introduced throughout the union, and it is not entirely facetious (and hopefully thought-provoking) to imagine that the nickname for the Union in 100 years' time could be 'England'.

The USA is the last superpower of the old type, and is now showing signs of forming the core of a new concatenation. For various reasons it is likely to drift further from Europe and closer to Latin America. NAFTA is only a first faltering step. At this very moment several states within the United States, headed by California, are moving rapidly towards Hispanicisation, and the consequences could be far-reaching. Americans must at least ponder the possibility that the penetration of their population by Hispanic culture may break down traditional fears of the gringo in the south, remove the mental barriers in the north against Hispanics, and open the way towards an ever-closer union of the two Americas.

Islam is defined by Huntington as a 'civilisation' – which is probably right – but it is extraordinarily diverse, politically diffuse and, stretching from Casablanca in the west to Timor in the east, geographically very disparate. Left to its own devices, it has no likelihood of early consolidation. However, crude discriminatory and hostile stereotypes of Islam abound, especially in America and in Russia, and unchecked external pressures of that kind could drive Islamic unification forward more effectively than any internal forces. It is in everyone's interests to tone down the prejudicial vocabulary and to discourage the climate in which fundamentalism and militancy thrive. A military attack by the USA or its allies on a Muslim country would be folly; it is the one thing that could accelerate either the unification of the Muslim world as a political force or the consolidation of competing Islamic activists.

Several other regions of the world defy easy prediction. India, in a sense, is already a vast concatenation and a budding world power, but it does not have much room for expansion. Africa is extremely poor and extremely fragmented. Without continuing assistance from 'the north', it does not seem to possess the capacity for effective development. Australia, New Zealand and South Africa all fit uncomfortably into the contiguous regions. It is not inconceivable that they might look to each other across the Southern Ocean rather than to their Asian, Polynesian or African neighbours.

By far the most interesting, not to say the most worrying, prospects are to be found in the Far East. China is both an ancient civilisation and a great power, clearly with unsatisfied ambitions. Its economic dynamism is phenomenal, and its apparent success in combining modern capitalist economics with rigid, dictatorial state authority has confounded many predictions. Japan is another global economic and financial power, second only to the United States but rapidly being overhanded by China. Its culture, though unique, has probably retained more affinities with its Chinese roots than the present pro-Western veneer might suggest. As the hatreds of the twentieth century recede, therefore, one cannot rule out the possibility that China and Japan may be reconciled, and in their reconciliation carry the rest of the Far East with them, including Korea. The Pacific region is rapidly catching up with its dominant Atlantic counterpart. American dominance then, established during the Second World War, is now slipping. After that, one has to ponder the significance of the most glaring geographical fact in the political economy of today's world: that the globe's emptiest, resource-richest yet least developed region – Siberia – lies immediately adjacent to the globe's most populous and most land-hungry region. The strategic goal of a Far Eastern concatenation, if it is realised, can hardly be in doubt.

Potential flashpoints and danger areas abound. One needs to talk of the Caspian, of Iraq and Iran, of Israel–Palestine, of Taiwan, Moscow, and perhaps of Washington itself.

The Caspian

The countries on either side of the Caspian Sea, which lingered long as a backwater of the USSR, have found new prominence. They are independent, so open to political overtures from outside, and they are all affected by the presence of huge oil reserves. Some, like Azerbaijan with its capital Baku, are oil producers. Others, like Georgia, are strategically important since they control territory through which future pipelines will have to pass. A further category, which includes Kirghiztan and Turkmenistan, is unstable due to the rise of new national movements. The dangers of conflagration arise from three interlocking factors. Firstly, there are numerous local conflicts – between Russia and Chechnya, between Georgia and its breakaway provinces of Abkhazia and South Ossetia, and between Armenia and Azerbaijan – which could be exploited by others. Secondly, American oil firms have been investing heavily in several countries like Uzbekistan where wayward dictatorships are in power. Thirdly, Russia still regards the region as part of its 'near abroad', where foreigners are not supposed to interfere. The Americans, in particular, will have to tread carefully if they are not to provoke an outburst.

Iraq and Iran

The Middle East is a region of many tensions which show no sign of abating. The Arab world is deeply divided between ultra-conservative but wealthy monarchies like Saudi Arabia and the Gulf states, and supposedly progressive regimes such as those in Egypt, Syria and Iraq, which have been drawn into the orbit of popular Arab nationalism but which in practice are run as military dictatorships.

Yet two countries – Iraq and Iran – have the distinction of having openly defied America's regional hegemony, and hence, in the eyes of radicals, are potential leaders. The Islamic Republic of Iran, which replaced the ousted shah in 1979, angered Washington when it openly identified the United States as the 'Great Satan'. Iraq, which at an earlier stage had been an American client, provoked the USA into open warfare during the Gulf War of 1990–91 by invading Kuwait. From 1980 to 1988 Iraq and Iran fought a bitter bloody war. The big question now is whether the two can ever be reconciled to form a potent focus of anti-Americanism.

Here, two factors are relevant. Firstly, Iraq is a highly artificial agglomeration, constructed by the British in the 1920s from three disparate Ottoman provinces. The Kurds in the north look to their compatriots in Turkey and western Iran. The Sunnis in the centre around Baghdad are another minority, but one which has traditionally held the reins of power.

The Shias of the south around Basra form a distinct majority, which if democracy were ever to arrive would gain the dominant voice. And the Iraqi Shias, though Arabs, are the religious cousins of the Shias in Iran.

Secondly, there have been noises on the extreme right of American Republicanism calling for a campaign to complete the unfinished business of the Gulf War – to end the ineffective sanctions regime and invade Iraq. The Project for the New American Century is a think tank established in 1997 whose members have included Dick Cheney and Donald Rumsfeld and which has strong connections with American Zionist circles. If this strategy were to gain favour with the incoming administration of President George W. Bush, the chances of a major regional shift of power would be much increased. Saddam Hussein is an unpleasant tyrant, but his secular regime is based on the Sunnis. It holds down the Shias and acts as a bulwark against Islamicist extremism. His removal would open up the possibility of a takeover by Shia Islamicists and of a new anti-American Iraqi–Iranian axis.

The Israeli–Palestinian Impasse

The repeated failure of Israel and the Palestinians to settle their differences and make peace is a festering sore. It reduces America's ability to act as an impartial arbiter in the rest of the region and it fuels ongoing resentments throughout the Muslim world. Friends of Israel tend to see her as a doughty champion of democracy, an oasis of Western values amid a surrounding desert of hostile tribes. Friends of the Palestinians tend to see them as an oppressed and poverty-stricken people, victimised by rich and powerful intruders who care nothing for international law or for resolutions of the United Nations. Each of these caricatures contains more than a grain of truth, but since 1967 the basic situation has not changed: it is the Israelis who are occupying Palestinian land, not the Palestinians who are occupying Israel.

All parties to the conflict agree that the best chance for a resolution lies in the formula 'land for peace'. Israel will have to return all or most of the territories it has occupied since 1967 in order to receive assurances about its right to exist in a secure environment. Such was the basis of the negotiations that proceeded through the 1990s, and which seemingly came within an ace of success at the Oslo talks between Prime Minister Barak and Chairman Arafat. Yet those who were outraged by Arafat's rejection of an apparently generous offer which would even have included East Jerusalem should realise that merely returning land to its rightful owners is no great concession at all. Something more than land must be relinquished. Israel is a nuclear power. It has first-class American-financed armed services of all varieties. It has taken control of everything from water resources and energy to communications, trade and the labour market. The Palestinians control nothing that the Israelis can't take away in an instant. That section of the Palestinian population which has succumbed to terrorism – just as part of the Jewish population once adopted terrorism under the British mandate – acts out of desperation and hopelessness. Israel will only be moving onto the path of genuine concessions when in addition to land it brings itself to share power and to treat the Palestinians as respected equals. This does not mean exact equivalence; it does not mean that the Palestinians must be given an A-bomb just because Israel has one. But it does mean that Israel must relax its monopoly grip on a number of key sectors, otherwise they will be creating a bantustan.

The solution equally requires a relaxation of the United States' unbending pro-Israeli stance. Ever since the demise of the USSR the Arabs have had no countervailing patron, and the whole framework of debate is extremely unbalanced. For reasons best not examined, the world's only superpower has chosen to lock itself into the interests of one tiny client country whose population is less than that of Lithuania. Worse still, the right-wing government of the United States has ignored the peaceable vision of its founding fathers, and has put its faith in guns, money, clandestine nuclear weapons, tendentious propaganda and an extreme security doctrine. Its version of democracy can only be likened to that of the old Northern Ireland, where the majority ethnic community could legally deny the minority all effective access to justice, dignity or equality and could militarily crush all reasonable or unreasonable forms of opposition. Sooner rather than later, this state of affairs will crumble. The manner of its demise will seriously affect the alignment of the three or four concatenations whose interests in the region will inevitably be affected.

According to the best estimates, the window of opportunity may close within fifteen or twenty years. The Israeli economy cannot maintain its present high efficiency if security considerations deprive it of a mobile Palestinian labour force. The flow of Russian immigrants has now stopped, and temporary measures, like the import of Chinese workers, look like desperation. More importantly, the Jews of Israel are rapidly losing the demographic race. As often happens, a poor population defends itself by high rates of reproduction, and the Arabs are building up an unassailable predominance. The dubious objective of a purely Jewish society within Israeli frontiers has already passed into history, and within a generation or so the Palestinians may outnumber the Israelis by a clear margin. Everything points to urgency in the search for a permanent solution before new pressures arise.

Taiwan

Ever since the communist takeover of 1949 the United States has maintained its guarantee of the independence of Taiwan, the last remaining territory of America's wartime ally, the Chinese Nationalist republic of Chiang Kai-shek. In the meantime, the People's Republic of China on the mainland has grown into a nuclear power, a permanent member of the UN Security Council and the world's fastest-growing major economy. What is more, since the restitution of Hong Kong in 1997 Taiwan has been the last thorn in the flesh of China's pride. Perhaps because Taiwan is so small in relation to the People's Republic its capacity to cause irritation has actually increased. And one should never underestimate the very strong nationalistic streak in the communist leadership.

There are three sides to the conflict – Beijing, Taipei and Washington. Rightly or wrongly, Beijing sees itself as the injured party, and is very unlikely to change its stance. It wants Taiwan back inside the fold, but unless provoked is willing to bide its time. Taipei lives under the most immediate pressure. Basically, it must choose one of three options. It could do nothing and prepare to defend the status quo at ever-increasing risk and cost. It could set a date for its reunion, and work for a Hong Kong-type arrangement of 'one country, two systems'. Or it could make a bid for permanent separation, declaring that it is no longer a province of China, but a completely separate entity with an independent future. Washington can no doubt advise, but in essence it is condemned merely to react to the consequences of Taipei's decisions.

With China, however, the Americans have to deal with a civilisational power bloc that is already established and is visibly putting on economic and military muscle. It is not, like Islam, a *potential* player in the world power game; it is already there, and is the most likely power to eventually topple the United States from its pedestal. The stakes are high, and as seen in the recent stand-off over a hijacked plane, the Chinese can play tough, while, judging by the experience of the last few decades, the Americans will do almost anything to avoid a confrontation. One of their criteria for military action seems to be that their adversary should be virtually defenceless. And China is not defenceless.

Russia

Russia is another ready-made power, but one, unlike China, in marked decline. Huntington rated Russia a single 'civilisation', but many do not. The late Soviet Union was an empire created by brute force; the Russian Federation, which only ten years back was lord of fifteen Soviet republics, of six European countries of the Soviet Bloc, and of a concatenation stretching from Angola and Mozambique to Afghanistan and Mongolia, is now just a rump. But it is a rump that occupies the largest single state territory in the whole world, and it still contains many internal colonies. Moreover, its imperial pretensions have not faded, as demonstrated by the entirely avoidable tragedy of Chechnya. And, though it retains both a space programme and a vast nuclear arsenal, it is surviving off international aid and a brittle economy whose only thriving sector, oil and gas, seems to have fallen into the hands of a tiny and undesirable coterie of so-called oligarchs. According to speakers at a recent seminar at St Antony's College – hardly a hotbed of anti-Russianism – progress towards democracy and a market economy is more superficial than real.

Moscow is the last place where foreigners have ever learned much about the realities of Russia, and ex-Sovietologists come from one of the most compromised of disciplines. One would be better advised to seek the opinion of people who have been on the receiving end of Muscovite rule, and that includes ordinary Russians who do not belong to the ruling establishment.

Three realities stand out. One concerns the predatory nature of Kremlin practices both inside Russia and outside it. Recent history is illustrative. Ten years of foreign investment in the 1990s radically transformed the Moscow skyline whilst not building a single all-weather road from one side of the federation to the other. (Don't believe everything which you see in Russian atlases.) The second reality is the chameleon-like mindset of all modern Russian leaders – including Gorbachev – whose formative years, and those of their families, were passed in an age of almost unimaginable lies and terror. (Anyone who knows about Auschwitz and Treblinka needs equally to learn about Kolyma and Kuropaty.) More attention should be given to the reasons why Gorbachev was extremely popular in the West but widely denigrated in Russia itself. Until recently Russian politicians could only survive if they learned to believe nothing but to blend instinctively into the flavour of the day. They could simultaneously persuade Gandhi and Genghis Khan of their best intentions, and they have had little trouble persuading the IMF of their creditworthiness. The third reality concerns democracy. If ever the principle of genuine choice were introduced into the politics of Russia's far-flung regions and autonomous republics, the federation would probably fall apart. This is the trickiest conundrum of all for anyone taking time off to reflect on the rise (and decline) of global powers in the twenty-first century.

Vladimir Putin, who won the presidency in 2000, is a very different animal from his recent predecessors in the Kremlin. He was a career officer of the KGB, and has publicly expressed the view that the collapse of the USSR was a 'catastrophe'. At the same time, he does not belong to the rump communist movement, and seems to accept that the old political and economic methods were ineffective. The result is that Putin's people are desperately trying to halt the centrifugal trends of the last decade, to exploit new levers of international influence, like energy, and to maintain Russia's status as a top-table player. Pressure is being exerted on the Russian media, on Russia's regions and on Russia's ex-Soviet neighbours in the CIS – in central Asia, in the Caucasus, and in Belarus and Ukraine – to toe the Kremlin's line. The imperialism of pipelines and of gas contracts has replaced the imperialism of tanks. If Putin succeeds, a cold wind will be felt both in the Far East and in Europe. If he fails, a huge geopolitical vacuum will develop. One may conclude that everyone else's interest lies in Putin neither failing completely nor in succeeding spectacularly.

Washington

Which leaves one last danger area: Washington. The United States is at the height of its power. It is hard to imagine that it can achieve a still greater degree of supremacy than that which fell into its lap through the unexpected collapse of the USSR. Yet some time, somehow, like 'all proud kingdoms', the power of the United States will pass away. Whether the Americans' day in the sun will be short or long will depend in large measure on their management of international relations in the immediate future. President Clinton's style in the first years after 'the end of history' was low-key, unassertive, conciliatory. His approach stood in marked contrast to that of his Republican opponents, especially of President Reagan, which was fine when facing up to a fellow superpower but perhaps less effective when dealing with rather more vulnerable partners. Unless the American giant can learn to be more nimble, to disguise its obvious advantages with tact and smiles, and to be restrained under provocation, it may well cause mortal offence without necessarily intending to. The incoming administration needs to cultivate the trust of the European Union – a potential economic rival but a long-standing partner – and despite all the obvious problems to resist the temptation to act outside the remit of the United Nations. For the time being, the future of the world will rest in Washington's hands. If Washington casts restraint to the winds, it will make enemies fast, and a growing circle of enemies will ensure that the 'New American Century' is short.

CODA:
WAITING FOR DINNER

STATE-MUNICIPAL Gastronomic Enterprise, No. 27. Category II. In other words, a restaurant. I was sitting at the corner table, waiting for dinner, and reading the menu. After some twenty minutes, the waiter walked across, briskly.

— Number Thirteen, I ordered, Pork chop (150 grammes), carrots, potatoes. 31 crowns.
— Sorry, sir, said the waiter, No pork chop.
— How's that? I asked.
— It's a meatless day, he replied.
— I thought Friday was the meatless day, I said.
— That's right, he agreed. Friday's the unofficial meatless day, for Catholics.
— But most of your people *are* Catholics, I said.
— That's right, he agreed. But under socialism, we have an official meatless day as well, on Wednesday.
— But today is Monday, I said.
— That's right, he agreed. It's just that today we don't have any meat.
— In that case, I said, I'll order Number Seven. Cod (125 grammes), cabbage, chips. 34 crowns.
— *Zaraz* (at once) . . . he said.

After some twenty minutes, the waiter walked across, briskly.

293

— Sorry, sir, he said. No cod.

— How's that? I asked.

— Fish is only delivered on Thursdays, he explained, so that the Catholics won't go hungry on Friday.

— In that case, I said, I shall order Number Sixteen. Plain Omelette (2 eggs). 22 crowns.

— *Zaraz* . . . he said.

After some twenty minutes, the waiter came across, briskly.

— Sorry, sir, he said. No omelette.

— How's that? I asked.

— No eggs, he replied.

— How's that? I replied, pointing to a lady opposite who was just finishing an omelette.

— Well, he explained, when there's no meat, and no fish, everyone orders eggs; so now there's no eggs.

— Look here, I said hungrily. I've been here for an hour without a bite. Give me anything you can find.

— Number Twenty-One? he suggested. Mushrooms-from-the-pan (200 grammes) and black bread (100 grammes). 25 crowns.

— Good, I said, and please bring the bill.

— *Zaraz* . . . he said.

After some twenty minutes the waiter came across, briskly, bringing a plate of mushrooms and a bill for 55 crowns.

— How's *that*? I said, showing him the bill.

— Well, he explained, in the evening when the band is playing, prices are doubled.

— But, I said, the band is not playing. I've not yet heard a note from them. How's that?

— Well, he explained, it's the musicians' break.

— Really, I said. I've been here for nearly an hour and a half and they've not even tuned up.

— That's right, he agreed. But musicians are like everyone else. Under socialism, everyone has the right to eat before he works. The musicians are at that table over there, and they too are waiting for dinner.

At that point, a hand rose above the musicians' table, summoning the waiter with the flourish of an empty bottle. The waiter disappeared. It was the time for action. I knew that my treachery would not be noticed for twenty minutes at least. So, putting 25 crowns and no tip on the table, I left the State-Municipal Gastronomic Enterprise No. 27, briskly.

(Looking back, I should not have been so unkind to the waiter, who was not to blame. I should have left him a note: 'Esteemed Gastronomic Worker! I have just slipped out to organise the Revolution. All our troubles will soon be ended. I shall wait on you with pleasure. You will sit at the corner table, and your pork chop will arrive without waiting – *zaraz!*)

NOTES

Introduction

1. *White Eagle, Red Star: The Polish–Soviet War of 1919–20* (London, 1972; New York, 1973), Foreword by A.J.P. Taylor: henceforth *White Eagle, Red Star* (1972).
2. *God's Playground: A History of Poland* (Oxford, 1981; New York, 1982): henceforth *God's Playground* (1981); *Europe: A History* (Oxford, 1996; New York, 1997): henceforth *Europe* (1996).
3. The prize example is Jean-Baptiste Duroselle, *Europe: A History of Its Peoples* (London, 1991).
4. London, 1999.

Prologue: The Legend of Europa

1. Stonehenge is an Anglo-Saxon name dating to *c.* AD 500. Before it, there would have been Latin, British Celtic and probably several pre-Celtic names, all lost.
2. Ovid, *Metamorphoses*, ii, lines 862 ff.; translated by A.D. Melville, (Oxford, 1986), p. 50.
3. Herodotus, *The Histories*, Book 1, 2.
4. Ovid, op. cit., line 875.
5. Possibly from the Assyrian word *ereb*, meaning the west.

I: The Idea of Europe

1. The following text has been produced by amalgamating a lecture called 'The Idea of Europe', presented in Budapest on 11 June 1998 to a conference jointly organised by the Budapest University of Economics and Michigan State University, with a lecture called 'Europe's Changing Identity', presented at the British Library's Centre for the Book on 25 February 1998.

2. Edith Hall, *Inventing the Barbarian: Greek Self-definition through Tragedy* (Oxford, 1989).

3. 'Concepts of Europe', *Europe* (1996), pp. 7–16.

4. See Robert Olby, *The Path of the Double Helix: The Discovery of DNA* (New York, 1994).

5. 'Hellas – Ancient Greece', *Europe* (1996), pp. 95–147.

6. 'The Bosporus, 4 November 1079 AUC', ibid., pp. 206–12.

7. 'The Christian Church, 325–787', ibid., pp. 257–84.

8. On the Church schism, ibid., pp. 328–32.

9. On symbols, including the swastika, ibid., pp. 194–5.

10. See E.H. Gombrich, *Norm and Form: Studies in the Art of the Renaissance* (London, 1978).

11. See R.S. Westman (ed.), *The Copernican Achievement* (Berkeley, Ca., 1974).

12. See Denys Hay, *Europe: The Emergence of an Idea* (Edinburgh, 1957).

13. 'Lumen – Enlightenment and Absolutism, *c.* 1650–1789', *Europe* (1996), pp. 577–674.

14. 'Western Civilization', ibid., pp. 19–31.

15. 'European Imperialism', ibid., pp. 848–54.

16. See ibid., pp. 764–82, 1293.

17. 'Monkey', ibid., pp. 793–4; also, on eugenics, pp. 859–60.

18. See Bertrand Russell, *Religion and Science* (Oxford, 1935); also John S. Hapgood, *Religion and Science* (London, 1972).

19. See Helen Litton, *The Irish Famine: An Illustrated History* (Minneapolis, 1994).

20. 'Caucasia', *Europe* (1996), pp. 734–5.

21. 'Lettland', ibid., p. 1017.

22. *Classocide* is a term adopted by certain repentant ex-communists: see Stephane Courtois et al., *The Black Book of Communism* (Cambridge, Mass., 1999).
23. Churchill at The Hague, quoted by Anthony Sampson, *The New Europeans: A Guide to the Workings, Institutions and Character of Contemporary Western Europe* (London, 1968), pp. 4–5.
24. Salvador de Madariaga, ibid.
25. As recounted to the author by Mr Bielecki.
26. 'Parnasse', *Europe* (1996), p. 784.

II: Fair Comparisons, False Contrasts

1. Special faculty lecture, University of Oxford, presented at Examination Schools on 22 November 1996.
2. *The Times*, 30 September 1865.
3. *Journal de Saint-Petersbourg*, as quoted by *The Times*, 10 October 1865.
4. See R.F. Foster, *Modern Ireland, 1660–1972* (London, 1989).
5. *The Times*, 10 October 1865.
6. Marc Raeff, 'A Reactionary Liberal: M.N. Katkov', *Russian Review*, XI, 53 (1952).
7. I am indebted to HE Patrick McCabe, Ireland's ambassador in Warsaw, for extensive notes on this subject.
8. *Co nasłączy, co nas dzieli* (What unites us, what divides us), *Gazeta wyborcza*, 22 March 1996.
9. See David Priestman, 'The Totalitarian Model and Its Critics', seminar paper, Oxford, 3 May 1993. 'The concept of Totalitarianism stands or falls ... only on the substance of the points of comparison between Communism and Fascism. If these points are real and predominate, then Totalitarianism is a waste of time.' For an extensive exposé of the points of comparison, see *Europe* (1996), pp. 945–8.
10. Zbigniew Brzeżiński and Samuel P. Huntington, *Political Power and Principle* (London, 1964).
11. *Europe* (1996), pp. 944–9.

12. Sir Isaiah Berlin, in G. Thomas (ed.), *The Unresolved Past: A Debate in German History* (London, 1990), pp. 18–19.

13. See *Europa, Europa: Das Jahrhundert der Avantgarde in Mittel- und Osteuropa*, an exhibition at the Kunst- und Ausstellungshalle, Bonn, May–October 1994, directed by R. Stanislawski and C. Brockhaus, catalogue (Bonn, 1994), 4 vols.

14. Edward Said, *Orientalism* (London, 1978); see also Edward Said and Christopher Hitchens, *Blaming the Victims: Spurious Scholarship and the Palestine Question* (London, 1988).

15. Peter Laslett, 'Family and Household as Work Group and Kin Group: Areas of Traditional Europe Compared', in R. Wall et al. (eds), *Family Forms in Historic Europe* (Cambridge, 1983), pp. 513–63.

16. Maria Todorova, 'Myth-making in European Family History: The *Zadruga* Revisited', *East European Politics and Society*, 4, 1 (1991), pp. 30–69.

17. Immanuel Wallerstein, *The Modern World-System: Capitalist Agriculture and the Origins of the European World Economy* (New York, 1974).

18. *Europe* (1996), pp. 812–35, especially pp. 829–33.

19. Friedrich Meinecke (1852–1954), author of *Die deutsche Katastrophe* (The German Catastrophe, 1946). See also Hans Kohn, *Nationalism: Its Meaning and History* (Princeton, NJ, 1965); Louis Snyder, *The Dynamics of Nationalism* (New York, 1964), and *The Varieties of Nationalism: A Comparative Study* (New York, 1976); Ernest Gellner, *Nations and Nationalism* (Oxford, 1983); Anthony Smith, *Theories of Nationalism* (London, 1971).

20. John Petrov Plamenatz (1912–75) *Man and Society: A Critical Examination of Some Important Social and Political Theories from Machiavelli to Marx* (London, 1963); also *Ideology* (London, 1970).

21. *Man and Society*, op. cit.

22. Ibid.

23. I am indebted to Professor Gilbert Rappaport of the University of Texas at Austin for the suggestion to add this section to the original

text. Tendentious histories of anti-Semitism abound as do references to 'Polish anti-Semitism', which is often presented as 'going with the territory' as if Polish–Jewish relations had no redeeming features. See Leon Poliakov, *A History of Anti-Semitism* (London, 1974); R.S. Wistrich, *Antisemitism: The Longest Hatred* (London, 1991); B. Lazare, *Antisemitism: Its History and Causes* (Lincoln, Neb, 1995).

24. Quoted by Larry Wolff, *Inventing Eastern Europe: The Map of Civilization on the Mind of the Enlightenment* (Stanford, 1994). Hobsbawm's paper was not apparently published in the conference symposium.

25. Edith Hall, *Inventing the Barbarian: Greek Self-definition through Tragedy* (Oxford, 1989).

26. Neal Ascherson, *Black Sea* (London, 1995), p. 49.

27. See C. Harrison et al., *The Ashmolean Museum: Complete Illustrated Catalogue of Paintings* (Oxford, 2004). For William Holman Hunt (1827–1910) see www.abcgallery.com/H/huntwh/huntwh11.html. Although the scene is presumably from Roman Britain, where Celtic Druidism had been exterminated by the Romans, a British family is shown living in a windowless hovel and wearing skins, protecting an exhausted Roman priest from presumably Druidical marauders outside.

28. See J. Neissen (ed.), *Religious Compromise, Political Salvation: The Greek-Catholic Church and Nation-building in Eastern Europe* (Pittsburgh, 1993); also P. Pallath (ed.), *Catholic Eastern Churches: Heritage and Identity* (Rome, 1994).

29. Wolff, op. cit.

30. 'Entering Eastern Europe: Eighteenth-Century Travellers', ibid., Chapter I, pp. 17 ff.

31. Michel Foucault, *Surveiller et punir: naissance de la prison* (Paris, 1975), pp. 9–11; also G.R. Scott, *A History of Torture* (London, 1994).

32. See C.H. Willberger, *Voltaire's Russia: Window on the East* (Oxford, 1972).

33. From Frederick II's 'Guerre des Confederés', quoted by Wolff, op. cit., p. 265.

34. John Ledyard (1788), quoted ibid., pp. 342–3.
35. Edward Gibbon, quoted ibid., p. 268.
36. G. Barraclough (ed.), *The Times Atlas of World History* (London, 1984), Introduction.
37. Quoted by Wolff, op.cit., p. 342.
38. F. Taylor (ed.), *The Goebbels Diaries* (London, 1982), p. 16.
39. Magdalena Zaborowska, *How We Found America: Reading Gender through East European Immigrants* (Chapel Hill, NC, 1995).
40. J. Wertheimer, *Unwelcome Strangers: East European Jews in Imperial Germany* (Oxford, 1987); also S.E. Aschheim, *Brothers and Strangers: The East European Jew in German and German-Jewish Consciousness, 1800–1923* (Madison, Wis., 1988).
41. Winston Churchill's Fulton speech, in R.R. James (ed.), *Churchill Speaks: Winston S. Churchill in Peace and War – Collected Speeches* (Leicester, 1981).
42. R.J.W. Evans, born 1943, MA, PhD, Regius Professor of History since 1998. I originally assumed that Professor Evans had learned Welsh, among many other languages, as an adult, only to find that he was raised in a bi-lingual home and has spoken Welsh since childhood. I stand humbly corrected.
43. Timothy Garton Ash, *The Uses of Adversity: Essays on the Fate of Central Europe* (Cambridge, 1989).
44. Jean-Baptiste Duroselle, *L'Europe: histoire de ses peuples* (Paris, 1990); translated as *Europe: A History of Its Peoples* (London, 1990).
45. 'The Waffen SS Divisions, 1933–45', listed in *Europe* (1996), Appendix III, pp. 1326–7.
46. Noel Malcolm, 'Pulling Europe Together', *Sunday Telegraph*, 13 October 1996.
47. *Europe* (1996), pp. 691–2, 699, 701.
48. Johann Wolfgang von Goethe, 'Der west-östliche Diwan', in *Selected Verse*, ed. D. Duke (Harmondsworth, 1972).
49. Churchill, quoted by Wolff, op. cit., Introduction, p. 3.

III: Western Civilisation versus European History

1. This text has been produced by amalgamating two similar lectures. One, called 'Western Civilisation versus European History', was presented at Harvard University on 6 April 1992; the other, called 'European History versus Western Civilisation', constituted the third of the Waynflete Lectures and was presented at Magdalen College on 14 May 1997.

2. W.H. McNeil, *History of Western Civilization: A Handbook*, 6th edition (Chicago, 1986; 1st edition, 1949); Robert E. Herzstein, *Western Civilization* (Boston, 1975); John B. Harrison et al., *A Short History of Western Civilization* (New York, 1971); J. Russell Major, *Civilization in the Modern World* (Lippincott, 1967); J. Kelly Sowards, *Makers of the Western Tradition* (New York, 1982); R.M. Golden (ed.), *The Social Dimension of Western Civilization*, 4th edition (New York, 1999); F. Roy Willis, *Western Civilization* (Lexington, 1973); Mark Kishlansky, *Civilization in the West* (New York, 1990); Marvin Perry et al., *Western Civilization: Ideas, Politics and Society,* 2nd edition (Boston, 1985); Glenn Blackburn, *Western Civilization: A Concise History* (New York, 1990); R.L. Greaves, *Civilizations of the West,* 2 vols (New York, 1986).

3. McNeill, op. cit., pp. v–vii, 243–8.

4. J. Mortimer Adler, 'Great Books, Past and Present', in *Reforming Education* (New York, 1977), pp. 318–50; also Harold Bloom, *The Western Canon: The Books and School of the Ages* (New York, 1994).

5. Gilbert Allardyce, 'The Rise and Fall of the Western Civilisation Course', *American Historical Review*, 87, 3 (1982).

6. Eugene Weber, 'Western Civilisation', in A. Mollo and G.S. Wood (eds), *Imagined Histories: American Historians Interpret the Past* (Princeton, 1998).

7. See J. Wertheimer, *Unwelcome Strangers* (New York, 1987); also S.E. Aschheim, *Brothers and Strangers: The East European Jew in German and German-Jewish Consciousness, 1800–1923* (Madison, Wis., 1988).

8. Larry Wolff, 'Teaching Eastern Europe without the Iron Curtain', *Perspectives*, 31, 1 (1993).

9. An example would be R.R. Palmer, *The Age of Democratic Revolution, 1760–1800*, 2 vols (Princeton, 1959, 1964); also Piotr Wandycz, *The Price of Freedom: A History of East Central Europe* (London, 1992).

10. John J. Kulczycki, 'Eastern Europe in Western Civilization Textbooks: The Example of Poland', *The History Teacher*, 38, 2 (Feb. 2005), pp. 153–77. The textbooks examined were: L. Hunt et al., *The Making of the West: Peoples and Cultures*, 2 vols (New York, 2001); S. Hause and W. Mattby, *Western Civilization: A History of European Society* (Belmont, Ca., 1999); M.L. King, *Western Civilization: A Social and Cultural History*, vol. II (Prentice Hall, 2003); D. Kagan et al., *The Western Heritage*, vol. II (Prentice Hall, 2003); M. Kishlansky et al., *Civilization in the West*, 5th edition (New York, 2003); and A. Esler, *The Western World: A Narrative History*, vol. II (Prentice Hall, 1997).

11. Kulczycki, op. cit.

12. Greaves, op. cit., vol. I p. 242.

13. Ibid., p. 304.

14. On Boudicca, see *Heroic Females or an Authentic History of the Surprising Achievements and Intrepid Conduct of Boadicea, Queen of the Iceni and Her Two Daughters* (London, c. 1805); J.M. Scott, *Boadicea* (London, 1975); Graham Webster, *Boudica: The British Revolt against Rome* (London, 1978); M.J. Trow, *Boudicca: The Warrior Queen* (Stroud, 2005).

15. Greaves, op. cit., vol. I, p. 266.

16. Ibid., p. 267.

17. Jan Nowak-Jeziorański (1914–2005), December 2004 – 'byle co', which means 'anything at all' or 'anything you like'.

18. Greaves, op. cit., vol. I, p. 240.

IV: Roller Coaster

1. This essay has been constructed from notes prepared for numerous

talks presented in 1996–7 for the launch and promotion of *Europe* (1996).

2. *Europe* (1996), jacket.

3. Herbert Albert Laurens Fisher (1865–1940), *A History of Europe* (London, 1936; revised and enlarged edition, London, 1938).

4. Inexplicably, this volume does not appear in the OLIS catalogue.

5. A. Gibson and W. Pickford, *Association Football and the Men Who Made It*, 4 vols (London, 1905).

6. Orlando Figes, *A People's Tragedy: The Russian Revolution, 1891–1924* (London, 1996).

7. *Europe* (1996), p. xi.

8. Ibid., pp. 1131–6.

9. Ibid., Samphire pp. 82–3, Brie p. 329.

10. Ibid., Appendix I, pp. 1203–4.

11. Ibid., Plate I, *Il ratto dell'Europa*: fresco from the House of Jason, Pompeii, first quarter of the first century AD.

12. Ibid., 'Phenology and Sägesignatur', p. 1220.

13. Sebastian Müntzer, 'Regina Europa', from *Cosmographia Universalis* (Basel, 1550–4), in ibid., p. xviii.

14. Including Theodore Rabb in the *New York Times*. The objection seemed to be that variant perceptions of the map of Europe, which ignored the convention that the north should be placed at the top of the page, were dangerously subversive.

15. *Europe* (1996), pp. 486–7.

16. Ibid., pp. 1234–5.

17. The prize went to Orlando Figes for *A People's Tragedy*.

18. R.J.E. Evans, now Regius Professor of History at Oxford.

19. *Europe* (1996), Responsa, p. 1019.

20. By Abraham Brumberg in the *Times Literary Supplement*.

21. J.M. Roberts, *The Pelican History of the World* (London, 1987); *The Penguin History of Europe* (London, 1997).

22. E.g. Timothy Garton Ash.

23. London: Pimlico, 1997.

24. Elżbieta Tabakowska, *O przekładzie na przykładzié* (Kraków, 2003).

25. New York: HarperCollins, 1998.

26. Norman Deyvis, *Evropa: Istoriya* (Ki'iv: Osnóvi, 2000).

V: Not Forever England

1. This essay has been assembled from the text of various talks presented in 1999–2000 following the publication of *The Isles: A History* (London, 1999).

2. Hugo (H.J.S.) Young (1938–2003): journalist on the *Sunday Times*, 1965–84, and the *Guardian*, 1984–2003; author of *One of Us*, a critical biography of Margaret Thatcher (London, 1989) and *This Blessed Plot: Britain and Europe from Churchill to Blair* (London, 1998).

3. Elizabeth I Tudor (reigned 1558–1603), queen of England, was daughter of Henry VIII and Anne Boleyn; Mary II Stuart (reigned 1689–94) and her younger sister Anne (reigned 1702–14), the first queen of Great Britain, were the daughters of James Duke of York, the future James II, and Lady Anne Hyde.

4. Kenneth O. Morgan, *The Oxford History of Britain* (Oxford, 1999), p. v.

5. *The Isles*, op. cit. Unlike the 'snapshots' in *Europe: A History*, those in *The Isles* were placed at the beginning of each chapter, not at the end.

6. Rudyard Kipling, 'The Roman Centurion's Song', *The Complete Verse* (London, 1990), p. 586.

7. Alistair Moffatt, *Arthur and the Lost Kingdoms* (London, 2000); see also his *The Sea Kingdoms: The Story of Celtic Britain and Ireland* (London, 2001); *Before Scotland* (London, 2005); and *The Borders* (Selkirk, 2002).

8. See Ragnhild Hatton, *George I: Elector and King* (London, 1978; republished, New Haven, Conn., 2001).

9. 'Rule Britannia', poem by James Thomson (1700–48), set to music by Thomas Arne in 1740.

10. Prince Philip, Duke of Edinburgh, Earl of Merioneth, Baron Greenwich, etc., was born on Corfu on 10 June 1921, the son of Prince Andrew of Greece and Princess Alice of Battenberg. According to the Royal Family's official website www.royal.gov.uk, his paternal family is 'of Danish descent'. But Wikipedia states both that 'it is uncertain what his original surname was' and 'he is a member of the

Danish Royal House of Schleswig-Holstein-Sonderburg-Glücks-burg'. In fact, the only uncertainty surrounds whether the family is Danish or German. The short answer is both. It is descended from the dukes of Oldenburg in northern Germany, and through a series of dynastic masterstrokes successively ascended the thrones of Denmark (1863), Greece (1863) and Norway (1905). By order in council, the British royal family's surname was first fixed as 'Mount-batten-Windsor' and subsequently as Windsor. The Duke lost out.

11. Noël Coward, 'Mad Dogs and Englishmen', *The Lyrics* (London, 1983), pp. 122–3.

VI: *Sicut Lilium*

1. First Waynflete Lecture, Magdalen College, Oxford, 30 April 1997. I am greatly indebted to Mr D.A.L. Morgan for comments and improvements on the original draft.
2. Edward Gibbon, *Memoirs of My Life and Writings* (1974; reprinted, London, 1994).
3. Song of Songs 2: 2–3a.
4. Bolton School, like many others no doubt, had adopted the Harrow school song as its own; it has since replaced it.
5. Gibbon, op. cit., p. 97.
6. Ibid., p. 105.
7. Unless otherwise noted, all biographical information derives from the *Dictionary of National Biography*, or from my *Encyclopaedia Britannica*, 11th edition (1910–11).
8. See 'The Contest with James II, 1687–8', H.A. Wilson, *Magdalen College* (London, 1898), University of Oxford, College Histories Series.
9. Peter Heylyn, *Microcosmus* (1621), *A Help to English History* (1675), *Ecclesia restaurata* (1661), *Cypriarius Anglicus* (1671), *France Painted to the Life* (London, 1657).
10. See G.M. Yould, 'The Career and Writings of Dr George Hickes, Non juror', Oxford University, DPhil thesis (1965).
11. Joseph Addison, 'The Campaign' and 'Ode' (hymn).

12. R. Chandler, *The Life of William Waynflete, Bishop of Winchester* (London, 1811).

13. R.D. Middleton, *Dr Routh* (London, 1938).

14. See M. Elwin, *Charles Reade: A Biography* (London, 1931).

15. See R.W. Clark, *An Eccentric in the Alps* (London, 1959).

16. See Harold Orlans, *T.E. Lawrence: Biography of a Broken Hero* (London, 2002).

17. Charles R.L. Fletcher, *An Introductory History of England* (London, 1904–23); *The Making of Western Europe* (London, 1912); *Mr Gladstone at Oxford, 1890* (London, 1908); *The Germans* (London, 1914); also (with Rudyard Kipling) *A History of England* (1911).

18. Charles Grant Robertson, *A Historical and Modern Atlas of the British Empire* (1905).

19. Charles Grant Robertson, *A History of Western Europe, 1453–1789* (London, 1929).

20. Private letter, 4 June 1997.

21. T.S.R. Boase, *Boniface VIII* (London, 1933); *St Francis of Assisi* (London, 1936); *An Oxford College and the Gothic Revival* (London, 1955); *Death in the Middle Ages* (London, 1972).

22. See William Griffin, *Clive Staples Lewis: A Dramatic Life* (London, 1986); also David Barratt, *C.S. Lewis and His World* (London, 1987).

23. See A.W. Wright, *G.D.H. Cole and Socialist Democracy* (Oxford, 1973).

24. J.M. Thompson, *A Historical Geography of Europe, 800–1789* (Oxford, 1929); *Robespierre* (Oxford, 1939); *Napoleon: His Rise and Fall* (Oxford, 1953).

25. J.M. Thompson, *Lecures on Foreign History, 1494–1789* (Oxford, 1956).

26. Ibid.

27. See James Patrick, *The Magdalen Metaphysicals: Idealism and Orthodoxy at Oxford* (Macon, Ca., 1953); R.G. Collingwood, *An Autobiography* (Oxford, 1951); David Boucher, *The Social and Political Thought of R.G. Collingwood* (Cambridge, 1989).

28. See R. Cole, *A.J.P Taylor: The Traitor within the Gates* (Basingstoke, 1993); Adam Sisman, *A.J.P. Taylor: A Biography* (London, 1994); Kathleen Burk, *Troublemaker: The Life and History of A.J.P. Taylor* (London, 2000); Chris Wrigley, *A.J.P. Taylor: Radical Historian of Europe* (London, 1951).

29. J.W. Stoye, *The Siege of Vienna* (London, 1964); *Europe Unfolding 1648–1688* (London, 1969); *English Travellers Abroad, 1604–67,* (London, 1952); *Marsigli's Europe, 1680–1730* (New Haven, Conn., 1994).

30. C.G. Hardie, *Studies in Dante* (Oxford, 1969); *Dante's Comedy as Self-analysis and Integration* (London, 1959).

31. Paul Johnson, *A History of the Jews* (London, 1987), *A History of Christianity* (Hemel Hempstead, 1990), *The Offshore Islanders* (London, 1992); Felipe Fernandez-Armesto, *Millennium* (London, 1995), *Civilisations* (London, 2001), *Food: A History* (London, 2002); Martin Gilbert, *Churchill*, 8 vols (1966–88), *The Holocaust* (London, 1987), *In Search of Churchill: A Historian's Journey* (London, 1995).

VII: Europe Overseas and Overland

1. Inaugural Lecture of the Adelaide Book Festival, University of Adelaide, 5 March 1998.

2. See Robert Hughes, *The Fatal Shore: A History of the Transportation of Convicts to Australia, 1787–1868* (London, 1985), *passim*.

3. See John Prebble, *The Highland Clearances* (London, 1963); also his *Culloden* (London, 1961) and *Glencoe* (London, 1966).

4. See Cecil Woodham-Smith, *The Great Hunger: Ireland, 1845–52* (London, 1962); E. Laxton, *The Hunger Ships: The Irish Exodus to America, 1846–51* (London, 1996).

5. See Nicholas Thomas, *Discoveries: The Voyages of Captain James Cook* (London, 2002).

6. *The Overlanders* (1946), written and directed by Harry Watt.

7. Henryk Skok, *Polacy nad Bajkalem, 1863–83* (Warsaw, 1974).

8. *Roman Sanguszko, zeslaniec na Sybir z r 1831 w swiette pamigtnika matki* ... (Warsaw, 1927).

9. See Robert Service, *Lenin: A Biography* (London, 2000).

10. See H. Chevigny, *Russian America: The Great Alaskan Adventure* (New York, 1965); California State Park Service, *Fort Ross Historical Park* (n.d.).

11. See Frank Mocha, *Poles in America: Bi-centennial Essays* (Wisconsin, 1978).

12. See W. Slabczyński, *Pawel Edmund Strzelecki: podróże, odkrycia, prace* (Warsaw, 1957).

13. L. Boyd, K. Houpt, *Przewalski's Horse: History and Biology of an Endangered Species* (Albany, NY, 1994).

14. For a Soviet perspective, see V. Alexandrov, *The Wonderland Called Siberia* (Moscow, 1979); L. Shinkarev, *The Land beyond the Mountains* (London, 1973).

15. Alan Woods, *Sex and Violence in Siberia* (Lancaster, 1968).

16. A.H. Brown et al. (eds), *The Cambridge Encyclopaedia of Russia and the Soviet Union* (Cambridge, 1982), *passim*.

17. Avraam Shifrin, *The First Guidebook to the Prisons and Concentration Camps of the Soviet Union* (New York, 1982), now superseded by an *Encyclopedia to the Gulag*, published by Memoriel in 1988.

18. Robert Conquest, *The Great Terror* (London, 1968); *The Nation Killers: The Soviet Deportation of Nationalities* (London, 1970); *Kolyma: The Arctic Death Camps* (London, 1978); *The Harvest of Sorrow: Soviet Collectivisation and the Terror Famine* (London, 1986).

19. See Keith Sword, *Deportation and Exile: Poles in the Soviet Union, 1939–48* (London, 1994).

20. Sławomir Rawicz, *The Long Walk* (London, 1956).

21. Hughes, op.cit., *passim*.

22. A saying of Marshal J. Piłsudski, himself a prisoner-exile in Siberia in the 1890s.

VIII: History, Language and Literature

1. George Borrow, *Wild Wales: Its People, Language and Scenery* (London, 1862, Nelson Classics edition, n.d.), p. 164.

2. Ibid., p. 165.
3. Matthew v: 3–12, 'Sermon de Jesus-Christ sur la Montagne'.
4. William Blake (1757–1827), 'The Sunflower', from *Songs of Experience* (1795).
5. Gilbert Highet, *Poets in a Landscape* (London, 1957), p. 1.
6. Gaius Valerius Catullus (*c.* 84–*c.* 54 BC), Carmen LXXXV, 'Odi et amo'.
7. Felice Cavallotti (1842–98), 'La Regina dei Fiori'. Despite his name, Cavallotti, sometime soldier of Garibaldi, was killed in a duel.
8. From Robert Graves, *The White Goddess: A Historical Grammar of Poetic Myth* (London, 1948).
9. Sophocles (*c.* 496–406 BC), *Antigone*, 332 ff.
10. Simonides of Ceos (*c.* 556–468? BC), 'On the Spartans at Thermopylae', of which there are innumerable translations. See Earl of Cromer, *Paraphrases and Translations from the Greek* (London, 1903), no. 33.
11. Norman Davies, *Rising '44: The Battle for Warsaw* (London, 2003), p. 613.
12. Ibid., p. 615.
13. Bede (673?–735), Book V, 23.
14. J. Macpherson, *The Poems of Ossian* (Edinburgh, 1805; reprinted, 1971), II, p. 385.
15. Quoted in *Europe* (1996), p. 200.
16. Ibid., p. 254.
17. From Aneirin (*fl. c.* 600), *Y Gododdin: Britain's Oldest Heroic Poem*, ed. A. O. H. Jarman (Llandysul, 1988), p. 7.
18. G. Jack (ed.), *Beowulf: A Student Edition* (Oxford, 1994), 'The Fight at Finnsburgh', lines 1106–27, pp. 93–4.
19. F. Gudmundson (ed.), *The Orkneyinga Saga* (Reykjavik, 1965), p. 15.
20. Dante Alighieri (1265–1321), *Paradise*, Canto XXXIII, 133–46, translated by John Ciardi.
21. Professor David Abulafia, of Cambridge University.
22. Alphonse de Lamartine (1790–1869), from 'Le Lac', in *Meditations poetiques* (1820).

23. Joachim du Bellay (1525–60), 'Sonnets', in *Recueil* (1549).

24. Juliusz Słowacki (1809–49), from *Journey to the East* (1836), quoted in *Europe* (1996), p. 1.

25. Joseph Freiherr von Eichendorff (1788–1857), from 'Das Zerbrochene Ringlein', in Leonard Forster (ed.), *The Penguin Book of German Verse* (London, 1959), p. 315.

26. Eichendorff, from 'Abschied', in ibid., pp. 311–12.

27. Eichendorff, from 'Der Umkehrende', in ibid., p. 317.

28. Elias Lönnrot (1802–84), from *Kalevala* (1849), quoted in *Europe* (1996), p. 818.

29. Vladimir Mayakovsky (1893–1930), from 'Conversation with the Inspector of Finances', in D. Obolensky (ed.), *Penguin Book of Russian Verse* (London, 1962), p. 381.

30. Federico García Lorca (1898–1936), from 'Romance de Guardia Civil española'.

31. From *Gospoda Nashego Iesusa Khrista Novyi Zavyet na Slavyanskom i Ruskom Yazykakh* (The New Testament of Our Lord Jesus Christ in the Slavonic and Russian Languages), parallel texts (St Petersburg, 1823), p. 23; quoted in *Europe* (1996), p. 459.

32. Taras Shevchenko (1814–61), 'Zapovit', quoted in *Europe* (1996), pp. 53–4.

33. T.S. Eliot (1888–1965), *The Waste Land* (facsimile), ed. Valerie Eliot (London, 1971), quoted in *Europe* (1996), p. 954.

34. Hugh Seton-Watson (1921–86), author of *The Russian Empire, 1801–1917* (Oxford, 1967), *Nations and States* (London, 1977), *Neither War nor Peace* (New York, 1962), *The New Imperialism* (London, 1967), etc.

35. 'Dreamtime' is the Aborigine concept for the past: hence 'White fella dreamin' stands for 'European historian'.

36. Giuseppe Tomasi di Lampedusa (1896–1957), *The Leopard* (London, 1961), p. 11.

37. *Il Gattopardo* (Milan, 1963), p. 24.

38. Charles Baudelaire (1821–67), 'Correspondences', in *Selected Verses*, ed. F. Scard (London, 1961), pp. 36–7.

IX: 1000 Years of Polish–German Camaraderie

1. *God's Playground* (1981), vol. I, pp. 493–5; see also K.L. von Poll-nitz, *La Saxe Galante, or the Amorous Adventures of Augustus of Saxony* ... (London, 1750).
2. See Konrad Jazdzewski, *Ancient Peoples and Places: Poland* (London, 1965).
3. See J. Wertheimer, *Unwelcome Strangers: The East European Jew in Imperial Germany, 1890–1914* (Oxford, 1987); also S.E. Aschheim, *Brothers and Strangers: The East European Jew in German and German-Jewish Consciousness, 1800–1923* (Madison, Wis., 1988).
4. Heinz Guderian, *Panzer Leader* (London, 1952), p. 38.
5. Józef Iwicki, *Listypolaka, Żolnierza armii niemieckiej z okopów I wojny światowej*, ed. A. Juzwenko (Wrocław, 1978).
6. E. Słoński, 'Ta co nie zginęta', *Zbiór poetów polskich XIX wieku* (Warsaw, 1965), IV, 855–6.
7. Johann Scheffler (Angelus Silesius, 1624–77), 'Ohne Warum', in Leonard Forster (ed.), *The Penguin Book of German Verse* (London, 1959), p. 173.
8. Joseph Freiherr von Eichendorff (1788–1857), 'Abschied', in ibid., p. 311.
9. See John Sack, *An Eye for an Eye: Jewish Revenge on Germans in Poland in 1945* (New York, 1993).
10. Andreas Gryphius (1616–54), 'Tränen des Vaterlandes', in Forster, op. cit., p. 131.
11. Günter Grass, 'Pan Kichot', in *Gedichte* (Neuwied/Berlin, n.d.), p. 27; translated by Norman Davies.

X: The Islamic Strand in European History

1. Presented as a lecture at the Institute Universitaire de Hautes Études, Geneva, 28 October 1998.
2. Edward Said, *Orientalism* (London, 1978).
3. Bassam Tibi, *Arab Nationalism: A Critical Enquiry* (London, 1981);

The Challenge of Fundamentalism: Political Islam and the New World Disorder (London, 1998).

4. Noel Malcolm, *Kosovo: A Short History* (London, 1998).
5. Noel Malcolm, *Bosnia: A Short History* (London, 1994).
6. Samuel P. Huntington, *The Clash of Civilizations and the Remaking of the World Order* (New York, 1990).
7. Professor Fouad Ajami, SAIS Johns Hopkins University, 'But they said, We will not hearken', www.coloradocollege.edu/dept/95/finley/ps425/mading/huntington2.html.
8. See Richard Fletcher, *Moorish Spain* (London, 1992).
9. R. Allison Peers, *Ramon Lull: A Biography* (New York, 1929).
10. Jonathan Riley-Smith, *The Crusades: A Short History* (London, 1987, *The First Crusade and the Idea of Crusading* (London, 1993); Steven Runciman, *A History of the Crusades* (Cambridge, 1954), *The Fall of Constantinople, 1453* (1990).
11. See John Stoye, *The Siege of Vienna* (London, 1964).
12. E.G. Parker, *A Thousand Years of the Tartars* (London, 2002).
13. Derek Hall, *Albania and the Albanians* (London, 1994).
14. See Note 4, above.
15. See Note 5, above.
16. M.S. Anderson, *The Eastern Question, 1774–1923: A Study in International Relations* (London, 1966).
17. H.D. Purcell, *Cyprus* (London, 1969).
18. Alistair Horne, *A Savage War of Peace: Algeria, 1954–62* (London, 1977).
19. Bernard Lewis, *The Emergence of Modern Turkey* (Oxford, 1968); Lord Kinross, *Atatürk: Rebirth of a Nation* (London, 1990).
20. John B. Dunlop, *Russia Confronts Chechnya: Roots of a Separatist Conflict* (Cambridge, 1998).
21. Walter Laqueur (ed.), *The Arab–Israeli Reader* (London, 1969); Bassam Tibi, *Conflict and War in the Middle East, 1967–91* (Basingstoke, 1993); M. Tessler, *A History of the Israeli–Palestinian Conflict* (Bloomington, Ind., 1994).

XI: The Jewish Strand in European History

1. 7th Maccabean Lecture, University College London, presented on 23 April 1998.
2. *Europe* (1996), pp. 199–200.
3. Gershon Hundert (ed.), *Polin: Studies in Polish Jewry. Vol. 10: Jews in Early Modern Poland* (Oxford, 1997).
4. John Dryden, 'Absolom and Achitophel' (1681), quoted in Walter Pater, *The Renaissance* (1873; reprinted, New York, 1959), p. 72.
5. *Europe* (1996), p. 595.
6. Niall Ferguson, *The House of Rothschild: Money's Prophets, 1798–1848* (London, 1998); *The House of Rothschild: The World's Banker, 1849–1999* (London, 1999).
7. Isaac Deutscher, *The Non-Jewish Jew and Other Essays* (London and New York, 1968).
8. See Robert Service, *Lenin: A Biography* (London, 2000).
9. See Bryan M. Rigg, *Hitler's Jewish Soldiers: The Untold Story of Nazi Racial Laws and Men of Jewish Descent in the German Military* (Lawrence, Kan., 2002).
10. Menahem Begin, *White Nights: The Story of a Prisoner in Russia* (New York, 1979).
11. Antoni Słonimski, 'Elegy for the Jewish Villages', quoted in translation in Eva Hoffman, *Shtetl* (London, 1998), p. 1.

XII: Misunderstood Victory

1. This essay was first published in *The Grand Coalition: A Report*, Warsaw Rising Museum (2005). A slightly shorter version of this article was published in the *Sunday Times* on 1 May 2005.
2. Czech Flight Sergeant Jozef František, fighting in Polish Squadron 303.
3. Antony Beevor, *Stalingrad* (London, 1998).
4. Antony Beevor, *Berlin: The Downfall 1945* (London, 2002).
5. Norman Davies, *Rising '44: The Battle for Warsaw* (London, 2003).

XIII: The Politics of History

1. This paper was prepared for a conference on 'Politics and History' at the Museum Powstania in Warsaw.
2. Howard Zinn, *A People's History of the United States* (London, 1980).
3. N. Chomsky and H. Zinn (eds), *The Pentagon Papers: The Defense Department History of United States Decisionmaking on Vietnam* (Boston, 1971–2).
4. Howard Zinn, *The Politics of History* (Boston, 1970).
5. T.A. Meade and M.E. Wiesner-Hanks (eds), *A Companion to Gender History* (Oxford, 2004).
6. M.B. Dubermen et al. (eds), *Hidden from History: Reclaiming the Gay and Lesbian Past* (London, 1991).
7. See Clive Ponting, *A Green History of the World* (London, 1991).
8. T. Clarke, *By Blood and Fire: The Attack on the King David Hotel* (London, 1981).
9. Jacob Neusner, *Who, Where and What Is Israel?* (Lanham, Md, 1989).
10. S.R. Sizer, *Christian Zionism: Road-map to Armageddon?* (Nottingham, 2004).
11. Irwin Stelzer (ed.), *Neoconservatism* (London, 2004).
12. Edwin Jones, *The English Nation: The Great Myth* (Stroud, 1998).
13. D. Streonoukoff, 'Moscow the Third Rome: Source of the Doctrine', *Speculum* (Jan. 1953), pp. 84–101.
14. A. Loewenberg, *The Annals of Opera* (London, 1978), pp. 784–6; see also *Europe* (1996), pp. 994–5.
15. *The Black Book of Polish Censorship*, translated and edited by Jane Leftwich Curry (New York, 1984).
16. Edwin Jones, *John Lingard and the Pursuit of Historical Truth* (Brighton, 2001).
17. Norman Davies, *The Isles* (London, 1999), pp. 36–8.
18. G. Schöpflin and G. Hosking (eds), *Myths and Nationhood* (London, 1997).

19. William Shakespeare, *Richard II*, ii 1, 43–53.
20. Norman Finkelstein, *The Holocaust Industry: Reflections on the Exploitation of Jewish Suffering* (London, 2000).
21. Phillip Knightley, *Philby: The Life and Views of the KGB Masterspy* (London, 2003); Kim Philby, *My Silent War* (London, 2003); John Cairncross, *The Enigma Spy* (London, 1997).
22. J. K. Zawodny, *Death in the Forest: The Story of the Katyn Forest Massacre* (Notre Dame, 1972); Allen Paul, *Katyn: The Untold Story of Stalin's Polish Massacre* (New York, 1991); Vladimir Abarinov, *The Murderers of Katyn* (New York, 1993).
23. Phebe Marr, *The Modern History of Iraq* (London, 1985); Peter Sluglett, *Britain in Iraq, 1914–32* (Oxford, 1976); Charles Tripp, *A History of Iraq* (Cambridge, 2000).

XIV: The Rise of New Global Powers

1. The basic version of this essay was prepared as a Cabinet Office memorandum, December 2000.
2. Samuel P. Huntington, *The Clash of Civilisations and the Remaking of the World Order* (New York, 1996). Now professor of political science at Harvard, Huntington was once an associate of Zbigniew Brzeżiński in the Carter administration.
3. Or rather, the simplified versions of the Fukuyama thesis. Like all academics, he hedged his basic idea with nuances and reservations. See Francis Fukuyama, *The End of History and the Last Man* (New York, 1992).
4. The question made realistic provision for the existence of 'multiple identity'. Everyone in Britain has several layers to their identity – they can be British and English, British and Welsh, British and Asian, British and Polish-Irish. For political purposes, the key thing is to know whether the British layer remains the strongest or not.

INDEX

and *Europe: A History* 64
and Greek-Orthodox Uniates 35
and Islam/Muslims 209, 212, 213,
    214, 217–18, 221
and Jews 32, 33, 39, 228
literature 150, 176
and nomenclature 262
and Ottoman empire 209, 212,
    257
parochial outlook in 43
and Poland/Poles 22–3, 23–4, 133–5,
    147–8, 198, 269
and propaganda 256–7
and Second World War 241, 242
settlement in California 135, 138–9
speculations about future of 290–2
and studies of European history 49,
    51, 53, 60, 64
see also Russian language
Russian Federation 141–2, 290
Russian language 175–6
Russian Orthodox Church 35
Russian Revolution 65
Russo–Polish War (1831) 133, 134

Said, Edward: *Orientalism* 204
St Paul's school 168, 175
St Peter's, Rome 68
St Petersburg 35, 36, 245, 263
    see also Leningrad
Sakhalin 133, 144
Samara/Ulyanovsk 263
Samoyeds 141
Sand, Georges 21
Sanguszko, Prince Roman 134
Sankt-Petersburgski Zhurnal 22
Sapporo 183, 184
Sarajevo 211
Saudi Arabia 215, 220, 274, 286
Saxe, Maurice de 189
Saxe-Coburg-Gotha 97
    House of 98
Saxelby, Emma 152
Saxony 200
Scandinavia 8, 11, 34, 57, 89, 90, 141,
    241
Schama, Simon 65
Schleswig-Holstein 63
Schuman, Robert 103
science 13, 15–16
Scotland 85, 89, 95, 96, 100, 103, 104,

120, 131, 140, 164, 166, 265, 268,
    282
    see also Britain
Scott, C.P. 252
Scottish Parliament 100
Scythians 6
Second World War (1939–45) 18, 35,
    37, 39, 68, 143, 210, 217, 218,
    233, 235 240–8, 269, 270–1
secularism 12–13, 14
Securitate 181
Ségur, Marquis de 35
Sephardim 225
Serbia 5, 209, 210, 211, 212
Serbo-Croat 178
Sétif 215
Seton-Watson, Professor Hugh 24, 183
Shadowlands (film) 122
Shakespeare, William
    King Lear 150
    Macbeth 184
    Richard II 264
Shamil 217
Sharon, Ariel 255
Shevchenko, Taras 179–80
Shias 220, 271–2, 274, 287
Shoah *see* Holocaust/Shoah
Sholokhov, Mikhail: *Quiet Flows the
    Don* 176
Siberia 133, 134, 135, 139, 140,
    141–6, 147, 285
Sicily 58, 94, 207, 221
    migrants from 38
Silesia 16, 172–3, 194, 196–7, 201
Silesius, Angelus 173, 196
Simpson, John 75
Sinaia 180–1
Sirmione 154
Six Day War 268
Slavic (Slavonic) departments 40, 176
Slavonic names 262–3
Slavs 11, 28, 31, 37, 146, 191, 265
    proto-Slavs 191–2
Sleeve, the 90
Słonimski, Antoni 170, 237
Słoński, Edward 195
Slovakia 266
Slovenia 209, 211
Słowacki, Juliusz 171–2
Służewiec 158
Smith, Anthony 31